THE
G·R·E·A·T
REFORMATION

R.TUDUR JONES

INTERVARSITY PRESS
DOWNERS GROVE, ILLINOIS 60515

Published in the United States of America by InterVarsity Press, Downers Grove, Illinois, with permission from Universities and Colleges Christian Fellowship, Leicester, England.

InterVarsity Press is the book-publishing division of Inter-Varsity Christian Fellowship, a student movement active on campus at hundreds of universities, colleges and schools of nursing. For information about local and regional activities, write IVCF, 233 Langdon St., Madison, WI 53703.

Distributed in Canada through InterVarsity Press, 860 Denison St., Unit 3, Markham, Ontario L3R 4H1, Canada.

Unless otherwise stated, quotations from the Bible are from the Holy Bible, New International Version. Copyright © 1973, 1978, International Bible Society. Used by permission of Zondervan Bible Publishers.

ISBN 0-87784-606-5

Printed in the United States of America

Library of Congress Cataloguing in Publication Data

Jones, R. Tudur (Robert Tudur)
    The great Reformation

    Bibliography: p.
    Includes index.
    1. Reformation.   I. Title.
BR305.2.J66   1985   270.6   85-23930
ISBN 0-87784-606-5

| 16 | 15 | 14 | 13 | 12 | 11 | 10 | 9 | 8 | 7 | 6 | 5 | 4 | 3 | 2 | 1 |
| 99 | 98 | 97 | 96 | 95 | 94 | 93 | 92 | 91 | 90 | 89 | 88 | 87 | 86 | | |

Maps

Preface

This book is addressed to the Christian reader who wishes to know a little by way of introduction about the Protestant Reformation. Some of the characters that participate in the drama will already be known to such a reader but the majority of them will be unfamiliar. This should be a reminder that we are describing one of the greatest upheavals in the history of Christianity and an upheaval in which thousands of people were passionately interested at the time. And the story too will remind us that the traditional description of the upheaval as the 'Protestant Reformation', as though it were one closely integrated movement, can be quite misleading. The reformation of the church in the sixteenth century took many forms and there is much to be said for talking about the 'Protestant Reformations' – in the plural. Even that description may not be entirely accurate, for there were non-Protestant Reformations too.

The Christian reader will be on the watch as he reads for every sign that the Spirit of God was at work powerfully and creatively in the lives of sixteenth-century people. There were memorable episodes in the story of those days when Christianity was granted a new opportunity to affect European life. But it is wise also to notice how mixed people's reactions were to the opportunity offered. It was an age when little people did great things which provoked Christians to praise God; there were also many shameful and cruel things which tempt the most sanguine to despair of mankind. But it is part of the rich legacy of the Protestant Reformers that they have taught us in all things to appreciate that God rules and that ultimately all things promote his glory.

I am grateful to the staff of the Inter-Varsity Press for their kindness and patience while this book was being prepared and to my colleagues Professor E. Stanley John and Emeritus Professor Glanmor Williams for valuable assistance and enlightenment.

R. Tudur Jones

1 Roman Catholicism in crisis

St. Peter's bark is tempest-tossed,
I fear the vessel may be lost.

Sebastian Brant (1457–1521).

For many centuries the Roman Catholic Church had sought to realize the dream of a united Christendom. It saw the pope, the bishop of Rome, as the vicar of Jesus Christ upon earth. Since the spiritual must take precedence over the material, the pope could claim supreme authority in Christendom. He exercised a moral rule which bound every prince and every kingdom. Only slightly inferior to the pope was the Holy Roman Emperor who was the embodiment of the secular unity of the Christian world. And a succession of able philosophers and theologians, known as the Schoolmen, the greatest of whom was Thomas Aquinas (c. 1225–74), sought to bring the whole wealth of knowledge within the confines of a Christian system of ideas.

And any visitor to western Europe in the Middle Ages would have been impressed by the unity that had been achieved. The church buildings and the services held in them were very similar everywhere. The universal use of Latin facilitated communication. The clergy, the monks and the nuns were easily identified everywhere. The statues of saints, the shrines, the crosses, the pilgrimages and the devotions of ordinary people testified to a real unity in Christendom. But Christendom was not the solid and stable unity which it claimed to be. Within the external unity there was a complex and rich diversity, and the Roman Catholic Church did not embrace all Christians by any means – the Greek Orthodox and the Coptic Christians were beyond its bounds. But from 1350 onwards there were

ominous signs that the very foundations of Christendom
were disintegrating.

WARS AND RUMOURS OF WARS

First of all, Christendom was assaulted by appalling
disasters. Famine often stalked the countryside, as it did
with tragic consequences between 1315 and 1317. In 1347–8
the plague – the Black Death, killed about two-fifths of the
population of Europe. Incessant warfare demonstrated
man's brutality towards man. Only in 1453 did the Hundred Years' War between France and England end. In the
early years of the fifteenth century Wales was devastated
during Glyn Dŵr's War of Liberation, as was a large part.of
eastern Europe by the Hussite wars of 1419 to 1435. For
thirty years after 1455 England was torn apart by the Wars
of the Roses. And Christian Europe shuddered as it
received news of the advance of Islam into the Balkans after
the fall of Constantinople in 1453. It was little wonder that
the European imagination was haunted by terrible visions
of death and judgment. Dürer's *Four Horsemen of the Apoca-
lypse* gave memorable artistic expression to the nightmares
of millions. And it was not surprising that so much late
mediaeval piety, with its concern for requiem masses,
chantries and the buying of pardons, should be obsessively
centred on the dead.

THE DIFFICULTIES OF THE PAPACY

In 1309 Pope Clement V made Avignon his permanent
home. It is true that in the two previous centuries popes
had spent more time away from Rome than in it. But the
move to Avignon was different. It lasted seventy years and
became known as the 'Babylonian Captivity'. At that time
Avignon was not a part of the kingdom of France, but all
the popes who made their court there were Frenchmen and
the majority of the cardinals were also Frenchmen. The
impression was therefore given that the papacy was now
subservient to France.

Worse was to come. On 17 January 1377 Gregory XI
moved the papal court back to Rome. But he died in March
1378 and was succeeded by Urban VI. The eleven French

cardinals who had participated in his election soon repented of their action, retired to Fondi, and in September 1378 they elected a rival pope, Robert of Geneva, who took the title Clement VII and set up court at Avignon. So the Great Schism began, with two popes, two courts and two sets of cardinals. It was a severe blow to the ideal of a united Christendom, for the states of Europe aligned themselves behind the pope most likely to favour their individual interests.

Councils

It seemed that the only way to restore unity was by convening a general council. The two colleges of cardinals summoned such a council to meet at Pisa in March 1409. It deposed both the ruling popes and then elected a new one, Alexander V. But since the two reigning popes refused to accept the council's jurisdiction, the church now had three popes. Only after the Council of Constance, which was in session from 1414 to 1417, did unity return to the church. The ruling popes were deposed and Martin V elected on 11 November 1417.

The impression had now been given that general councils were more powerful than the popes. Long before this, Pope Innocent III (1198–1216) had proclaimed that the pope is 'set between God and man, lower than God but higher than man, who judges all and is judged by no one'. Such astonishing claims seemed hollow in the aftermath of the councils of Pisa and Constance. But there were thinkers who were prepared to challenge such high papal claims as a matter of principle. Thus, long before the Great Schism, John of Paris in his book, *On royal and papal power* (1302–3) had argued that both church and state are equal in sovereignty, each having its own restricted sphere. More radical was Marsilius of Padua (*c.* 1275–1342), author of one of the most remarkable of mediaeval books, the *Defender of the Peace*. He denied the right to use coercion in religious matters. Power, he argued, derives from the general body of citizens or believers. Thus the secular ruler derives his authority from his subjects, just as the pope derives his authority from the general body of the faithful. It followed logically from this conviction that a general council of Christian believers possessed an authority superior to that of the pope.

This was indeed explosive material, but even the men who had argued that only a council could heal the breach in the church did not propose to transform the papal monarchy into rule by permanent council. Despite the convening of several councils after the one at Constance, by 1450 conciliarism was dead and papalism had successfully reasserted itself.

A decadent papacy
The Roman Catholic Church, with its 700 dioceses, was a massive and powerful institution. The head of such an institution had at his service immense power, prestige and wealth. In constitutional matters, the fifteenth century popes had successfully repelled the challenge to their authority that came from councils. But in other ways the authority of the pope was being eroded. The popes were becoming increasingly embroiled in local Italian politics. Italians had an absolute majority among the cardinals from the time of Pius II (1458–64) onwards and these men were far more concerned about the fortunes of their families than with the welfare of the universal church. Half the popes between 1447 and 1517 had fathered illegitimate children and the papal court itself became a hotbed of conspiracies, plots and intrigues. And the moral degradation reached its lowest point in the person of Rodrigo Borgia – Alexander VI. At the same time, pope Nicholas V and his successors became munificent patrons of the arts. But again this served to show the secularization of the office and it illustrates how the service of the gospel played but a subsidiary role in the lives of these men.

THE BURDENS OF WEALTH

Pope John XXII (1316–34) had issued a number of bulls (official pronouncements) severely condemning the ideal of absolute poverty promoted by Francis of Assisi (1182–1226). Poverty, the pope taught, is to be understood in a spiritual sense, not as the literal renunciation of money and possessions. It was the kind of teaching that could be taken to justify ostentation among churchmen. Papal revenue came from two sources, the estates over which the pope ruled as prince, and the payments made to him by all the countries of Christendom for 'spiritual' services. Even so, the popes, almost without exception, were burdened with debts and new ways of raising revenue had to be devised, such as, for example, exploiting the new alum mines at Tulfa, selling indulgences, or selling offices of profit in the papal court for annuities. But despite all their financial difficulties, the princes of the church lived a life of splendour and luxury if they had access to fruitful sources of revenue. The trouble was that in order to secure such revenue it became the practice to combine benefices, emoluments and offices in the hands of one man. This was called 'pluralism' and, since no man can be in two places at once, it meant absenteeism. True enough, canon law insisted that the holder of a benefice should provide a substitute when he himself was absent, but this legal obligation was discharged very perfunctorily.

By the end of the Middle Ages the financial administration of the church was in chaos. At one end of the scale prelates enjoyed immense incomes while at the other there was abject poverty. Some idea of the variations in the value of dioceses may be gained from the fact that Winchester with an income of £3,880 was more than three times the value of the four Welsh dioceses put together, while the 138 dioceses of the kingdom of Naples were so poor that it would have required two hundred of them to produce an income equivalent to that of Winchester. There was very real hardship among parish clergy while the practice of pluralism meant that the pastoral and educative ministry of the church had all but collapsed in many parts of Europe.

A FAILING MINISTRY

Financial disorder and rapacity among the higher clergy, were not the only reasons for the failure of the church's ministry in the parishes. Very few resident curates in parishes had received any education. Attempts were made to improve the quality of training for these men, but in the main these were fruitless. And those who did graduate took their degrees in arts and in law rather than theology. This fitted men for administrative and legal posts rather than for providing enlightened teaching. And episcopal scrutiny of candidates for ordination was lax. Thus, for example, the curia at Rome conducted very large general ordinations, as when on 31 December 1471, 105 were given various orders in circumstances which made any effective screening of the candidates impossible. Of course, there were all over Europe men of great learning devoted to high ideals, but they were the exceptions and only rarely did their work affect the daily spiritual life of parishoners.

The church was also plagued by immorality. The papacy and the cardinals set an appalling standard. But it is clear that the Roman Catholic Church's insistence on celibacy, especially among unwilling people, created unnecessary moral scandals. Thus, towards the end of the fifteenth century in the diocese of Constance some 1,500 children were born annually to priests. The Church condoned their behaviour by exacting a cradle fee for each child and a concubinage fee from each offending clergyman.

The traditional system of discipline was subjected to strains that often rendered it ineffective. Thus the income of a monastery could be diverted to supplement the earnings of an absentee cleric. If that cleric was the nominal head of the house, upholding discipline was very difficult. Then again the practice of exempting monasteries from the jurisdiction of the local bishop often meant exemption from effective supervision. Thus, in England at the time of the dissolution of the monasteries there were 285 exempt houses.

All in all, the Roman Catholic Church, and the Christian faith itself, were facing a momentous crisis as the fifteenth century drew to a close.

2 Pioneers of reform

Finally, I entreat you all to persevere in the truth of God.

John Hus (1373–1415), in his last letter to his friends, 29 June 1415.

From 1350 onwards the church showed many alarming signs of decadence. Yet over the same period a deep desire for reform expressed itself in a variety of ways. The Conciliar Movement, which sought to restore the unity of the church under one pope, was an example of a concerted effort to reform Christendom. The work of Nicholas of Cusa (1401–64) illustrates the burning enthusiasm of an individual churchman. One of the ablest men of his age, he was made cardinal in 1448, and two years later became the pope's personal ambassador in Germany. From December 1450 to April 1452 he engaged in a vigorous campaign in Germany to remove abuses. His progress met with bitter, and sometimes violent, opposition. But he set the highest possible standards for the parish clergy, as well as for monks and nuns, and although his success was limited, he made it abundantly clear to the papacy that radical reform could not long be delayed.

REFORMING THE MONASTERIES

At their commencement, the monastic orders had been centres of reforming enthusiasm but decline set in and they fell on sad days. Yet there were among them people who cherished the high ideals of the original founders and worked hard to reassert them. One manifestation of this zeal for reform was the 'observantine' movement. Thus, from 1368 onwards, reforming Franciscans encouraged the formation of houses dedicated to the strict observance of their founder's rule. So there emerged two groups of

Franciscans, the Observants and the Conventuals. Similarly the Dominicans developed an Observant branch while the Augustinian monasteries of Germany and the Netherlands formed a Congregation of Reformed Augustinians, and it was to this order that Martin Luther belonged. Similarly, Windesheim, a house of Augustinian Canons founded in 1387, became the centre of a 'congregation' of houses which sought to maintain the highest possible ideals. Its members were often invited to initiate reform in decadent monasteries. As a result of these efforts, there were in many parts of Europe religious houses which were centres of good discipline and warm spirituality.

THE CONTRIBUTION OF LAY PEOPLE

A close relationship between state and church was one of the outstanding characteristics of the mediaeval period. Since the church wielded immense authority, kings and princes took an avid interest in church appointments within their realms. Gradually they secured effective influence, and sometimes outright control over such appointments. So it was in England where the first Statute of Provisors (1351) asserted the right of the Crown to present candidates to benefices. The kings of France also, from the time of Philip the Fair (1268–1314), were eager to weaken the pope's control over the church in their kingdom. Policies of this kind, of course, did lead to the appointment of royal favourites and to the generous use of leading churchmen in the service of the state. On the other hand, lay interest in the church did contribute to the removal of abuses. It was frustration at the inability of churchmen to put their house in order that moved the assembly of the French States-General at Tours in 1484 to put the reform of the church on its agenda. In Spain similarly the formidable Francisco Ximénez de Cisneros (1436–1517), Cardinal Archbishop of Toledo, overcame monastic opposition to his reforms not only by securing the co-operation of the pope but also by ensuring the unwavering support of King Ferdinand and Queen Isabella.

Lay discontent with the church was widespread but uneven. The financial demands of the church were felt to be excessive and the privileges that clergy enjoyed were considered unjustifiable. At Worms and Geneva in 1500 some one-tenth of the inhabitants were clergy, and they were immune both from taxation and the jurisdiction of the secular courts. One way in which lay people sought to supply the spiritual nourishment that was not provided by the clergy was by appointing public preachers. Effective and solid preaching was much appreciated. There was no more admired preacher in the period immediately before the Reformation than Johannes Geiler von Kaysersberg (1445–1510), whose preaching fascinated the citizens of Strasbourg. And he had high hopes that a thorough reform of the church was in the offing. The growing popularity of preaching was reflected in the readiness of well-to-do burghers in many European towns to endow preacherships. They felt that that was a more fruitful use of their money than to endow chantries. And it was also an indication that in the cities a demand was emerging for a more educative piety.

WYCLIF AND HUS

Most of the reform movements of the late mediaeval period assumed the validity of the doctrine and teaching of the church. With John Wyclif (1329–1384) we come to a writer whose significance lies in a grasp of principles that were to be adapted, clarified and amplified by the Protestant reformers. Wyclif was both a brilliant Oxford academic and a close associate of men in high places. His idiom is that of the mediaeval scholastic, but the content of his thinking entitles him to be called 'the morning star of the Reformation'. For him the Bible is an infallible authority, superior to the church and its traditions. And the Bible must be made accessible to the public – hence his interest in promoting English versions of the Bible. And no ordinance is of greater value in disseminating knowledge of the Bible than preaching. It follows that the church itself should be judged in the light of the New Testament. The true church of God consists of those predestined to eternal life, not necessarily those who claim membership in the visible church. One excellent proof of Christian calling is holiness of character and by this standard large numbers of clergy fail miserably. Wyclif argued for the dissolution of the monastic orders and severely criticized the papacy for the way in which it manipulated political power for unspiritual ends. He had sharp things to say about contemporary worship and the way in which images, pictures, the cult of the saints and of the Virgin Mary had been thoroughly debased. And as for the teaching that the merits of the saints formed a heavenly treasury, this was but a 'fantasy', while to assert that this treasury was at the disposal of the pope was, in his view, 'blasphemy'. His influence was to penetrate English religious life through the Lollard movement and was also to be indirectly influential at the other end of Europe, in Bohemia.

John Hus (1373–1415) was a native of southern Bohemia and was educated at the University of Prague. He was ordained in 1401 and the following year became rector of the university and preacher at the Bethlehem Chapel. Prague had been under the spell of the great reformist preaching of Conrad of Waldhausen from 1360 to 1369, Jan Milic from then until 1374, and Matthew of Janow, who died in 1394. Hus entered into this dynamic tradition. In 1401 Jerome of Prague (c. 1371–1416) returned from Oxford bringing copies of Wyclif's books with him. Hus became a great admirer of Wyclif's views and at first Archbishop Zbinek of Prague gave him his support. But sympathy gave place to repression and in July 1410 Hus was excommunicated and his views condemned. He clung to his convictions and had to retire from public life, but this gave him the opportunity to produce his most significant book, *The Church*, which was finished in July 1413. He looked forward to the opportunity to defend his views before a wider public and so rejoiced when summoned to present them at the Council of Constance. He arrived at the city on 3 November 1414, fortified with a safe-conduct that had been issued by the Emperor Sigismund. But the safe-conduct was not honoured and Hus was arrested and brought to trial the following June. On 6 July 1415 he was declared a heretic and handed over to the secular power for punishment and that afternoon he was burnt at the stake. On 30 May 1416 his compatriot, Jerome of Prague, suffered the same fate at the hands of the council. Hus's death was particularly ironic because he had held that the church had no right to punish heresy with death – and, in any case,

Hus did not for a moment consider himself a heretic. Spiritual authority rests not in an earthly institution but in the whole body of believers destined to eternal life. Like Wyclif, Hus preserves a strong moral emphasis and argues that the immorality of a priest invalidates the sacrament which he administers. Hus also emphasizes the supreme authority of Scripture. Yet he did not reject transubstantiation, that is, the teaching that the substance of the bread and wine in communion are changed into the body and blood of Christ at the words of consecration. His was a mediating position as is shown by the fact that Luther, when writing to Spalatin in February 1520, said, 'Without knowing it I both taught and held the teaching of Hus: in short, we were all Hussites without knowing it'. It is interesting to note that for over a century voices have been raised in the Roman Catholic Church demanding a reconsideration of the verdict delivered against him at Constance.

VIGOROUS DISSENT

The story of the Waldenses is a noble one. The movement was founded in the twelfth century by Valdés, a merchant of Lyon in France, who parted with his wealth and became an itinerant preacher. He died in Bohemia in 1217. His followers gradually increased and became the most widespread of mediaeval dissenting movements. It was little wonder that they were subjected to prolonged and vicious persecution. They emphasized the value of the simple life and adherence to a strict morality. For them, the Roman Catholic Church had forfeited the right to be considered the true church because of its luxury, its institutionalism and its compromises with the world, and so its sacraments had become invalid. The Waldenses rejected the cult of the saints, prayers for the dead and belief in purgatory. Above all they were animated by a resilient faith in God. When they heard of the Protestant Reformation they realized that here was a movement which gave powerful expression to the testimony for which they had suffered over many generations, and so it became the oldest of the mediaeval evangelical movements to join the company of the Protestant churches.

Towards the end of the fifteenth century other vigorous movements were seeking renewal. To these we must now turn.

3 Signs of renewal

I see a golden age dawning in the near future.

Desiderius Erasmus (c. 1469-1536).

By the end of the fifteenth century there were rising hopes in many quarters that a Christian revival was at hand.

Sometimes these hopes took a dramatic form and were closely linked with a belief that history was moving towards a cataclysmic climax. Such was the movement associated with Girolamo Savonarola (1452-98). He was a product of the Observant movement among the Dominicans, and after his migration to the priory of San Marco in Florence in 1482 his fierce demands for strict asceticism began to attract public attention. From Lent 1491 onwards his preaching combined a prophetic emphasis on the near approach of the day of God's vengeance with stern calls to moral reformation. His reputation as a prophet was enhanced when his dire predictions seemed to be fulfilled in the fall of Lorenzo the Magnificent and the French invasion of Italy in 1494-5. The Florentines seemed to be overwhelmed with a spirit of repentance when they destroyed large quantities of their luxury articles in the 'burning of the vanities'. But Savonarola's popular support soon faded when Pope Alexander VI proceeded against him. He was put on trial, condemned to death and burnt. His brave and colourful career was a paradigm of the fate that awaited even a thoroughly medieval reformer in the Italy of 1498.

PRACTICAL PIETY

Dramatic protests were not the idiom of the Modern Devotion; it concentrated rather on the quality of spiritual life. Its founder was Geert Groote (1340-84) although it was his disciples and admirers who organized the movement. A

group of clerics intent on following a communal life formed
communities, first at Deventer and then at Windesheim.
The Brethren of the Common Life, as they came to be
called, were especially interested in the pastoral care of
schoolboys and established hostels at various centres of
learning to offer this service. The flavour of the piety promoted by the Brethren was distilled into Thomas á
Kempis's classic, *The Imitation of Christ*, written at the monastery of St Agnietenberg, near Zwolle, where Thomas
spent virtually all his time from 1399 to 1471 when he died.
The Modern Devotion sought a deeper and more Christo-
centric spirituality based on a firm commitment to the Bible.
Its adherents had little patience with any form of learning
that did not serve this purpose and it is a mistake to think of
the Brethren as patrons of humanism. With one or two
exceptions, the Brethren did not themselves teach in
schools nor did they directly support schools. Nor did their
type of piety find its fruition in Protestantism. It was the
spirituality of the mediaeval monastery made more
accessible to people generally, but there was in it little of
the concern for producing an attractive and viable lay piety
which was later to become so prominent among Protestants.

Groote had been a student of the work of Meister Eckhart
(*c*.1260–*c*.1327), but later reacted against the views of that
notable mystic. Mysticism has always been given an
honourable place in Roman Catholic spirituality, and the
mystical tradition continued into the fifteenth century in
the work of men like John Gerson (1363–1429) and Nicholas
of Cusa (1401–64). Luther, in his early years as a reformer,
thought highly of the work of another mystic, John Tauler
(*c*.1300–61). But there is a distinct difference between
Luther's spiritual man, born of faith alone, and the spiritual
man as described by men like Gerson and Tauler, who
carries in himself a divine kernel which, despite sin, sus-
tains man's connection with the divine. The spirituality of
the Modern Devotion, and that of the great mystical tradition, found its fruition in the piety of the Roman Catholic
Reformation rather than in Protestant piety.

THE ACID OF UNCERTAINTY

In the fifteenth century there were hundreds of thousands of people in Europe who panted for a relevant spirituality and a dynamic theology to lighten the darkness of their lives. The failure of the church to meet this passionate yearning was the most significant single factor in preparing the way for the Prostestant Reformation. Even so, the Protestant Reformation could not have made its contribution to alleviating people's spiritual hunger were it not for its radical gospel message. Revivals, after all, do not occur in a social or psychological vacuum. The fifteenth century without any doubt was a pious age. In a world harried by demons and dominated by terrible plagues and natural disasters that were attributed to the vengeance of a wrathful God, people felt a desperate need to seek help from the vast company of saints, and especially the Virgin Mary. Relics were reverenced. One had to go on pilgrimages to visit their shrines, to say appropriate prayers and to make suitable offerings. Loved ones, when they died, did not move into a realm of peace but into purgatory where they would suffer purifying torments over vast periods of time. It was a relief, people felt, to buy an indulgence or pay for a requiem mass which, so the ecclesiastical experts said, would shorten their stay in the flames. With the mediaeval belief in purgatory went a desperate obsession with death. Death was not, as it was to be later for Bunyan, a crossing of the last river to the sound of heavenly trumpets, but rather an initiation into centuries of agony. The rich could leave money for thousands of masses to be said for the repose of their souls. But what of the poor? It seemed as though their poverty in this world was to be punished in the next.

Shot through this pathetic piety was a deep uncertainty. Did these various prescriptions for alleviating the lot of the departed really work? Purgatory had to do with sin and its temporal punishment. The church claimed that it had authority to mediate forgiveness through the sacrament of penance. Sin needed to be confessed to the priest and, at his suggestion, repentance could be manifested by a money offering, or the recitation of prayers, or abstention from some luxury, or, if the matter were more serious, by a pilgrimage to Canterbury or Compostella or Jerusalem. But did such actions really secure God's forgiveness?

Another question was whether any kind of secular life was worth living at all. Good people insisted that only monks, nuns and clerics lived a life that was really pleasing to God. There was an unremitting denigration of lay life. It was widely suspected that the craftsman and the labourer, as well as the lawyer and the banker, lived a life that was inferior to that of the clergy. Family life itself was under a cloud because of the widespread conviction that God preferred people to be virgins. From all these questions it became evident that by the fifteenth century the means which the church had developed to deal with spiritual distress were, in fact, making it more acute. A new piety, firmly rooted in the New Testament, was desperately needed.

CHRISTIAN HUMANISM

Some of the humanists had sensed this. They felt that a new age was dawning and that the era of superstition and fear was ending. The French humanist, François Rabelais (c.1495–1553), expressed their sense of relief when he exclaimed, 'Thank God we are out of the Gothic night'. The humanists sought to simplify Christianity, to exalt reason, to emphasize morality rather than ritual. Their authority for engaging in such a programme was the original charter of Christianity – the New Testament. Desiderius Erasmus (c.1469–1536) was the most distinguished exponent of this vision. This illegitimate son of a Dutch priest became a scholar of international repute, flattered by popes, princes and universities as a sage and prophet. In 1516 he published his critical edition of the Greek New Testament, a momentous event in the history of biblical scholarship because it was a necessary tool for anyone who wished to penetrate beyond the Vulgate, the Latin translation of the Bible which was the official version of the Roman Catholic Church. Erasmus also prepared editions of the works of the early Christian fathers, a labour which made it possible for scholars to compare the church as they knew it with the church as it existed in the first three centuries. He also showed his prowess as a writer for a more extensive public in his *Praise of Folly*, wittily exposing human weakness and vice, while in his *Colloquies* he brilliantly castigated the superstitions of popular piety. In a more serious vein, he offered a guide to Christian living in his *Enchiridion*.

Erasmus, then, was a reformer, but a careful one. He much prized the patronage of the rich and great. He tried to provide his readers with a historical picture of Jesus and a lucid account of real Christianity as he understood it. For Erasmus, Jesus is the pattern whom we should emulate. Christianity is not a matter of performing mechanical acts of devotion nor yet of building imposing castles in the air in the manner of the Schoolmen. Christianity is a simple thing. It is following Jesus in a spirit of love and tolerance. The church needs to be cleansed of all those accretions that have obscured the original simplicity of its message. And this can be done by persuasion and education.

For a time Erasmus's influence was immense. In England, his friends, John Colet (*c*.1467–1519), Dean of St Paul's and Thomas More (1478–1535), were in warm sympathy with his aspirations. In France, he was admired by Guillaume Budé (1468–1540) and Lefèvre d'Étaples (1455–1529). In Spain, Cardinal Ximénez was one of his most ardent patrons. In Germany and in Holland Erasmus's influence had a crucial contribution to make in the development of both Protestantism and reforming Roman Catholicism.

Distinguished and influential as Erasmus was, his was not the only form of Christian humanism. In Germany, humanists like Rudolf Agricola (1444–85) and Conrad Celtis (1459–1508) combined their enthusiasm for the classical world of Greece and Rome with a deep interest in the German past. Similarly in Wales, William Salesbury (*c*.1520–*c*.1584), a typical humanist polymath, combined classical study with a renewed commitment to his native Welsh. Nor was the Old Testament and the Hebrew past forgotten. The notorious Reuchlin affair ensured that critics of Hebrew learning would be dismissed as obscurantist fools. Reuchlin (1455–1522) was Germany's foremost Hebrew scholar. When a converted Jew, Pfefferkorn, developed acute symptoms of anti-Semitism and demanded the destruction of all Hebrew books, his views, to the great alarm of the humanists, were endorsed by the emperor.

Reuchlin disagreed with such a policy and when he was viciously attacked for his views, he defended his reputation in a collection of commendatory testimonials, *Epistles of Distinguished Men*. This was followed by a spoof under the title *Letters of Obscure Men*, composed without Reuchlin's connivance by two young humanists, Crotus Rubeanus and Ulrich von Hutten. It was a merciless attack on mediaeval obscurantism.

Humanist groups became a feature of life in many countries and not least in Germany. There was a group at Nuremberg led by Willibald Pirckheimer (1470–1530), and one at Strasbourg of which Sebastian Brant (1457–1521), the author of the *Ship of Fools*, and Jacob Wimpfeling (1450–1528) were active members.

Humanism was an ambivalent movement. It provided the Protestant Reformers with significant intellectual equipment. But its fundamental convictions were very different from those of the leading Reformers. Humanism was an élitist movement with a strong faith in the mediaeval principle that men will achieve bliss and heaven if they do their best and follow the light of reason. The Protestant Reformation was a frightening experience for many humanists. It compelled them to choose. Many joined the various Protestant movements while others preferred to remain in the Roman Church. But even that choice proved tragic for Erasmus and his followers because when the Roman Catholic Reformation came, it had no place for him and his ideals. In 1559 Pope Paul IV put all Erasmus's works on the *Index* (of forbidden books).

So the stage was set for a spiritual upheaval more momentous and more radical than any that had been proposed by mediaeval and humanist reformers.

4 The gate of paradise

Now I felt as though I had been reborn altogether and had entered Paradise.

Martin Luther (1483–1546).

Luther is one of the most fascinating of Christian leaders. His character and career abound in striking contrasts. He was proud of his Saxon peasant roots, yet his voice echoed in the ears of princes. He never tired of emphasizing the freedom of the Christian man and yet he himself was so wedded to the routine of daily life that he hardly missed a lecture in thirty years. Kings, princes and popes were shaken by his writings, but he never met his own prince, the Elector Frederick. He had a European reputation, but apart from a journey or two, he spent his whole life in a small area of Germany, 'on the edge of civilisation', as he put it. No one expressed with greater urgency the belief that human diligence can contribute nothing to salvation, yet he himself was a man of phenomenal industry, immersed in preaching, teaching, writing letters, and publishing books and pamphlets at the rate of one a fortnight for a quarter of a century.

Martin Luther was born on 10 November 1483 at Eisleben, the eldest of the seven children of Hans and Margaret Luther. In the Spring of 1484 the family moved to Mansfeld and Hans Luther became a successful industrialist. In 1489 young Martin began his education at the Latin School, next to St George's Church in the city centre of Mansfeld. About Easter 1497 he was moved to a school at Magdeburg where he lodged in a hostel maintained by the Brethren of the Common Life. By 1498 he was attending a school at Eisenach. At these schools he was provided with the necessary qualifications to undertake a university career.

In April 1501, Luther matriculated at the University of

TOWNS OF LUTHER'S GERMANY

GERMANY

R. Elbe

R. Rhine

Hannover

Berlin

Magdeburg
Jüterbog
Wittenberg
Torgau

Eisleben
Eisenach
Erfurt
Leipzig
Dresden

Cologne
Bonn
Marburg
Schmalkalden
Zwickau

R. Elbe

Frankfurt
Coburg

Mainz
Worms
Heidelberg

Speyer
Nuremberg

Strasbourg
Stuttgart
Regensburg

Augsburg
Munich

R. Rhine

Basel

SWITZERLAND

AUSTRIA

0   50
Miles

Erfurt, a distinguished seat of learning. He was an assiduous student and graduated B.A. in 1502 and M.A. in 1505.

His father hoped that Martin would prepare himself for a lucrative career in the world and so, in May 1505 the young graduate registered for a course in the Faculty of Law at Erfurt. Then came an astounding change of direction; the budding lawyer became a monk. What drove him into the monastery? Later accounts of the spiritual shock that made a monk of him are not easily reconciled in detail. There is no doubt that there was a frightening experience at the heart of it, for in an open letter to his father in *Concerning monastic vows* (1521) he asserted that 'walled around with the terror and agony of sudden death I vowed a constrained and necessary vow'. He suffered an accident on 16 April 1503 when he slipped not far from Erfurt and his dagger pierced his leg. The severe bleeding that continued while his friend ran for help drove him in desperation to cry to the Virgin, 'Help, Mary'. And it may well be that the vow he had so hurriedly made was brought vividly to his mind on 2 July 1505 when he was driven into such a panic by a thunderstorm at Stotternheim, near Erfurt, that he cried, 'Help, St. Anne, and I will become a monk'. He felt he must fulfil the vow and so, having sold all his books, he entered the cloister on 17 July 1505. It was the house of the Augustinian Eremites, an order of mendicant friars belonging to the reformed congregation which a century or so previously had dedicated itself to a strict observance of the rule.

LIFE IN THE MONASTERY

After a year's probation, Luther made formal profession as a monk in September 1506. He was told to prepare himself for ordination and was duly ordained deacon in February 1507 and priest in April. On the occasion of celebrating his first mass, a memorable day in the life of a priest, he had to face his father for the first time since becoming a monk. His father made an impressive showing, accompanied by an escort of twenty horsemen and making a handsome donation to the monastery. When Martin sought to explain to him what heavenly signs had driven him into the cloister,

Hans Luther expressed his doubts and reminded his son that there was a commandment which said, 'Honour thy father and thy mother'. His first mass behind him, Luther settled down to the routine of monastic life and to advanced study. Then suddenly, in October 1508, he was transferred to the Augustinian monastery at Wittenberg to help Johann von Staupitz by lecturing on Aristotle. It was at this time too that he took his first theological qualification, the *Baccalaureus Biblicus*. Then in the Autumn of 1509 he returned to Erfurt to lecture on the standard textbook of theology, the *Sentences* of Peter Lombard (c.1100–60).

Luther at both Erfurt and Wittenberg belonged to Augustinian monasteries that had accepted reform. There was tension between this type of monastery and those which were unreformed. The Vicar-General of the Reformed Augustinians, Johann von Staupitz (1469?–1524) had persuaded the pope to issue a bull sanctioning the union of the two branches. But Erfurt was opposed to the merger and sent Luther, together with Johann Nathin, to present objections to the Archbishop of Magdeburg. That availed nothing, so Luther was sent on the same mission to Rome. Luther's stay there was very brief, perhaps no more than three weeks. 'In Rome I was a frantic saint', he wrote later. 'I ran through all the churches and catacombs and believed everything, their lies and falsehood.' The visit left an indelible scar on his heart. 'Godlessness and evil are great and shameless there. Neither God nor man, neither sin nor modesty, are respected'.

In the Autumn of 1511 he migrated once again from Erfurt to Wittenberg and soon began his career as a preacher, exercising his gift among his fellow-monks. In May 1512 he was appointed sub-prior of the monastery. Staupitz was overwhelmed by his monastic duties and wished to retire from his chair as Professor of Biblical Studies. He wanted Luther to be his successor. In order to be qualified for this post Luther was graduated Doctor in Theology on 19 October 1512, and throughout his life he believed that his doctorate conferred upon him the responsibility to proclaim and defend God's truth. At 6 a.m., Tuesday, 16 August 1513, he began his first series of lectures as a professor, and chose as his text the book of Psalms.

THE GREAT STRUGGLE

Luther had joined the monastery to save his soul by attaining the perfection which would please God. He observed the laws of his order to the letter and added further discipline of his own. He fasted for days, spent sleepless nights in prayer and whipped himself. But peace of mind eluded him. The more he tried, the further he felt from pleasing God.

He had been taught that in baptism the believer had been granted free and full forgiveness and after that the Christian, with the assistance of sacramental grace, must strive to do good acts that will gain merit before God. Again and again, mediaeval theologians had emphasized the principle, 'Do what you can'. Even the slightest effort, they said, would bring an access of divine grace. With the assistance of this grace a greater effort became possible and the greater the effort, the greater the grace granted. And this grace was dispensed by the church through its sacraments. For the soul, weary with the struggle against sin, the sacrament of penance was especially helpful. Full confession to the priest would lead to absolution and so to release from the guilt of sin. Of course, satisfaction had to be made for the temporal debt that sin entails, and that meant the performance of some sacrificial act. The penitent should have no anxiety about the sufficiency of the spiritual benefits at the disposal of the church. Jesus Christ, the Virgin Mary and the saints had produced such a superabundance of good works that their merits were infinite. The pope had this Treasury of Merits at his disposal and through indulgences and the sacrament of penance he was able to supplement the meagre merit of the penitent sinner. It seemed that with such assurances there was no room for anxiety.

With Luther, however, it was quite otherwise. 'Do what you can', said the textbooks. But what could he do to please the holy God? So holy and majestic is God that the sinner cannot do even the simplest act without revealing that he is a sinner. And so Luther felt himself to be confronted by the wrath of God in all its intensity. God pursued him with terrors and trials, and to the sinner in this predicament 'it seems that he is alone: God is angry with only him, and

irreconcilably angry against him.' Where was a gracious
God to be found?

Luther turned to his superior, Staupitz, whose patience
and good humour most helped him when everyone else
had been driven to exasperation. And even more helpful to
the anxious monk was his theological emphasis on the
value to the sinner of the work done by Christ in fulfilling
the terms of God's covenant with man. It is not God who is
angry with you, he told Luther, but you are angry with
God. Trust God's forgiveness and throw yourself upon
Christ, he said. But in the end he could not understand
Luther's anguish. Even so, he put Luther on the path
which led to the light by urging him to study the Bible
closely. And it was the Bible that spoke to Luther's condition.

It was the thought of God's utter righteousness that had
driven him to despair. How then could the Psalmist in
Psalm 31:1 beseech God 'deliver me in your righteousness'?
Even more mysterious was Paul's confident assertion (in
Romans 1:17) that God's righteousness is revealed in the
gospel. If this 'righteousness' was that implacable justice in
the presence of which sinful Martin Luther was reduced to
stark terror, how could the gospel be good news if it
revealed that same justice to a sinful world? But Paul, he
noticed, adds that the just shall live by faith. But if a person
is just, he can rely upon his good actions. He lives in virtue
of his own righteousness; he is in every way acceptable to
the just God. But Luther came to see that the sinner relies
not on his own good actions but on the mercy of God
whereby the believing man is considered just through Jesus
Christ. As Luther himself described the moment of
illumination,

> what Paul means is this: the righteousness of God,
> revealed in the Gospel, is *passive*, in other words that by
> which the merciful God justifies us through faith, as it is
> written, 'The righteous will live by faith!' At this I felt
> myself straightway born afresh and to have entered
> through the open gates into Paradise itself.

When did this illumination happen? This question has
provoked a lively and fascinating controversy in which

scholars have suggested a variety of dates extending from 1508 to 1519. Indeed, the words just quoted come from a fragment of autobiography which Luther wrote in 1545 and there he dates the turning point in 1519. The difficulty with such a late date is that he was expounding the essential nature of justification by faith alone in the Commentary on Romans which was composed in 1515–16. Luther admitted that it was only gradually that Scripture yielded its meaning to him, for he was not one of those who 'with one glance at Scripture exhausted the total spirit of its contents'. So it was over a period of years that he gradually developed the full wealth of his evangelical theology and its key concept of justification by faith alone. As a result we may never discover precisely when the crucial discovery was made.

What we can be certain of is that in those years of spiritual struggle in the monastery Martin Luther was developing the evangelical theology that was to shake western Christendom to its foundations.

5 True forgiveness

36. Any Christian whatsoever who is truly repentant has, as his due, plenary remission from penalty and guilt, even without letters of indulgence.

Martin Luther, *Ninety-five Theses* (1517).

On the eve of All Saints' Day, 31 October 1517, about noon, Luther, accompanied by his friend, John Agricola (1494–1566), walked from his monastery at one end of Wittenberg to the Castle Church at the other and there nailed a Latin poster on the door. The door was the public notice-board and the poster was an invitation to a debate on the ninety-five topics listed. Dr. Martin Luther would preside. The debate was not held as intended but before many months had passed thousands of people all over Europe were engaged in animated argument about the topics, for within a fortnight printed copies of the poster had been distributed by Johann Grunenberg, Luther's printer, and translated for those who could not read Latin. So was the memorable document, the *Disputation on the power and efficacy of Indulgences*, or, more popularly, *The Ninety-five Theses*, launched.

It was pastoral concern that moved Luther to act. People had come to make their confessions to him but showed no signs of sincere repentance for their sins. On the contrary, they produced copies of indulgences that they had bought and obviously thought of them as licences to sin with impunity. Luther declined to grant them absolution.

An indulgence, or letter of pardon, was by this time a printed certificate setting out the spiritual benefits conveyed through it on the authority of the pope and declaring how these benefits could be got. The particular indulgence that provoked Luther to act had been announced by Pope Julius II in 1510 and revived by Pope Leo X. Leo had appointed Albert, the archbishop of Mainz (1490–1545), chief commissioner to promote the sale of the indulgence in parts of Germany and since he was deep in debt to the pope, it was agreed that he should have half the proceeds. The other half was to go to the pope to help pay for the magnificent new basilica of St. Peter's in Rome. In his instructions to the pardon-sellers Albert extolled the graces available to those who bought the indulgence. It secured 'complete remission of all sins', ensured 'participation in all the possessions of the Church universal', its petitions, intercessions and prayers, and the benefits of this indulgence extended, on payment of an appropriate sum of money, to souls in purgatory. The man who sold the indulgence in the area nearest Wittenberg was the Dominican, Johann Tetzel (c.1465–1519), whose crude oratory was especially offensive to Luther. The Elector of Saxony had prohibited the sale of the indulgence in his territory but Tetzel was able to come to Juterbog which was sufficiently near for the people of Wittenberg to go over the border to buy the letters of pardon which so incensed Luther. He wrote to Albert of Mainz on 31 October 1517, enclosing a copy of his theses, and protesting vigorously about the instructions he had given to the pardon-sellers. It was a grave offence to teach people that salvation could be bought and sins forgiven through letters of pardon even if such sins included 'reviling the blessed mother of God'. It was no less a perversion of truth to teach simple people that 'the moment the money jingles in the box souls are delivered from purgatory'. Such assertions were not figments of Luther's imagination; he was echoing the words used by Tetzel when he commended the indulgence to the public.

The Ninety-five Theses challenged the presuppositions, the validity and the wisdom of the trade in indulgences. A true Christian who is truly repentant has remission from both the guilt and penalty of sin because he participates in the benefits of Christ (Theses 16–17). He has no need of letters of pardon and it is misleading to teach that buying indulgences is a good act when it is manifestly better to give the money to the poor (Theses 41–5). At most the pope can only remit punishments imposed by the church during this mortal life (Theses 20, 21, 24, 25); his authority cannot

possibly extend beyond the grave to purgatory (Theses
13–19, 22, 25). In any case, 'The Pope can remit no guilt,
but only declare and confirm that it has been remitted by
God . . .' (Thesis 6). Nor is there any such thing as a
treasury of the accumulated merits of the saints. The 'true
treasure of the Church is the holy Gospel of the glory and
the grace of God' (Thesis 62). And there is no more pointed
question in the theses than that in Thesis 82, if the pope can
release souls from purgatory for the payment of money,
➤ 'Why does not the Pope empty purgatory for the sake of
most holy love and the supreme need of souls?' It is a
fundamental mistake, says Luther, to suppose that the
burden of the uneasy conscience is thrown off by performing what the church calls penance. Jesus, says the first
thesis, did not say, 'Do penance', as the Latin Vulgate
translation has it, but, 'Repent' and by that he meant 'the
whole life of believers should be one of penitence'. It was a
very grave matter indeed that sinners should be lured into a
false security by the pardon-sellers. 'All those who believe
themselves certain of their own salvation because of letters
of pardon, will be eternally damned, together with their
teachers' (Thesis 32).

The theses were not intended to be a theological dis-
quisition; they were topics for debate. So Luther confined
himself to specific points. He does not challenge the doctrine of purgatory. He does not question the scriptural basis
of the sacrament of penance. He does not demand the
abolition of indulgences. Nor does he mention faith and
justification. But Luther's *Explanations of the Ninety-five
Theses*, published in August 1518, show how the theses are
deeply influenced by his evangelical principles, as when he
writes,

> And this is the confidence that Christians have and our
> real joy of conscience, that by means of faith our sins
> become no longer ours but Christ's upon whom God
> placed the sins of all of us. He took upon himself our sins
> . . . All the righteousness of Christ becomes ours . . . He
> spreads his cloak and covers us . . .

GROWING CONTROVERSY

Tetzel was infuriated by the theses and issued 106 counter-
theses, and Luther answered in his *Sermon on Indulgence and
Grace*. Far more formidable than Tetzel was John Eck (1486–
1543), professor of theology at Ingolstadt. He published an
attack on Luther under the title *Obelisks* to which the reformer replied in his *Asterisks*.

Meanwhile Luther had to attend the triennial meeting of
the General Chapter of the Augustinians at Heidelberg. It
was to begin on 25 April 1518. The Pope's first reaction to
the controversy over indulgences was to dismiss it lightly
as a typical quarrel among monks. He had now changed
his tune and commanded the General of the Augustinians,
Gabriel della Volta, to bring his monks to heel. He had
passed the message to Johann von Staupitz, Luther's
superior, but Staupitz took the view that it would be good
for the friars to hear what the new evangelical views were.
Hence Luther's appearance at Heidelberg on 26 April with
28 theses for debate. Short as the theses are, they are
extremely significant. He attacks the scholastic principle
that salvation begins with 'doing what in us lies'. On the
contrary, says Luther, while 'a person is doing what is in
him, he sins and seeks himself in everything'. This should
not cause despair for the Law is intended to humble a
sinner and to drive him to the grace of Christ. Some suppose that by their own efforts they can raise themselves to
see God in his glory. But the way to salvation involves
confronting God in the weakness and humanity of Jesus
Christ. 'For this reason true theology and recognition of
God are in the crucified Christ . . .' 'He who does not know
Christ does not know God hidden in suffering' and such a
person 'prefers works to suffering, glory to the cross,
strength to weakness, wisdom to folly, and, in general,
good to evil.' Man does not have an independent standing
before God and 'sinners are attractive because they are
loved; they are not loved because they are attractive.' So
Luther's remarkable 'Theology of the Cross' emerged into
the light of day at the Heidelberg disputation and takes its
place alongside his understanding of law and gospel,
righteousness and faith, human sin and the divine
initiative, in the fabric of his evangelical thinking.

ROMAN DIPLOMACY

Rome did not approve of Staupitz's leniency. On 7 August 1518 Luther received a citation summoning him to Rome. On the 23rd the Pope ordered his ambassador to Germany, Cardinal Thomas Cajetan (*c.* 1465–1534) to arrest Luther. As so often in this story, the demands of politics halted theological controversy. The Pope was eager to ensure the support of the Elector Frederick, Luther's prince, in his campaign to prevent Charles of Spain from succeeding his grandfather, Maximilian, as Holy Roman Emperor. So it seemed politic to the Pope to flatter Frederick by having Luther's case heard by Cajetan on German soil. This could be conveniently arranged since the Imperial Diet was meeting that Autumn at Augsburg.

Luther reached Augsburg on 7 October 1518, tired and ill. On the 12th he had his first interview with Cajetan and it soon became clear that accommodation was impossible. Cajetan demanded unqualified submission; Luther demanded a fair hearing by an impartial tribunal. With the connivance of Staupitz who took the precaution of absolving Luther from his monastic vows and so releasing him from the solemn promise to render absolute obedience to Staupitz, Luther slipped out of Augsburg secretly on the night of 20 October and made for Nuremberg on a borrowed horse. Luther was in extreme peril and he daily expected to hear that he had been excommunicated. Much depended on the attitude of the Elector Frederick. If he withdrew his patronage, Luther would have to flee Wittenberg. But the Elector made it clear that Luther would not be evicted out of the Electorate of Saxony to please anyone.

A new attempt was made by Rome to subdue Luther. The pompous Saxon noble, Charles von Miltitz (*c.*1490–1529) was sent as a special envoy to confer the coveted distinction of the Golden Rose upon Frederick and to cajole Luther into submission. But the interviews which began on 5 January 1519 proved quite fruitless. And there was an ominous turn to international events. On 12 January 1519 the Emperor Maximilian died and in due course his grandson, Charles V, was elected in his place. The papacy now had no further need of the good offices of the Elector of Saxony.

PUBLIC DEBATE AT LEIPZIG

There was one man in Germany who believed that he could overcome Luther and that was John Eck (1486–1543). He had challenged Luther's colleague, Andrew Bodenstein (1480–1541), usually known from his birthplace as Carlstadt, to debate. Eck published his theses in December 1518 and the debate opened at the Pleissenburg Palace, Leipzig, on 27 June 1519. During the first week Eck argued with Carlstadt and got the better of him. During the second week he faced Luther to debate the primacy of the pope. By some clever manoeuvring Eck got Luther to admit that at least some of the views held by Hus were Christian even though they had been condemned by the Council of Constance. Luther was disappointed at his own performance and confided to George Spalatin (1482–1545), the Elector's secretary, that the debate 'began badly and ended worse'. Eck, he believed, had carried the day completely. But Luther's pessimism was premature. Eck's victory was superficial while Luther's leadership was confirmed as he realized that he did after all stand in the tradition of Hus and that the Bible provided him with the authority to challenge the pretensions of the papacy and of church councils.

The struggle was but beginning.

6   The unforgettable stand

My conscience is captive to the Word of God.

Martin Luther, at Worms, 18 April 1521.

The Leipzig debate triggered off an extensive pamphlet warfare which revealed the bitterness of the opposition and the rapidity with which Luther's views were spreading. It also drove Luther to study with renewed intensity the implications of his standpoint. September 1519 saw the publication of his commentary on *Galatians*, with its powerful exposition of the nature of saving faith. By February 1520 he had realized the implications of the critical work done by Lorenzo Valla (1407–57) on the *Donation of Constantine*, one of the documents used by the papacy to justify its temporal government. Valla showed that these were forgeries and that there had been no transference of sovereignty from Constantine the Great to the Pope, as the documents alleged. Luther by now had come to realize that the breach with Rome could not long be delayed.

The year 1520 was to prove a momentous one in his career. On 15 June the papal bull, *Exsurge Domine*, was signed. It bewailed the pestiferous heresies that were being disseminated in Germany and listed forty-two articles allegedly taught by Luther contrary to Roman Catholic truth. The faithful were urged to take every possible action to curb the evil and Luther himself was given sixty days in which to retract his views. He did not do so and on 3 January 1521 the bull of excommunication, *Decet Romanum*, was published.

While Rome was thus preparing to purge itself of its troublesome reformer, Luther was consolidating his evangelical position. In June 1520 he published the *Treatise on Good Works*, which introduced a fundamental change into the understanding of Christian morality and gave a new dignity to the everyday life of the layman. The church had distinguished between those 'religious' good works, such as going on pilgrimages or buying indulgences, which were especially pleasing to God, and other good works. Luther argued that there is no biblical justification whatsoever for such a distinction. All the good works demanded by the Ten Commandments are equally pleasing to God if performed through faith in Christ.

THE REFORMATION MANIFESTOS

Germany had many grievances against the papacy and Luther's friends at Wittenberg pressed him to give public voice to them. This he did in his appeal *To the Christian Nobility of the German Nation concerning the Reform of the Christian Estate*. It was published in August 1520. The papacy, he asserted, has sought to protect its privileges by surrounding itself with three walls, namely, the teaching that 'the spiritual power is above the temporal', the dogma 'that only the pope may interpret the Scriptures', and, 'if threatened with a council, their story is that no one may summon a council but the pope'. In demolishing these three walls, he flatly denied the distinction between priests and laymen, 'except for the sake of office and work', otherwise 'all Christians are truly of the spiritual estate'. As for the second wall, not a single letter of Scripture gives the pope a monopoly over its interpretation. The Holy Spirit is given to pious hearts and so all Christians are priests and well fitted to judge what is 'right or wrong in matters of faith' on the basis of Scripture. It follows that Christians who exercise temporal power are perfectly entitled to seek the reformation of the church, if need be by summoning a council. Luther shows in a passionate and thunderous indictment of contemporary Roman Catholicism that the church in Germany was in desperate need of reform. So he appeals boldly to the leaders of German political and social life to take action as Christians to promote reform.

If the papacy had entrenched itself behind three walls, its inner citadel was the sacramental system. Luther launched his main attack on that in his book, *The Babylonian Captivity of the Church*, published on 6 October 1520. Like the Jews in Babylon, Christian Europe had been held captive by the papacy through the seven sacraments. At the very centre of

the system was the Lord's Supper, whose scriptural simplicity had been obliterated by withholding the cup from
the laity, by the doctrine that the substance of the bread
and wine was transformed into the body and blood of Jesus
Christ at the word of consecration, and by the teaching that
the mass was a sacrifice. He brings all three doctrines to the
touchstone of Scripture and finds them wanting. The
Lord's Supper is 'a promise made by one about to die', and
it is a promise of the forgiveness of sins 'confirmed by the
death of the Son of God'. And access to the promise is
gained, not by good works of any kind, but by faith alone.
There is no ground whatsoever in the Bible for speculations
about changes in the substance of the elements, nor for
thinking of the mass as a meritorious work. Since a sacrament contains a promise and a sign and must be
instituted by Christ, only two of the seven Roman Catholic
sacraments are valid, namely baptism and the Lord's Supper. Although Luther included penance as a third sacrament at the beginning of the book, he felt that it must lose
that status since there is no visible sign connected with it.
The *Babylonian Captivity* is a brilliant piece of communication and delivered a powerful blow at the very foundations of papal pretensions.

In the summer of 1520, Rome was preparing to launch
the final attack upon Luther, yet he himself, amidst all the
commotion, enjoyed inner peace. And he expressed it
memorably in *The Freedom of the Christian Man*, published in
November 1520. Miltitz was still trying to secure Luther's
submission and suggested to him on 12 October that a
devotional work, together with a courteous letter to the
Pope, might prove helpful. And that is how the treatise on
freedom came to be written. In the prefatory letter to Leo X,
he distinguished between the pope and his court. The
papal court deserves nothing but condemnation while Leo
was 'worthy of being pope in better days' and he encloses
his treatise 'as a token of peace and good hope'.

The righteousness and freedom of the soul do not rest on
external conditions. They depend on the Word of God, that
is, 'the Gospel of God concerning his Son', which can be
received only by faith. So 'true faith in Christ is a treasure
beyond comparison which brings with it complete salvation'. In these plain and simple words, Luther provides the

key to his own inner peace. By being united with Christ through faith, he is freed from the bondage of circumstances. Christians have been made kings and priests through Christ. As kings they 'are exalted above all things'. Even more excellent is their priesthood whereby they are made worthy 'to appear before God to pray for others and to teach one another divine things'. So by the gospel man has been set free from the tyranny of the Law and of the world and the Christian 'will be filled by the Holy Spirit with the love which makes us free, joyful, almighty workers and conquerors over all tribulations, servants of our neighbours.' This is Luther, servant of the Word of God and man of faith, laying bare the secret of his heart and in doing so making Christian liberty one of the foundation stones of the spiritual reformation over which he presided.

THE CONFRONTATION

If Luther's heart was at peace, there was excited turmoil round about him. Charles V was at Worms in 1521, meeting his Imperial Diet for the first time. He meant to stifle the Lutheran heresy once and for all. But how was this to be done? Luther's prince, the Elector Frederick, had no intention of throwing Luther to the wolves. Nor would he allow Luther to appear before the Diet without the most explicit guarantees for his safety. It would be politic on the Emperor's part to grant them because, as the Papal Nuncio, Jerome Aleander (1480–1542), wrote on 8 February, 'The whole of Germany is in open revolt. Nine-tenths of it shouts for Luther, and the other tenth . . . cries, "Death to the Roman Curia" '. In the councils of the Emperor there were violent quarrels, with the Elector of Saxony and the leading anti-Lutheran, Joachim of Brandenburg (1499–1535), shouting in each other's faces and unsheathing their swords.

Eventually Luther was summoned to appear before the Imperial Diet at Worms. On 26 March 1521, the imperial herald, Caspar Sturm, arrived at Wittenberg, bringing with him the summons and a safe conduct. On 2 April Luther set out on his 440-mile journey, travelling in a covered wagon and accompanied by his colleague on the faculty, Nicholas von Amsdorf (1483–1565) and others. He arrived at his lodging at Worms, the Hospital of the Knights of St John, on 16 April. On the following day, at 4 p.m., the marshals, Ulrich von Pappenheim and Caspar Sturm, arrived to take him to the episcopal palace for his first appearance before the Diet, leading him through side streets in order to evade the crowds. When he entered, he was asked two questions by Johann Eck (not his old Leipzig antagonist but the secretary of the bishop of Trier); whether the books on the table were his and whether he wished to retract the contents of any of them. Luther admitted that the books were his but asked for time to consider his reply to the second question. The Emperor granted his request and so at 4 p.m. on 18 April, Luther made his reply to the question, 'Do you wish to defend all your acknowledged books or to retract some?'. Luther spoke in Latin and in German. Although firm – even bold – he spoke humbly, quietly and modestly. He distinguished between the different kinds of books that he had written. Some dealt with faith and morals and they contained truths admitted by all. Others were critical of the papacy and attacked admitted evils in the church. He could not retract these without strengthening the tyranny which oppressed Germany. A third kind of book had been aimed at individuals and he admitted that he may have been inexcusably violent in his language in these, but that was because he was so concerned 'about the teaching of Christ'. He admitted that his writings had caused dissension, but if they contain manifest errors, he will gladly bow to the judgment of the Diet. Eck replied at length and asked Luther for a simple answer to the question, 'Do you wish to retract?' Luther replied, 'Unless I am convinced by the testimony of the Scriptures or by clear reason . . . I am bound by the Scriptures I have quoted and my conscience is captive to the Word of God. I cannot and will not retract anything, since it is neither safe nor right to go against conscience.' Then he added in German, 'I cannot do otherwise; here I stand; may God help me'.

Something quite extraordinary was happening at Worms when this solitary professor faced, without flinching, the distinguished and powerful leaders of Empire and Church in the name of the Word of God. He was now resolute. Further discussions at Worms failed to persuade him to recant. At 10 a.m. on 26 April, Luther started on his return journey.

Shortly after leaving Mohra, his ancestral home, his troop was attacked and he himself kidnapped. The kidnapping was the work of friends but organized by the Elector. That night he was taken to the castle of the Wartburg, overlooking Eisenach, where he was to spend almost a year in protective custody.

Back at Worms, the Emperor on 26 May appended his signature to the edict which made Luther an outlaw by putting him under the ban of the Empire. All loyal subjects were prohibited from having any dealings with Luther and everyone was to make an effort to secure his arrest.

Although he was now both an excommunicated heretic and an outlaw, Luther was safe and able to continue his reforming work. In fact, it is proper now to speak of the success of Luther's stand.

OPPORTUNITIES TAKEN

What social and cultural factors helped to ensure Luther's success?

There was, of course, Luther's own personality. His burning conviction, his grasp of theology, his penetrating mind and his rare courage, all made their contribution. But he was also a powerful communicator. Through the medium of Latin he addressed an international academic audience, and through German he addressed a people whose frustration with Rome and the demands it made upon their money was already tinged with what would later be called nationalism. And in the pulpit, Luther's profound understanding of Scripture coupled with an instinctive flair for conveying its substance to a mixed congregation made him a preacher of unique influence.

The printing press was still a comparatively new invention. Luther proved an expert at exploiting it to bring his message to the growing literate class in Europe. And he was not alone. Around him were men who conveyed Luther's message by means of the cartoon, the stage play and the ballad.

It was significant in the early years that so many humanists, led by Erasmus himself, should feel that

Luther's protest was part of their campaign for a simpler Christianity, based on the New Testament, that would cleanse the church of scholasticism and obscurantism.

In the social life of those years there were many features that made people sympathetic to Luther's message. On the one hand, the peasants, uneasy with the loss of ancient rights and hard-pressed by their superiors, interpreted the Reformer's emphasis on Christian freedom as a call also for a greater social freedom. On the other hand, in the cities, merchants and burghers were becoming increasingly critical of ecclesiastical restrictions and eager to express their civic pride by asserting their independence from their mediaeval overlords. For them, Luther's teaching came as a liberating doctrine.

The political events of the years between 1518 and 1521 similarly worked in Luther's favour. His own prince, the Elector Frederick, was not only a very significant influence in imperial politics but a man who still adhered to the mediaeval conviction that a prince was in duty bound to protect his subjects. And he acted upon that conviction, using his considerable political sagacity to defend Luther from the threats of both pope and emperor. Moreover, Frederick was being considered by Pope Leo X as a possible candidate to succeed the Emperor Maximilian. As it happened that emperor was succeeded by his grandson, Charles V of Spain. But in the diplomatic negotiations it was not in the interest of any of the parties to antagonize Frederick. So Luther was given a valuable respite to carry on with his work between 1518 and 1520.

So it was that the conjunction of these factors enabled Luther to speak the word that transformed an opportunity into a reformation.

7 Zwingli's call to action

> Christ is the only way to salvation for all who ever were, are and shall be.

> The third of the *Sixty-seven Theses*, 27 January 1523.

While Luther was engaged in his momentous struggle for reformation in Germany, a similar work was developing in Switzerland under the leadership of Huldrych Zwingli.

Zwingli was born on 1 January 1484 at Wildhaus, some 40 miles from Zurich, the son of Uly and Margaret Zwingli. Life was plain but not poor and the Zwingli family played a leading role in local life. The home was crowded with eleven children and Huldrych was sent to live with his uncle, Barthelemy Zwingli, the vicar of Wesen, who laid the foundations of the boy's education. He went on to enjoy the advantages offered by schools at Basel and Bern before becoming a student at the University of Vienna in 1498. He migrated to the University of Basel in 1502 and it was there that he graduated. He had been deeply influenced by his humanist teachers and not least by Thomas Wyttenbach (1472–1526), later the initiator of the Protestant Reformation at Biel, who introduced him to the new methods of Bible study. By the end of his university training, Zwingli emerged as a young man inspired by modern trends in scholarship but acquainted also with scholastic learning.

GRIPPED BY THE SCRIPTURES

In 1506 Zwingli became the vicar of Glarus. He was a busy and popular parish priest but found time to continue his studies. He had missed the opportunity to learn Greek at college, so in 1513 he began to study it. So excited was he at being able to master the language that he learnt all the epistles of Paul by heart in Greek.

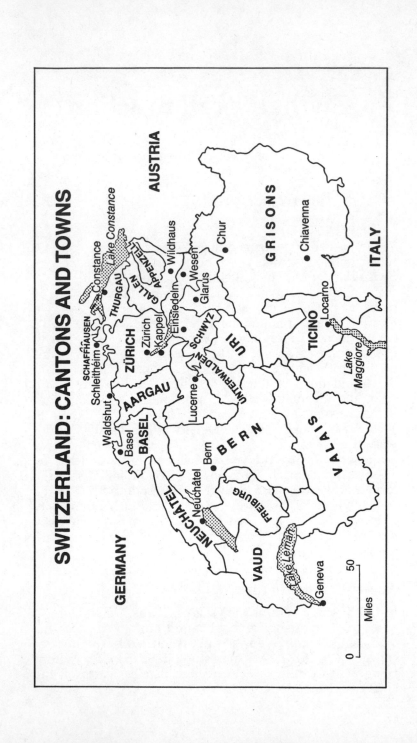

SWITZERLAND: CANTONS AND TOWNS

At Glarus, however, Zwingli was plunged into a spiritual crisis. His close study of the Bible raised the question of its authority in his mind. In his book, *The clarity and certainty of the Word of God*, published in September 1522, he wrote that 'some seven or eight years ago, I undertook to devote myself entirely to the scriptures'. That would place the resolution in 1514–1515. He was hampered, he adds, because 'the conflicting philosophy and theology of the schoolmen presented difficulties'. But he was gradually persuaded by his Bible study that the Word of God possesses an authority above all other books. He had reached that conclusion by 1516 and it was the principle that was to govern the development of the Reformation of Zürich. It was at Glarus, too, that he came to appreciate the evils that attended mercenary service by Swiss men in foreign armies. He served as chaplain with these troops in 1512, 1513 and 1515 and saw the appalling slaughter of 10,000 of his countrymen at the battle of Marignano, 14 September 1515. He became a severe critic of the system although the pope granted him a pension for his services to the soldiers who fought in his armies. In 1517 Zwingli renounced this papal pension as a protest. It was at Glarus also that Zwingli faced a moral crisis. He succumbed to sexual temptation and although that was a common enough failing among Swiss clergymen at the time, Zwingli could not condone it in himself.

But new spiritual powers were working in him.

THE PREACHED WORD

The people of Glarus were infuriated by Zwingli's criticism of the mercenary system and he had to leave the church although he remained the legal incumbent. He took up a post as chaplain at the Benedictine Abbey of Einsiedeln, just 18 miles away. Only two monks now resided there but pilgrims still came in large numbers to offer their devotions to the abbey's Black Madonna. It was these crowds who were first shaken by Zwingli's powerful expository preaching. Among the pilgrims at Einsiedeln were the men of Zürich and so impressed were they that they wanted Zwingli to move to their city. So he was given an invitation to become people's priest at the Great Minster in the city.

He accepted the invitation, resigned his charge at Glarus, and on 27 November 1518 moved to Zürich in order to start work there on 1 January 1519. Zürich at that time was a republic of some 7,000 population, governed by two councils and it was one of the thirteen allied Swiss states. It was a prosperous but licentious city; as Bullinger put it in an acid comment, 'Zürich was to Switzerland what Corinth was to Greece'. It was thoroughly Roman Catholic. Its three parishes were served by 57 priests, the 24 canons of the Minister and some 200 men and women in the religious orders.

Zwingli opened his ministry there by announcing his intention to deliver a course of sermons expounding the New Testament and beginning with the Gospel of Matthew. The congregations found it exciting and novel to be taken to the text of the Bible and to have its meaning explained in the light of the principle that the Bible is its own best commentary. Zwingli always maintained that he had discovered his evangelical principles before he had heard of Luther, but in 1519 the reading of Luther's books was a valuable assurance to him that he was not alone. The quality of his spiritual life was also enriched in 1519 by the serious illness which he suffered. He had returned from holiday that August when he heard that the plague had broken out in Zürich, and so had ministered with great devotion to the sufferers. But he himself was struck down in September. He recovered after being desperately ill and the poems which he composed at that time reveal him as a man overcome by a profound feeling of gratitude, joy and dependence upon God.

Gradually, the biblical principles proclaimed in Zwingli's sermons led to action. He himself showed his dissatisfaction with episcopal control over the city by resigning his post on 12 November 1521 and accepting a new authorization, this time from the city council.

CONTROVERSY

What ground was there in the Bible for the Roman Catholic practice of abstaining from meat during Lent? In his sermons Zwingli had distinguished between the demands of the gospel and the rules of the church. Under which head-ing did fasting during Lent come? The great Protestant printer, Christoph Froschauer (c. 1490–1564) decided to put the question to a practical test. During Holy Week he regaled his workers with sausages. The authorities were alarmed at such a breach of regulations but Zwingli, who was present when the offence occurred, preached a sermon in defence of Christian freedom on 29 March. This sermon was published on 16 April and by that time a commission appointed by the city council had vindicated Zwingli's view.

Almost simultaneously another question about Christian liberty was raised. Are priests free to marry? 'No!', said the church unequivocally. But Swiss clergymen took little notice of the rule. In this matter, Zwingli himself exercised his freedom by marrying, albeit secretly, Anna Reinhart, in the Spring of 1522. He did not publicly regularize the marriage until 5 April 1524. But he had begun to agitate for reform in this matter on 2 July 1522 when, with ten other priests, he sent petitions to the bishop and to the Swiss Diet seeking the abolition of compulsory celibacy. In view of the silence of the authorities he published on 23 August 1522 his book *A first and final explanation*, defending himself passionately from the charge of heresy and insisting that church regulations need to be justified by reference to Scripture.

Zwingli was working with a fully developed evangelical doctrine which agreed in essentials with that of Martin Luther. Excitement increased in Zürich during the latter half of 1522 as people came to realize this. But Zwingli was also facing physical danger from the opponents of reform and it was imperative that he should win the support of the Council at Zürich. The Council agreed to consider the whole question of reform in a public debate to be held on 29 January 1523. In preparation for this Zwingli drew up sixty-seven theses. Together they form a vigorous and succinct expression of the main principles of the Reformed faith – in fact, the very first of its kind, – and assert the primacy of the gospel, the sole lordship of Jesus Christ as teacher, saviour and mediator. No human laws may abrogate the gospel freedom of believers; the church, like any other institution, is subject to the secular powers 'provided they are Christian', and priestly confession, absolution, the cult of the saints and the existence of purgatory are all denied. A distinguished and representative audience of 600 gathered at the City Hall to listen to the debate. The bishop of Constance declined to be directly represented, on the ground that matters of theology should not be submitted to the judgment of laymen, and this gave Zwingli the opportunity to make the very significant point, in the context of the development of the Protestant Reformation in Switzerland, that the civic community was in every way qualified to sit as judges in the debate. And the field was left open to him to expound his theses. The debate was a great success for the reformers.

The same day the city authorities published a decree 'that Mr. Ulrich Zwingli continue and keep on as before to proclaim the holy gospel and the pure holy Scripture' and that all other preachers should teach in consonance with the same standards. So the work of reformation proceeded apace, fully supported by the secular power.

8 From loneliness to social tumult

We caught two hares and a few partridges – a worthy occupation for men with nothing to do.

Luther, writing from the Wartburg to Spalatin, 15 August 1521.

. . . it has been the custom heretofore that no poor man was allowed to catch venison or wild fowl, or fish in flowing water, which seems to us . . . selfish and not according to the Word of God . . . .

From the fourth of the *Twelve Articles* drawn up by the peasants in March 1525.

After being taken to the Wartburg castle, Luther was transformed from an emaciated monk into a rustic 'Sir George', a disguise to conceal his identity. The secret was well kept and admirers, like the artist Albrecht Dürer, were allowed to grieve over his supposed fate at the hands of the Emperor's minions.

After the immense strain of the Diet of Worms and the preceding years, the stay at the Wartburg provided Luther with a period of tranquillity to compose himself. But he was rarely at ease. The food did not agree with him and he was sometimes physically ill and psychologically oppressed by visions of the devil. He appreciated the Elector's concern for his safety but chafed at his inability 'to stand up in public for the Word of God'. But his zeal for the Word found several most fruitful means of expression. He continued his literary work, his exposition of the Psalms, and the homilies on the Epistles and Gospels. Even more epoch-making was his new translation of the New Testament. He began working on it in November 1521 and had completed the first draft before he left the Wartburg. Then, with the help of George Spalatin, Philip Melanchthon, the Professor of Greek at Wittenberg, and others, the text was revised and sent to the printer, Melchior Lotther of Wittenberg. The whole work finally appeared in September 1523, and the very first copy was sent to Hans von Berlepech, governor of Wartburg castle. Many translations of the Bible into German had appeared before but Luther's was to prove the greatest of them. This was not because he was an able Greek scholar but because he was a master of both official and colloquial German and had a finely-tuned ear for the cadences of the language. And he possessed a profound spiritual grasp of the substance of Scripture. As soon as he had finished the New Testament, he began work on the Old, assisted by a panel of experts which included Caspar Cruciger (1504–48), Caspar Aquila (1488–1560), Matthew Goldhann (or Aurogallus, *c.* 1490–1543) – all of them professors of Hebrew, as well as Justus Jonas (1493–1555) and Luther's own minister, John Bugenhagen (1485–1558). At their weekly seminar, held in Luther's house, they gradually produced the translation which, together with the 1523 New Testament, formed the whole German Bible published in 1534. It was a magnificent accomplishment. Not only was it a landmark in the history of German literature but for Luther himself it meant that ordinary people could now consult the Bible for themselves without being at the mercy of the theologians. Not that Luther, of all people, despised theology. In fact, he warmly approved the first systematic attempt to expound his theology made by his friend Philip Melanchthon in his *Loci Communes* of April 1521. But the public had a right to judge the theologian by the standard of truth found in the Bible.

RADICALISM

During Luther's absence at the Wartburg, the enthusiasm of his supporters flowered into a demand for immediate reformation. Luther's colleague at the University, Andrew Bodenstein of Carlstadt took the lead and precipitated the first crisis in the movement. He himself advocated a spiritual piety which despised the Roman emphasis on material things as aids to devotion. At the same time, thirty of the forty monks at the Augustinian covent abandoned their profession, and among them, Gâbriel Zwilling (c.1487–1558). By August 1521, Luther was discussing with Melanchthon how best to reform the Mass in consonance with his evangelical principles and in November 1521 published his book *On the Abrogation of the Private Mass*. It was typical of Luther that he wished to move slowly. Carlstadt, however, was impatient and at Christmas, Holy Communion was celebrated with an evangelical liturgy. Both Zwilling and Carlstadt criticized the use of images and condemned vows of celibacy with the result that there was an outbreak of image-breaking in the town.

By the end of December 1521 the two radicals had been joined by the 'Zwickau Prophets', Nicholas Storch, Mark Stübner and Thomas Drechsel, who had migrated from the industrial town of Zwickau and caused great excitement with their call for a complete break with the Roman Catholic Church. Luther had visited Wittenberg surreptitiously in December and became increasingly distressed with the spread of radicalism. Despite the Elector's prohibition, he decided to return and arrived on Thursday, 6 March 1522. The following Sunday he began a remarkable series of sermons during which he restored his authority as the leader of the Wittenberg reformation. He deplored anarchy and insisted that Christian freedom is best served by loyalty to the Word of God. It was in his second sermon that he made the oft-quoted declaration:

I will preach, speak, write, but I will force no one; for faith must be voluntary. Take me as an example. I stood up against the Pope, indulgences, and all papists, but without violence or uproar. I only urged, preached, and declared God's Word, nothing else. And yet while I was asleep, or drinking Wittenberg beer with my Philip Melanchthon and Amsdorf, the Word inflicted greater injury on popery than prince or emperor ever did. I did nothing, the Word did everything.

A ROYAL CRITIC

Reverence for the Word of God did not prevent Luther from indulging his partiality for strong language. In 1521

Henry VIII of England replied to Luther's *Babylonian Captivity* by publishing his *Assertion of the Seven Sacraments*. Luther's reply, *Against King Henry* (1522) not only poked fun at the title 'Defender of the Faith' conferred on Henry by Leo X, but abused the king as a 'fool' and a 'crowned donkey'; hardly the language to make a convert. But by 1525, when it seemed possible that Henry might become an ally, the Reformer thought it wise to apologize.

CHANGES AT WITTENBERG

Luther was convinced that preaching and teaching would restore the pristine purity of the church. It would be a process of purification, not the establishing of a new church. There was a strong pragmatic element in Luther's reformation. He crossed his bridges as he came to them. So, in the realm of worship, he accepted some of the changes introduced by Carlstadt. On 29 October 1525 the Wittenberg City Church used Luther's German Order for Communion for the first time. It was published at the end of the year as *The German Mass* and became the pattern for the churches of North Germany and Scandinavia. Luther found a place in the liturgy for hymns and in 1523 began composing some himself. His powerful rendering of Psalm 46, 'A safe stronghold our God is still' (as Thomas Carlyle rendered it) became the battle-hymn of Lutheranism. So popular was hymn singing that some 47 Lutheran collections were issued during Luther's lifetime. As for the order for baptism, it was in 1526 that Luther issued his own version. The main thrust of Luther's changes in matters of worship was to simplify the traditional forms, to give pride of place to preaching, to emphasize freedom to preserve whatever usages or ornaments that were not prohibited by the Bible and to make room for congregational singing.

THE PARTING OF THE WAYS

Protestantism was indebted in many ways to the New Learning. But the relationship between Reformation and Humanism was often very tense. The prince of humanist scholars, Desiderius Erasmus (*c.* 1469–1536), had cautiously welcomed Luther's stand at the beginning, but his sympathy soon cooled. In September 1524 Erasmus published a book, *Free Will*. It was an elegant restatement of the scholastic principle, 'do what in you lies' and so merit salvation by doing good works. Erasmus, in other words, was challenging Luther's fundamental conviction that man is unable on account of his sin to contribute to his own salvation and is therefore, says the gospel, justified before God by faith alone through grace. Luther could not be silent. In December 1525 his reply appeared under the title, *The Bondage of the Will*. Luther, quite justifiably, considered it one of his best books and despite its strong academic quality, it had a wide circulation. Erasmus took it as a personal insult and replied at great length in his *Defence of the Diatribe*. Luther made no reply. He was quite dis-illusioned with the great humanist and would have no more to do with him. Though it is misleading to say that the controversy marked the final break between Lutheranism and humanism, it does mark a parting of the ways and it defines the frontier between the modest reforms espoused by Roman Catholic humanists and the more thorough changes desired by evangelical humanists.

DEVASTATION

In 1524 Melanchthon, a fervid student of astrology, was oppressed by the belief that the configurations of the stars portended a great tumult. Luther mocked astrology but was a keen observer of omens and believed that the end of the world was not far off. Such anxieties added emotional fuel to the excitement that accompanied the growth of the evangelical Reformation. Poor people dreamt dreams of emancipation and when prophets appeared preaching the imminent collapse of the oppressive social system, their message fell on attentive ears. And Luther's message, in particular, stirred men's hopes. Thomas Münzer (*c.* 1490–1525) preached a gospel of social revolt and accused Luther of being the toady of princes. For that matter, Carlstadt was echoing similar ideas with his emphasis on the value of simple country life. But country life in the sixteenth century was not idyllic. For over a century in many parts of Europe the oppressed in country areas and in the towns had expressed their exasperation in riot and rebellion.

By 1524 the peasants in Thuringia, Swabia and Franconia were banding together for an armed struggle and were producing lists of demands, of which the most influential was the declaration known as the *Twelve Articles*, adopted in Swabia and published on 16 March 1525. It is a plea, and a singularly moderate one, for the removal of abuses, the institution of equitable laws, and the restoration of lost rights. Luther reacted in his *Admonition to Peace* of May 1525. It was a moving plea for peasants and lords to get together to settle their differences amicably.

But Luther was too late. Everywhere the peasants had risen in revolt against their lords and there had been widespread devastation. He vented his feelings in his tract *Against the robbing and murdering hordes of peasants*. The lords and princes are exhorted to extinguish the rebellion by every possible means and anyone who dies fighting on the side of the rulers will be a 'true martyr in the eyes of God' while anyone who perishes fighting on the side of the peasants 'is an eternal brand of hell'. The lords and princes needed no encouragement. On 15 May at Frankenhausen, Münzer's peasant army was overwhelmed by the combined forces of Philip of Hesse, the Elector of Saxony and Duke George of Saxony. Münzer was captured and beheaded after suffering barbaric torture. Scores of thousands perished in the ensuing bloodbath.

Luther was not alone in his stand. Melanchthon's *Confutation of the Articles of the peasants* is more moderate in language than Luther's tract, but the underlying assumptions are the same. Evangelical freedom must not be construed as a justification for violence or social upheaval. But the consequences of Luther's intervention affected Lutheran attitudes for generations. Even within the churches, the congregational democracy which had begun to emerge in the early years now faded away. It was a sad episode in Luther's career.

9   The Word of God remains for ever

We are not heretics.

The Confession of Augsburg, 1530.

Just when the disturbances of the Peasants' War were at their height, Luther got married. The ceremony was at the Black Cloister on 13 June 1525 and John Bugenhagen officiated. The bride was Catharine von Bora (1499–1552), a nun of noble birth who had fled with eight others when they abandoned their convent at Nimptsch. It was to be a happy marriage of which six children were born. The Luthers' was a busy and exceptionally hospitable home, a precursor of the thousands of Protestant clerical homes which have made such a remarkable contribution to European life and culture.

The princes had shown no mercy in suppressing the peasants but there was one who said to his servants, 'If I have wronged any of you, I beg you to forgive me for God's sake; we princes do many evil things to poor people.' They were the words of Frederick, Elector of Saxony, who died on 5 May 1525 when the tumult was at its worst. Ever since 1517 he had been Luther's protector and Protestantism owes him an immense debt. And yet the only sign he gave of accepting Luther's teaching was accepting Communion in both kinds on his deathbed. He was succeeded by his brother, John the Constant, who reigned from 1525 to 1532. He was a firm adherent of the Reformation and emblazoned his livery and ensigns with the letters V.D.M.I.Æ, from the Latin words *Verbum Dei manet in aeternum*, that is, 'The word of God abideth for ever'. He in turn was succeeded by his son, John Frederick, who reigned from 1532 to 1554.

DISAPPOINTMENT

As a result of the breach with Rome, the traditional discipline of the church collapsed. Luther suggested to the Elector of Saxony that he should initiate a visitation within his territories in order to gather information about conditions in the parishes. These visitations were conducted by Luther, Melanchthon, Jonas, Spalatin and others. The visitations of 1527 revealed extensive disorder. Many of the clergy were unfit for their office; some were immoral, others were ignorant. It became obvious that the Reformation as a theological and spiritual renewal had left these people untouched.

REMEDIES

Melanchthon threw himself enthusiastically into the task of creating an educational system. He had organized a school at Eisleben in 1525 and a few months later he planned an educational system for Nuremberg. In 1527 he was helping Philip of Hesse with his plans for the new university that opened at Marburg that year. Then in 1528 he drew up a set of articles stating the Lutheran faith and formulated a plan for the organization of schools. And so the Saxon territories were provided with a general public educational system backed by law, the first of its kind in Europe. Melanchthon's articles show clearly that he was working with a coherent theory of education. Education is rooted in Scripture and faith and so the context of culture is the work of God in salvation. Education is to serve the cultivation of the whole person. All in all, it was a fine system, often copied by Protestants elsewhere. By 1555 some 135 similar plans had been published and at least 56 cities had sought guidance from Melanchthon in creating their educational systems. In this way, Melanchthon had a deep and lasting influence on European culture.

Just as education became the responsibility of the state, so did the discipline of the church. The appointment of ministers in Saxony became the responsibility of the Elector and to ensure that high standards were maintained he was also responsible for nominating superintendents and consistories. In this way some episcopal functions devolved upon the Elector. Thus the German Lutheran system, with its close connection between Church and State, evolved from the Saxon experience. And as for the promotion of piety, Luther himself made a singular contribution through his expositions of the Creed, the Ten Commandments and the Lord's Prayer. His *Great Catechism* proved too cumbersome and so in July 1529 he published his *Enchiridion* or *Short Catechism*. It was a masterpiece, second only to the Bible in the influence it had on German piety.

THE IMPERIAL THREAT

The Imperial Diet at Worms in 1521 had declared Luther an outlaw. But how was this ban to be executed? How could he and his followers be brought to book? In order to meet the threat of Lutheranism, the Roman Catholic princes in July 1524 formed the League of Ratisbon and the Protestants, under the leadership of Philip of Hesse and Elector John of Saxony, replied by forming the League of Torgau in June 1526. The division between the two sets of territories was accentuated by the resolutions at the Diet of Speyer, June to August 1526. Common action between Roman Catholics and Lutherans was now imperative because of the Turkish invasion of Hungary. So it was agreed that 'every state shall live, rule, and believe as it may hope and trust to answer before God and his imperial majesty.' It was meant as nothing more than a convenient truce, but the Lutherans took it as a licence to accelerate the work of reformation in their lands. Moreover, the Roman threat was suspended for a while since the Pope and the Emperor were locked in the bitter conflict which culminated in the terrible sack of Rome on 6 May 1527.

Once peace was restored, the Lutheran position became precarious again. At the second Diet of Speyer in March 1529, the compromises of the previous diet were abrogated. It was this resolution to eliminate the Lutheran heresy that provoked John of Saxony and his allies to reject the Roman Catholic proposals and to assert once again the principle that they be allowed to live and govern 'as we trust to answer before God and his Roman Imperial Majesty'. This was the 'Protest' of 19 April 1529 which gave us the word 'Protestant' to describe the evangelical parties. So the lonely stand of Luther at Worms had grown in eight years into the protest of princes. But the Emperor rejected it.

PROTESTANT DISUNITY

The Protestants found it difficult to form a united front. There were several Reformations developing in different places and the leaders were conscious of both their fundamental unity and their quite real differences. For Luther, the whole Reformation struggle was primarily a doctrinal one. He was ready enough to compromise on many points, but he would not modify his theology no matter what political or social consequences might follow. The sticking-point came over the understanding of the sacramental nature of Holy Communion.

Is the body of Jesus Christ present in the bread and wine on the Communion table? Luther firmly believed that it is. At the same time he rejected the scholastic doctrine that the substance of the two elements is changed into the real body of Christ during the canon of the Mass. Zwingli, on the other hand, held that the body of our Lord is in heaven and that it cannot possibly be present on the altar. Not that Zwingli denied a real presence. What he denied was a corporal presence in the elements. He asserted the real spiritual presence of our Lord in the mind and heart of the believing communicant.

Luther adopted a hostile attitude towards Zwingli and asserted 'that I cannot regard Zwingli and all his teaching as Christian at all.' Philip of Hesse was anxious about the growing Roman Catholic threat and wished to bring Zürich into a united front with the German Protestants. So he invited representatives of the two views to meet in conference. Only with the greatest reluctance did Luther and Melanchthon agree to go. On Friday, 1 October 1529, the conference or 'Colloquy', as it is usually called, opened at the castle at Marburg. The main participants were Luther, Melanchthon, Zwingli and Oecolampadius (1482–1531) of Basel. They were supported on the Lutheran side by Jonas, Cruciger, Osiander and others, and on Zwingli's by Martin Bucer (1491–1551), Caspar Hedio (1494–1553) and Jacob Sturm (1498–1553), all three of Strasbourg. The twenty-five year old Landgrave Philip of Hesse listened intently as an observer, and his presence prevented the theologians from extremes of bad temper. Luther drew up fifteen articles and all present agreed with them. For that matter, they agreed with the fifteenth as well in what it said about Communion, except for the statement that the real body and blood of Christ are corporally present in the bread and wine. They agreed that 'both parties shall cherish Christian charity for one another', but the Lutherans insisted on adding 'so far as the conscience of each will permit'. So the articles were signed but Luther maintained an ungenerous attitude to Zwingli to the end. The Colloquy did not produce the unity which the Landgrave desired but it did point the way towards a more amicable relationship in the future.

THE POLICY OF THE EMPEROR

The Emperor had achieved peace with both Rome and France and was crowned at Bologna on 24 February 1530. He now felt free to devote his attention to the elimination of heresy in Germany. On 20 June 1530 the Imperial Diet was formally opened at Augsburg. The Elector of Saxony had asked the theologians to produce a statement of their faith to be presented to the Emperor. Luther could go no nearer Augsburg than the castle at Coburg because he was an outlaw under the ban of the Empire, so the Saxon delegation was led by Melanchthon who found the responsibility a crushing strain. Nevertheless he composed a statement of Lutheran belief that became one of the historic documents of Protestantism, – the Augsburg Confession. The Emperor would not have it read at a plenary session of the diet, so, on 25 June 1530, about 3 p.m., in the private chambers of the Emperor at the bishop's palace, in the presence of some 200 high dignitaries, Dr. Christian Beyer, chancellor of Electoral Saxony, rose to read the Confession and took his seat again after some two hours. Among the nine signatories were the Elector of Saxony, Landgrave Philip of Hesse, Margrave George of Brandenburg and the city of Nuremberg. Lutherans have always considered this event as a moment of high drama, and quite rightly so. The Confession, although it is silent on several points of doctrine that might prove provocative to Roman Catholics, is a magisterial expression of the evangelical faith. It was not the only confession submitted to the Emperor. On 8 July Zwingli's confession was presented and three days later Bucer and Capito presented the Tetrapolitan Confession on behalf of the cities of Strasbourg, Memmingen, Lindau and Constance. Considerable discussions between the various parties followed these submissions but in the end the Edict of Worms was reaffirmed on 22 September and the Protestants given a period of grace until 15 April 1531 before imperial action would be taken against them. In order to defend themselves they formed the Smalcaldic League in 1531. But as a result of a temporary truce agreed upon at the Diet of Nuremberg in July 1532, the Protestant cause was given a further respite and preserved from the perils of war.

10 Advance and dissent at Zürich

The Word of God . . . is certain and cannot fail us; it is clear and does not let us wander in darkness. It teaches itself, it explains itself and it brings the light of full salvation and grace to the human soul.

Zwingli (1484–1531),*The clarity and certainty of the Word of God.* 6 September 1522.

Having secured the support of the secular authorities for the principle of the primacy of Scripture in January 1523, Zwingli was in a favourable position to press for further reform. In his books, *Commentary on the Sixty-seven Theses* (June 1523) and *Essay on the Canon of the Mass* (August 1523) he had focused attention on the use of images in churches as well as the nature of the Eucharist. These were the topics discussed in the second disputation, held from 26 to 29 October 1523 in the presence of a large audience of 900 persons. In the debate Zwingli was supported by Leo Jud (1482–1542) and the Roman Catholic side was defended, not without ability, by Martin Steinli and Conrad Schmid. The Council was not wholly convinced by Zwingli and he was asked to form a panel to provide a more adequate exposition of the points at issue. But official opinion was changing. A private debate in the presence of clergymen and a few others, 20 January 1524, dealt with the Mass. The authorities during the Spring decided to permit further reform and by June 20 the visible signs of mediaeval Roman Catholic devotion had been removed. Images, pictures, candles, altars, were disposed of; frescoes were white-washed, saints' relics buried and organs broken up. According to Bullinger, 'The superstitious lamented; but the true believers rejoiced in it as a great and joyous worship of God.'

On 12 April 1525 the Council abolished the Mass and that evening it was celebrated for the last time and replaced on the following day by evangelical Communion. In November 1525 the monasteries were suppressed and their wealth transferred to support social welfare and education. On 19 June 1525 a theological college, the Carolinum, was opened and was to have extensive influence in future years through the men educated in it. Since German now replaced Latin as the language of the church, there was urgent need for a translation of the Bible. Luther's New Testament was available and was revised in 1524 the better to suit the spoken German of Zürich. The whole Bible appeared from Froschauer's press in 1530 and was the joint production of Leo Jud, Conrad Pellican, Theodor Bibliander and others.

CONSERVATIVE OPPOSITION

Although he was able to carry the day for reform, Zwingli faced considerable opposition. Some of the aristocrats resented their loss of influence and sought the support of the anti-clerical party which disapproved of Zwingli's growing influence in the city. The deputy town clerk, Joachim Am Grüt co-ordinated the specifically Roman Catholic opposition. There was growing hostility in the Swiss Confederation too, because the five Inner States (Uri, Schwyz, Unterwalden, Zug and Lucerne) agreed at a meeting at Beckenreid on 8 April 1524 to stand by the 'Old Faith' and resist all changes. And they had their sympathizers inside Zürich among the 'pensioners', those who looked for gifts of money to the Emperor, the Pope or France. One proof of the resolve of Zwingli's supporters to crush every possible form of sedition was the execution of a highly respected citizen, Jacob Grebel, on 29 November 1526, as a recipient of pensions. And there were also slanderous attacks on Zwingli's character and even threats to his life.

THE RADICAL AWAKENING

In 1520 Zwingli had held the view that the true church must be a suffering community, guided by the Word of God and at odds with the world, which will never 'be a friend of Christ'. But as he came to realize that the secular authorities could be persuaded to support a generous measure of reform, he retreated from this position in the hope that moderation and patience would lead to a general reformation embracing perhaps the whole of Switzerland. Young scholars like Conrad Grebel (1498?–1526) and Felix Mantz (1498–1527), who were studying Greek and Hebrew under Zwingli, soon became uneasy with their teacher's leadership. They wanted thorough and quick reform. Their impatience was made public during the second Zürich disputation of October 1523. Grebel pressed for immediate action against images and the Mass. Zwingli replied that the Council would decide how best to deal with these matters. It was in reply to this statement that Simon Stumpf made his oft-quoted declaration, 'Master Ulrich, you do not have the right to place the decision on this matter in the hands of my lords, for the decision has already been made, the Spirit of God decides'. The group which had now been joined by Balthasar Hübmaier (c. 1480–1528), the pastor of Waldshut, was bitterly disappointed by Zwingli's prevarication.

They, together with their supporters, began to hold regular Bible-study groups and still had hopes of influencing Zwingli. They pressed upon him plans for a more thorough reformation which would lead to the organizing of a church of believers 'according to evangelical truth and the Word of God', with ministers supported by voluntary gifts, and dispensing the Lord's Supper with biblical simplicity. In short, they hoped to gather at Zürich a Free Church, untrammelled by state interference. Zwingli would have none of it. In consequence the radicals began to organize themselves as nonconforming congregational fellowships. And their nonconformity obviously stemmed from their insistence that obedience to biblical authority should be more consistently applied than was the case with Zwingli.

THE PRICE OF DISSENT

The crucial step, which made nonconformists of them, was taken on 21 January 1525. The nature of baptism had been a matter of growing concern among them since early in 1524

when William Reublin of Wytikon, later to be one of the
most energetic Anabaptist evangelists in south Germany,
preached against the baptism of infants. The radical groups
became convinced that there was no scriptural warrant for
infant baptism, rejected their own baptisms and considered
the possibility of undergoing a new baptism on profession
of their personal faith. And that is what happened on 21
January 1525 when George Blaurock (c. 1491–1529), after
being baptized by Conrad Grebel, went on to baptize the
other members of the group. It was a historic step. It marks
the emergence of the Swiss Brethren and the effective
beginning of the Anabaptist movement. At the same time,
it was a fundamental challenge to the type of state-
patronized reformation of the kind promoted by Luther
and Zwingli, and defended in the latter's *Justice, human and
divine* (June 1523).

From Zwingli's point of view, the radicals were challenging the very basis of the reformation at Zürich. Gradually the
authorities became more repressive. They were alarmed at
the welcome which ardent preachers like Grebel, Mantz
and Blaurock were enjoying in the neighbourhood. Their
preaching was accompanied by spiritual effects of the kind
that were to characterize the revivalism of later generations.
They created a profound conviction of sin, followed by
repentance, conversion and believers' baptism. So baptism
for these converts was not an academic theological matter;
it was deeply embedded in profound spiritual experiences
and provided people with an escape from the terror of sin.
But such enthusiasm was truly alarming both to Roman
Catholics and the promoters of the Reformation. Thus the
Roman Catholic authorities in the canton of Schwyz
arrested Hippolytus Eberli and he was burned at the stake
on 29 May 1525, the first Swiss Anabaptist martyr.

Meanwhile, at Zürich Zwingli sought to restore unity by
argument and compulsion. Discussions were held with the
radicals in December 1524 and January 1525, but the Council was not impressed by the case they made for themselves. Grebel and Mantz were ordered to desist from their
dissenting activities, those who were not citizens of Zürich
were expelled, and parents who had unbaptized infants
were to have them baptized immediately or suffer banishment. During the following months the Anabaptists

were in and out of prison. In the main, they adhered firmly to their convictions. An exception was the gentle Balthasar Hübmaier. He had been rebaptized by Reublin at Easter 1525 but was later imprisoned and subjected to torture and in January 1526 he recanted his views, a lapse which caused him bitter grief for the remainder of his short life.

Blaurock and Mantz were put on trial on 18 November 1525 and sentenced to indefinite imprisonment. On the 8 March 1526, the city authorities decreed that anyone found guilty of rebaptizing anyone else should be 'put to death by drowning'. Blaurock and Mantz succeeded in escaping from prison but were rearrested. Blaurock was not a citizen and was sentenced to receive an exceptionally brutal beating and afterwards expelled. Mantz, the indefatigable evangelist, was finally silenced when he was condemned to death on 5 January 1527 and executed by drowning in the river Limmat that afternoon. He was the first Anabaptist to suffer martyrdom at the hands of Protestants. Grebel, weakened by imprisonment, died of the plague in the summer of 1526. In his dealings with the radicals, Zwingli adopted a stern attitude. There are many passages in his books against them, *Baptism* and *Refutation of the tricks of the Anabaptist*, which reveal his apprehensions. He shared with the other magisterial reformers a firm conviction that the support of the state was vital to the Reformation. Hence his fear that the activities of the radicals could provoke the authorities to put an end to his work.

POLITICS

The Swiss Roman Catholics were eager to stem the tide of reform. The Swiss Diet on 20 March 1526 ordered a disputation to be held on the religious question at Baden. It duly met on 18 May. Since the proceedings were under the chairmanship of John Eck (of Leipzig fame), and Zwingli declined to be present, the conclusions were unfavourable to the reformers. Although Zwingli was not branded a heretic, he and his views were held to come under the same imperial and papal condemnations as those of Luther.

As Protestantism spread, its supporters in the Swiss cantons drew closer together for mutual defence. Thus by February 1529 their Christian Civic Union included eight

members, led by Zürich, Bern, Basel and Strasbourg. The
Roman Catholics, led by Lucerne, retaliated by forming the
Christian Alliance on 23 April 1529. There was much acri-
mony between the two groups, especially over the rights of
religious minorities, and it was this question that provoked
Zürich to declare war on 8 June 1529. No great harm
followed since an uneasy peace was patched up in the first
Peace of Kappel, 26 June 1529. The increasing militancy, at
this time, of the Roman Catholic powers under Emperor
Charles V worried Zwingli and, with the help of Philip of
Hesse, he tried to create a united front of the Protestant
powers. But despite the Colloquy of Marburg and his political efforts, Zwingli was not able to achieve the desired
unity. The Roman Catholic cantons in Switzerland were
anxious lest the Protestant economic blockade might be a
prelude to an attack on their religious freedom and declared
war on Zürich. In the battle of Kappel, 11 October 1531, a
needless and untidy skirmish, Zwingli was killed. His body
was burned and his ashes scattered to the wind. It was an
ignominious end to a remarkable career.

ZWINGLI AND LUTHER

Zwingli rightly takes his place as one of the outstanding
figures of the Protestant Reformation. The reformation of
which he was the leader differed from Luther's while
having much in common with it. Luther worked in a mon-
archical principality; Zwingli worked in a republic with an
elected government. Luther relied on the patronage of
princes while Zwingli had to pay attention to the moods of
the civic authorities. Both reformers were agreed on the
importance of justification by faith alone and the authority
of the Bible, but disagreed about how precisely biblical
standards were to be applied in detail. And both disagreed
on the question of Christ's presence in the Eucharist. In
Zwingli we have the roots of that 'Reformed' tradition that
was to be developed and enriched by Calvin.

11 Militant Protestantism

> . . . we find upon consultation of our registeries and
> soul-books that . . . you have turned away from us
> many souls through your writing, teaching and
> preaching.

Luther's influence as described in the satirical
Lucifer's Letter to Luther, 1524.

Europe in the sixteenth century was much more
fragmented than it is in the twentieth century. Thus Germany consisted of about 250 separate states, and in matters
of religion each of these entities made its own decisions.
Those that embraced Protestantism had much in common
with one another but there were also variations among
them. And it was inevitable that a very large number of
people would be implicated in the work of reform. It is
entirely proper that Luther's mighty personality should
dominate the history of the early years of the evangelical
protest but as the years passed by a whole army of men and
women contributed to the story. A review of the territorial
expansion of Protestantism in Germany and the adjacent
territories will make it possible to name some of the people
who deserve to be remembered.

SIGNIFICANT GAINS

Luther's work was done in Electoral Saxony. Contiguous
with this territory was Ducal Saxony. While Duke George
reigned there was no hope of initiating religious change for
he was implacably opposed to Luther and Lutheranism. It
was a hard blow to the papal cause when George died in
1539 and was succeeded by his brother, Henry the Pious,
who immediately introduced the Protestant Reformation
and did so with great ceremony. He got Luther to preach to
a huge congregation at Leipzig in May 1539. Despite sharp

opposition from the Roman Catholics, Protestantism flourished and the University of Leipzig became a stronghold of Protestant scholarship.

Two powers that were to play significant roles in the history of Protestantism were Hesse and Prussia. The ruler of Hesse after 1518 was the Landgrave Philip the Magnanimous (1504–67). Luther had made a deep impression on Philip at the Diet of Worms and he had asked to be instructed by Melanchthon. He openly embraced Protestantism and after the truce between Roman Catholics and Lutherans at the Diet of Speyer in 1526 he set to it to reform Hesse. He held a synod at Homberg in October 1526 in which the eloquent Frenchman, François Lambert (1486–1530) advocated a church constitution combining congregational self-government with oversight by councils. Luther disapproved of such a scheme and the Landgrave himself assumed the functions of a bishop and instituted reforms using Electoral Saxony as a model. On 1 July 1527 the University of Marburg was opened and soon began to make a fine contribution to evangelical scholarship. Although Philip was an unstable character, he remained a firm adherent of the Protestant cause.

Prussia was the territory conquered by the Teutonic Knights. In 1511 Margrave Albert (1490–1568) became grand master of the order. In 1522, during the Diet of Nuremberg, he first made contact with Luther's theology through the preaching of Andreas Osiander. In 1525 he resigned from the Teutonic Order, transformed Prussia into a secular duchy and formally introduced Protestantism on 6 July 1525. In 1523 Luther had commended John Briessmann (1488–1550) to the Margrave and, apart from a stay in Riga (1527–31), he served at the cathedral at Königsberg from his arrival in September 1523 until his death. He was assisted in the work of reform by the bishop of Samland, George von Polentz (1487–1550), a Saxon aristocrat who had given up a distinguished diplomatic career and devoted himself after 1522 to transforming his diocese into a Lutheran stronghold with himself as superintendent. The acquisition of Prussia to the Protestant ranks was of considerable significance, although the prestige of Prussia as the Protestant nucleus of the German Empire belonged to the distant future.

CITY REFORMATION

Cities which were also free territories and had their own forms of self-government play a vivid role in the history of sixteenth century Protestantism.

Nuremberg was a large city of perhaps 30,000 inhabitants, a busy trade centre governed by a small council of 42 members, patricians and aristocrats who had long mastered the art of maintaining control over the citizens. The concern of the rulers for the city's spiritual welfare had been manifested in the pre-Reformation period by their assumption of control over the monasteries and over clerical appointments.

Luther had stayed there in 1518 on his way to meet Cajetan at Augsburg and had preached there on the way back. In 1518, Wenceslas Link (1483–1547), Luther's colleague at the monastery and the university at Wittenberg, had settled at Nuremberg and had drawn considerable attention with his plain, evangelical sermons. He soon gained the sympathy of the humanist group which called itself the Sodalitas Celtica out of respect for the poet Conrad Celtis (1459–1508). It included people like Willibald Pirckheimer (1470–1530), the artist Albrecht Dürer (1471–1528) and the town clerk Lazarus Spengler (1497–1534), the distinguished supporter of Lutheranism in the city. Luther's stand at Worms had deeply impressed Nuremberg's five delegates there and, despite the city's eminence in the Empire, as the place where the imperial regalia were stored and one of the venues of the Diet, it was prepared to allow the propagation of evangelical ideas. Lutheran sympathizers were appointed provosts of the two parish churches of St. Lorenz and St. Sebald, Hektor Pomer (1495–1541) and George Pester (1470?–1536). Other Lutheran preachers were appointed also, the most forceful of them being Andreas Osiander (1498–1552) – uncle to Thomas Cranmer's wife – who worked there from 1522 to 1549.

Under the influence of men like these, changes were soon introduced. At Easter 1523 Communion was administered in both kinds and a year later German became the language of worship. The Council permitted ministers to eliminate unacceptable practices and ornaments and also it introduced changes of its own, such as banning the Passion Play on Good Friday 1524.

The city had to keep a wary eye on the Emperor but it adopted the view that imperial declarations which permitted the preaching of the pure gospel in accordance with the Bible were to be understood as abrogations of the Edict of Worms and a licence to proceed with reform. In order to decide finally the city's official position in doctrine, a public disputation was held from 3 to 14 March 1525 in which the Roman Catholic standpoint was defended by Lienhard Ebner and the evangelical view by Osiander. The Council decided for the reformers, the Mass was abolished and the monasteries dissolved. Nuremberg was especially successful in reorganizing social welfare and education. All church property was to be administered from the Common Chest and the Great Almonry, and they were responsible also for paying the stipends of ministers, the pensions of monks and nuns, the salaries of teachers, and grants to the poor. From these sources also the resources for the upkeep of the improved school system came.

Thus at Nuremberg the Protestant Reformation started early and developed under the patronage of the City Council. The civic concern for good order, however, meant that there was no room for dissent. Unacceptable pamphlets were confiscated and dissenters, like Hans Denck, were expelled. Anabaptism was discouraged but only one of its leaders, Wolfgang Vogel, was executed. Otherwise, Nuremberg acted with moderation in promoting religious change.

Nuremberg became a stubborn supporter of the evangelical position. Thus, when Melanchthon was being tempted at Augsburg in 1530 to compromise with the Roman Catholics, Nuremberg insisted that he stand fast by his principles. And the final church order that was adopted in 1533 by Nuremberg served as a model for securing uniformity of doctrine and organization in other parts of Germany.

EVANGELISTS AND MARTYRS

Through the exertions of devoted preachers, as well as by eager imitation, towns, cities and states all over Germany joined the Protestant ranks. It was a time of exciting and extensive spiritual upheaval.

Nicholas von Amsdorf (1483–1565) was one of Luther's closest friends, his companion at Leipzig in 1519 and at Worms in 1521. From 1524 he was pastor of St. Ulrich's at Magdeburg and the first Protestant superintendent. His work there was so well-regarded that he was invited to reform other cities, such as Goslar in 1528 and Einbeck in 1534. His installation as bishop of Naumberg by Luther, 20 June 1542, was the beginning of an unhappy interlude and he was glad to move from there back to his old haunt at Magdeburg in 1547.

The Reformation was introduced into Breslau in 1525 by the accomplished humanist, John Hess (1490–1547), who at the beginning was assisted by the lay evangelist, Caspar Schwenkfeld (1489–1561), who later became one of the exponents of radical reformation.

In Bremen the pioneer was Henry of Zutphen (1468–1524) who started work at the Chapel of St. Ansgar in November 1522. He had already suffered imprisonment at Antwerp and had been released by a huge crowd. His brief ministry at Bremen was remarkably successful but when he was on a preaching mission in Holstein he was attacked by a drunken mob and burned at the stake at the village of Heide. His colleague, Jacob Propst was heartbroken as a result, for he, together with John Esch and Henry Voes, had shared Henry's imprisonment in the Low Countries. Esch and Voes were burned at Brussels, 1 July 1523, – the first evangelical martyrs. Propst gained his freedom by recanting, a moment of weakness which he regretted throughout his long life of service which ended with his death on 30 June 1562. He it was who persuaded Luther to publish his commemorative pamphlet, *The burning of Friar Henry*.

Hamburg became Protestant in 1523 and in 1528 was able to secure the services of John Bugenhagen, Luther's pastor at Wittenberg, to supervise the reform. Bugenhagen of Pomerania (1485–1558) was minister of Wittenberg city church from 1523 until his death, as well as professor of Theology at the University from 1535. He was a gracious pastor of souls, as Luther well knew, but combined with this ability a gift for organization which he was able to exercise in many places in northern Germany and Denmark.

Urbanus Rhegius (1489–1541), humanist and poet, was the pioneer of the Reformation in both Augsburg in the south and Brunswick-Luneburg in the north. At Mecklenburg the impetus came from the local dukes who began to initiate change in 1524. John Brenz (1499–1570) began to introduce the Reformation at Schwäbisch-Hall in 1522 and his work there became the model for change in the Duchy of Würtemberg.

12 New evangelical strongholds

The city of hope.

Anabaptist description of Strasbourg.

Although it did not rank as one of the great commercial centres of Europe, like Nuremberg or Frankfurt, Strasbourg was a flourishing city handling the trade that passed through it from Italy to the north and making its own contribution to economic wealth with its textiles, wine and garden produce. And it was to play a unique role in the history of the Protestant Reformation since it was accessible to the various new ideas that were fermenting in Europe at the time. Humanism thrived there in the persons of Sebastian Brant, Jacob Wimpfeling, Jacob Sturm and others.

Preaching was to be a crucial influence on the emergence of Protestantism at Strasbourg. In 1521 Matthaus Zell (1477–1548) announced his intention to preach the pure gospel from his pulpit in the St. Laurence chapel at the cathedral. The bishop, Wilhelm von Hohenstein, initiated legal proceedings against him but the magistrates refused to depose Zell because of the public support for his sermons. In 1523 Wolfgang Capito (1478–1541), the son of a blacksmith and a brilliant academic, came to Strasbourg as provost of St. Thomas's, was soon converted to the evangelical position by Zell and started preaching himself. 'The people crowded around with wonder that a provost should preach and concern himself with such trifles', said the chronicler. There was little the city authorities could do to stop the rise of Protestantism since the new men appointed to vacant livings soon embraced evangelical views. Distinguished among the converts was Caspar

Hedio (1494–1553), preacher at the cathedral, and Martin Bucer (1491–1551), a native of Selestat in Alsace who had been deeply impressed by Luther's performance at the Heidelberg disputation and had successfully sought release from his monastic vows. Bucer was to make a very personal contribution to the story of the Reformation with his passionate ecumenical search for Christian unity. He arrived in Strasbourg in May 1523. On 21 February 1524 the parishoners of St Aurelie, led by the influential Gardeners' Guild defied higher authority and chose him as their pastor. This set a pattern and in August 1524 the magistrates decided to take the appointment of preachers into their own hands. So the ordinary people had played a formative part in initiating the Reformation and by 1525 the city authorities had become its patrons.

The city authorities moved slowly. The first step towards abolishing the Mass was taken at Easter 1525 but only after a long popular campaign did final abolition come in February 1529.

In the main the Protestant leaders at Strasbourg were tolerant men and large numbers of refugees from persecution elsewhere made the city their sanctuary. In constitutional matters, Bucer's attempt to persuade the Council to erect a system in which religious and secular life would be closely bound together, with the clergy having substantial powers, came to nothing and in 1534 the city adopted a constitution in which doctrine, discipline and finance were to be under the control of lay committees – in other words, a state church in miniature. In educational and social matters, the Reformation at Strasbourg coincided with remarkable and effective improvements. By 1531 the Councils had instituted a fine system of education which gave every child the opportunity to climb from the elementary school, through grammar school to university. Concern for social welfare had long characterized the city leaders and only indirectly did Protestantism contribute to the improvements of the system which enabled Strasbourg to cope efficiently with the flood of refugees that came to the city.

AUGSBURG

Luther had visited Augsburg in 1518 and John Frosch, his host at the priory and a Wittenberg graduate, became a warm supporter. It was he, together with Urbanus Rhegius (1489–1541), who first administered Communion in both kinds in 1524. The city Council tolerated evangelical preachers while seeking not to offend the Emperor. It was difficult to hold such a balance because of the growing influence of Zwingli's supporters and of the Anabaptists. The latter were dispersed and when the Diet was held in Augsburg in 1530, the Emperor prohibited evangelical preaching and the Council dismissed the preachers. But the Council found it difficult to withstand the growing public clamour for reformation and the threat of disorder. After much discussion the city did embrace Protestantism in July 1534, banned Roman Catholic preaching and secularized church property. Augsburg is an interesting example of the way in which city authorities could be made to accept Protestantism under pressure from public opinion.

BERN

Many of the characteristics of the Protestant Reformation in the German cities may be observed in Switzerland too.

The progress of the Reformation at Bern illustrates how evangelical preaching, combined with trenchant literary propaganda and lay criticism of church abuses, could bring about change. The pioneer preacher was Berchtold Haller (1492–1536), born in Würtemberg and educated at Cologne, who became assistant preacher at the church of St. Vincent in 1515 and embraced evangelical views in 1521. It was in October of the year that Dr. Sebastian Meyer came to the Franciscan priory and supported Haller's efforts. When Hugo von Landenberg, the bishop of Constance, admonished his flock in a letter to beware of Zwinglian views, Meyer replied in his robust *Earnest Admonition* (1522) in which he exposes the rapacity of church bureaucrats, the addiction to ceremonialism and empty titles, and the quarrelsomeness of the monastic orders. And for what purpose? 'Dear layman, it is all done with one purpose in mind, – to get at your pocketbook, which enables them to have full

gullets and live indulgent lives.' Even more abrasive were
the productions of Nicholas Manuel (died 1530), poet,
soldier and statesman. During Lent 1523 his play, *The
Corpse-eaters*, was performed in the city. It is a satire on the
exploitation of the cult of the dead. The priest at the
opening of the play explains why he likes dead people, for
'They are our food and pay.' Unless he and his like are to
lose their life of ease, they must be 'Quiet about the Gospel', in case lay people discover the truth! The play is a
vivid reminder that the Protestant Reformation was not all
sermons and academic disputations. Lampoons, satires,
broad farces and comic songs also made their contribution.

The evangelical leaders, assisted from April 1527 by
Franz Kolb (1465–1535), persuaded the city to embrace Protestantism. In 1525 Haller ceased saying Mass. Although
the Peasants' War led to a nervous reaction and the
expulsion of Meyer, public demand for reformation continued to rise and the municipal elections of 1527 went in
favour of the Reformers. The Council ordered a public
disputation which lasted from 6 to 25 January 1528. The
Roman Catholic representatives were not able to match the
strong Protestant team, consisting of Zwingli, Capito,
Bucer, Oecolampadius, as well as Haller and Kolb. The
debate centred on the Ten Theses drawn up by Haller and
opening with the thesis:

> The holy Christian Church, whose only head is Christ, is
> born of the Word of God, and abides in the same and
> listens not to the voice of a stranger.

These theses served as the basis for the edict of 7 February
1528 which abolished episcopal jurisdiction and initiated
Protestantism at Bern. In January 1532 a church order and
system of discipline were adopted to give the church there
its Reformed character.

BASEL

At Basel the architect of the Reformation was Johannes
Huszgen (1482–1531), usually known by his humanist pen-
name as Oecolampadius, the man whom both Luther and
Calvin called 'the noblest of men'. He was the son of a

merchant, born at Würtemberg and educated at
Heidelberg, Tübingen and Basel. He grew into an
exceptionally learned humanist, a friend of Erasmus and
Reuchlin, tutor to Landgrave Philip of Hesse. He moved to
Basel in 1515 to work as Erasmus's literary assistant and
after a brief absence returned to become a professor of
Theology at the University there in 1523. That year, too, he
adopted the evangelical position and began to exercise con-
siderable public influence as acting vicar of St. Martin's.
With regard to the sacrament of Communion, he sided with
Zwingli. He began to reform the liturgy at his church
towards the end of 1525 but the printed form which
appeared the following year still contained distinctively
Catholic elements.

The city authorities were reluctant to support a full
Reformation until after the disputation at Baden, 18 May to
8 June 1526. It was hoped that a successful debate there
would lead to a general Swiss reformation in which all the
cantons would participate. Haller together with Oecolampadius stated the Protestant case against John Eck,
the Roman Catholic theologian, but at the end the voting
went against the Reformers. But Oecolampadius now hard-
ened his attitude to Roman Catholicism and became sterner
in his condemnation of the Mass. Excitement increased and
on 9 February 1529 the supporters of Protestantism took
matters into their own hands, demolished images and cru-
cifixes, removed pictures from the churches and demanded
of the Council a form of worship like that used at Zürich. It
had little choice but to comply. Under the leadership of
Oecolampadius, who became the chief preacher at the Minster as well as 'Antistes' (Superintendent) of the clergy, the
Reformed Church at Basel was put on a firm evangelical
foundation as regards moral teaching and theology. In
worship a number of Roman Catholic practices were
retained and such religious offences as blasphemy and
denial of the clauses of the Apostles' Creed were
punishable by banishment or even death.

In these various ways, Protestantism took root in many
German and Swiss cities, pioneered by individual
preachers who formed groups and parties able to influence
the wielders of civic power. And the change occurred over
a comparatively short period, eleven years in Constance,

thirteen years in Nuremberg, nine years at Rostock and ten years at Ulm. That so great a change as that from Roman Catholicism to Protestantism should have happened so often with so little disruption was a remarkable achievement.

13 A challenge to Christendom

The law that condemns heretics to the fire builds up both Zion in blood and Jerusalem in wickedness.

Now it is apparent to everyone, even the blind, that the law which demands the burning of heretics is an invention of the Devil.

Balthasar Hübmaier (1485?–1528) in 1524.

In the countries where Protestantism struck the deepest roots, its success owed much to the patronage of governments. The close co-operation between the church and the civil powers could be traced back to the time of Constantine the Great in the fourth century. The relationship had been consolidated during the Middle Ages and embodied in the concept of 'Christendom', the all-embracing Christian social organism in which the secular and religious aspects of European life were fused into a unity. It was therefore assumed by the authorities that a good government would patronize and defend true religion. As Christian people renewed their familiarity with the Bible in the sixteenth century, an uneasiness grew about this marriage between church and state. And a minority were moved to make a fundamental challenge to Christendom. If the state-sponsored reformations of people like Luther, Zwingli and Calvin sought only to remove some of the obvious weaknesses of traditional Christendom, had the time not come to institute a kind of reformation which rejected the concept of state-sponsorship and boldly set about erecting free churches? This is the challenge to which we turn now as we glance at the 'Radical Reformation'.

VARIETY

This upsurge of radical enthusiasm was not a single unified movement. It had no centralized organization. It was pluralistic and took many forms. It had a large number of active leaders and they generated among their fellows a dedication which made missionaries of a high proportion of them. These leaders were inveterate wanderers, partly from choice and partly from necessity, for their principles made fugitives of them. These groups were scattered all over Europe from Italy to England and from Spain to Poland. They did not have a uniform organization. The majority were congregationalists, for necessity dictated the simplest of structures. But some, like the Hutterite Brethren, set up a church that was also a social and economic community. A very small minority sought to erect a church that was both a community and a kingdom, as did the revolutionaries in Münster, while at the opposite extreme individuals like Sebastian Franck thought of the true church as an invisible, inward and spiritual fellowship. A study of these radical reformers reveals vividly how varied were the forms of reformation being canvassed from 1521 onwards. And the variety extended to matters of theology as well.

COMMON BELIEFS

Those who advocated a voluntary and free reformation had no formal creed to unite them nor did they all embrace one system of doctrine. Yet despite the considerable differences between them on many points of theology, they did hold some beliefs in common. Thus, they were all critical of the Roman Catholic Church. They were all disappointed with the state-sponsored attempts to reform it. They distinguished sharply between the sphere of the state and that of the church and held that it was quite unbiblical for the state to coerce people in matters of faith, for faith is nurtured by God, not by human compulsion. Only a very small minority of the radicals held that state compulsion could ever be justified in matters of religion. Numerically, the largest bloc among the radicals was the Anabaptists who far outnumbered all the others. They rejected infant baptism and insisted that baptism, in order to be a true sacrament, must be administered on confession of personal faith. So the practice of believers' baptism was a potent bond of unity between them as well as a mark to differentiate them from others. And since their rejection of their own infant baptism drove the authorities to fury against them, they were united by the anguish of persecution. Many of them in their teaching emphasized the significance of suffering as a unique hallmark of Christian obedience.

They were divided among themselves about the seat of authority in matters of life and faith although they firmly rejected the Roman Catholic emphasis on tradition. The vast majority – including virtually all the Anabaptists, – shared with other Protestants a deep conviction that the Bible had prime authority in matters of faith. Indeed, it was their complaint that Luther and Zwingli had not applied their own principle of 'scripture alone' (*sola scriptura*) with sufficient rigour and had allowed the state rather than the Bible to settle too many questions. But other radicals were inspirationists who asserted the prime authority of the Holy Spirit. These looked more to the glories of the future rather than to any attempt to reproduce the beauties of the New Testament church. Then there were those who shared much of the humanist faith in human reason and saw it as the seat of authority. Some of these turned the edge of their rationalism against the doctrine of the Trinity as defined by the councils of the fourth and fifth centuries. The Anabaptists, however, were Trinitarians.

While the majority of radicals were orthodox Protestants with regard to the central doctrines of the Christian faith, they differed from both Protestants and Roman Catholics and disagreed among themselves on the understanding of the nature of the church, the role of the magistrate, the legitimacy of war, the relation of good works to justification, the nature of the sacraments and the way in which the divine Logos became incarnate.

At many points, therefore, the testimony of the radicals provides a lively counterpoint to the dialogue between Roman Catholic and state-sponsored Protestant.

BEGINNINGS

Demands for a more thorough application of evangelical principles, leading to some public disorder, were voiced in Wittenberg during Luther's enforced absence at the Wartburg in 1521. The leader of the agitation, as we have seen, was his senior colleague, Andrew Bodenstein of Carlstadt. However this outburst of radical enthusiasm soon subsided when Luther reasserted his authority after his return from the Wartburg. In Zürich similarly, as we have seen also, the movement led by Grebel, Mantz and Blaurock was suppressed by the authorities only to spread beyond the borders of Switzerland. These trials compelled the Anabaptists to ponder over their significance in the Christian's life and they integrated a doctrine of suffering into their theology. It makes a moving counterpoint to Luther's 'Theology of the Cross'.

THE WAY OF SUFFERING

Many Anabaptists, following the teaching of leaders like Hans Denck, Hans Hut and Balthasar Hübmaier, distinguished between three kinds of baptism, namely, baptism by the Spirit, baptism by water and baptism in blood. They insisted that suffering was a positive and enriching aspect of Christian discipleship. This teaching had affinities with late mediaeval penitential mysticism but official opposition to the Anabaptists compelled them to meditate very realistically upon the spiritual significance of the anguish which they themselves had to undergo at the hands of their persecutors. And their deep faith in the value of their suffering contributed towards the unflagging persistence of their evangelism.

SPREADING THE MESSAGE

The Swiss Brethren soon extended their mission beyond the neighbourhood of Zürich. In the years between 1525 and 1529 they met with remarkable success. During those years, in the lands lying between Strasbourg in the west and Vienna in the east, Thuringia in the north and the Tyrol in the south, some 500 Anabaptist congregations came into existence. The vast majority of them had no more than 25 members each, but there were also substantial churches, such as the 360 at Waldshut, the 300 at Augsburg and the 100 at Strasbourg. But of course even the small congregations must have had a larger circle of sympathizers in addition to the enrolled membership.

SATTLER AND SCHLEITHEIM

The movement produced some fascinating leaders, fitting successors of the Swiss pioneers. The ex-monk Michael Sattler (c. 1490–1527) had escaped from Austria to Zürich in 1525 and it was there that he abandoned Lutheranism to become an Anabaptist. On his expulsion from the city in November 1525 he made his way to Strasbourg and then to Horb, near Rattenburg, where he exercised a vigorous and influential evangelistic ministry. He realized how important it was to provide the scattered congregations with a measure of stability in the face of the emotional enthusiasm that had emerged on the fringes of the movement. He was the leading spirit at the conference of Anabaptists held at Schleitheim, in the canton of Schaffhausen, on 24 February 1527. The gathering accepted a declaration drawn up by Sattler, the *Brotherly Union*, addressed to the 'children of light . . . scattered everywhere'. This Schleitheim Confession, as it is now commonly known, is not a full statement of Christian faith but concentrates on points that were of concern at the time. It asserts the belief in believers' baptism, the importance of excommunication (or the 'ban') as the instrument instituted by Christ to preserve the purity of his church, and defines the unity of the church of validly baptized true believers. Then it goes on in its fourth article to assert the need to make a separation from 'the wickedness which the devil planted in the world', while the fifth article shows how soon the Anabaptists had come to possess a mature doctrine of the function of the pastor in the community. The sixth article deals with the 'sword', which, it says, has been ordained by God 'outside the perfection of Christ' and is rightly used by the civil magistrate for the punishment of evildoers. But 'in the perfection of Christ' no other sanction is permissible than the ban. The last article declares that it is

wrong for Christians to swear an oath under any circumstances. In this way, Sattler sought to bring the congregations of the brethren in south Germany and Switzerland to
a common mind on some issues.

While Sattler was at Schleitheim, the authorities became
aware of his activities and he and his wife were arrested
and brought to trial on 15 May 1527 together with a dozen
members of their congregation. They were charged with
such things as disobeying the emperor, denying the Real
Presence in the Eucharist, rejecting the validity of infant
baptism, refusing to swear oaths and advocating pacifism.
Despite suffering considerable abuse from the members of
the court, Sattler defended himself with ability and an
unfailing courtesy which exasperated both the bench and
the public gallery. He was found guilty and, after being
subjected to revolting barbarities, was burned at the stake
on 20 May 1527. His wife was executed by drowning a week
later. His martyrdom, together with his courage, left an
indelible mark upon contemporaries and forced his tor-
mentors to consider seriously whether it was not more
advisable to seek the conversion of dissenters than to provoke public sympathy by making martyrs of them.

AN ADVOCATE OF TOLERATION

Balthasar Hübmaier (?1485–1528) was not a man of steel,
but the gentleness which made him abhor violence adds to
the attraction of this former professor at the University of
Ingoldstadt, who later became a preacher at Regensburg
Cathedral, and in 1521 parish priest at Waldshut on the
northern border of Switzerland. He had embraced the
teaching of Zwingli but by 1525 he had become convinced
that personal faith was a necessary precondition of baptism
and in consequence that it should not be administered to
infants. He himself was baptized by William Reublin and
some 360 of his parishoners followed his example. During
the Peasants' War his sympathies were with the rebels and
he had to leave Waldshut for Zürich. After a public debate
with Zwingli and others he agreed to recant his views on
baptism but when the time came to do so in the
Fraumunster, his conscience forbade him to comply. He
was imprisoned and tortured and once again agreed to

withdraw his views, which he did to his lasting regret, as he showed in his *Short Apology*.

He now left Zürich and found peace in Moravia. He settled down at Nicolsburg under the patronage of the two counts of Liechtenstein, Leonard and John, in 1526. Here, over the space of a few months, he published a series of seventeen pamphlets expounding his views with learning, graciousness and occasional brilliance. His peace was soon disturbed by the advent of Hans Hut and his fiery gospel. Dissension followed and Ferdinand of Austria, the overlord of the territory, demanded his extradition. Although sorely tempted to recant his views, he stood his ground and was burned at the stake at Vienna on 10 March 1528 with words of forgiveness and the name of Jesus on his lips. Three days later his wife was executed by drowning in the waters of the Danube. Although Hübmaier was not a typical Anabaptist, the movement produced no finer spirit and his arguments for religious toleration make him a notable pioneer of liberty of conscience.

VISIONS OF CATASTROPHE

If Sattler and Hübmaier represented the more prosaic side of Anabaptism, there were others who were inspired by apocalyptic visions. The belief that the world was approaching its end was common enough; it weighed upon Luther's mind. But in some Anabaptist circles the belief gave rise to excited expectations.

Thomas Münzer (c. 1490–1525), although not himself an Anabaptist, had linked his own brand of rebellious radicalism with a militant gospel. When he was parish priest of Allstedt in 1523–4 he had recruited a local militia to defend the parish and its Protestantism from outside interference. He was implicated in the Peasants' War and saw it as a sign of the imminence of the Kingdom of God. He used extremely inflammatory language as he called the oppressed people to engage in battle. 'Let not the sword of the saint get cold', he wrote, and he devised a revolutionary banner for the peasants which bore a white flag with a sword or, alternatively, a white banner bearing the rainbow of the covenant. When Landgrave Philip of Hesse was moving to extinguish the peasant uprisings, Münzer

deployed his soldiers at Frankenhausen. The peasants had
the advantage over the prince on the first day, 14 May 1525,
but were scattered on the following day when bombarded
by the Landgrave's artillery. Münzer was captured after the
battle, recanted his views and was beheaded on 27 May.

FROM VIOLENCE TO NON-RESISTANCE

It was typical of Hans Hut's eccentricity that he should be
present with the army at Frankenhausen selling books to
the peasants. He was a man of irrepressible energy whose
tempestuous oratory drew people to him. Deeply
impressed by Münzer's predictions of the imminent end of
the world, the calamity at Frankenhausen only served to
strengthen his faith in that message. Indeed, just four days
after Münzer's execution he was himself preaching that
'The subjects should murder all the authorities, for the
opportune time has arrived: the power is in their hands.' A
year later, 26 May 1526, he was at Augsburg and accepted
rebaptism at the hands of Hans Denck. He now became the
Anabaptist 'apostle of Austria' combining a new emphasis
on non-resistance with a stirring call to the faithful to await
God's fearful vengeance on all oppressors. He caused dissension among Hübmaier's people at Nicolsburg and so
deepened a growing schism among the radicals. Finally
he was arrested and imprisoned at Augsburg and died of
suffocation after a fire in his cell on 7 December 1527.
Eschatology provided much of the agenda for the 'Martyrs'
Synod' held at Augsburg in August 1527 and attended by a
host of Anabaptists, including Hut and Denck. Was it
proper to expect the second coming in 1528? How should
Anabaptists prepare for the event? What should their
attitude be to the secular authorities? Was it not the
appropriate time to ordain many new missioners for work
in southern Germany? These were the questions discussed
at Augsburg. But the authorities, assisted by the city's
Protestant leader, Urbanus Rhegius, began to round up the
Anabaptist leaders, Hut among them. And so the Martyrs'
Synod gained its name.

APOSTLES OF LOVE

Hans Denck became disillusioned by what he saw and heard at Augsburg. His preference was for a spiritualistic understanding of the Bible and he, like Hübmaier, objected to the literalistic eschatology of Hans Hut. Denck (c. 1495–1527) was an accomplished scholar who, after attending the universities of Ingoldstadt and Bern, taught school at Nuremberg. His unreadiness to attribute an objective value to the sacraments led to his expulsion and he migrated to Augsburg where he was rebaptized in the autumn of 1525 by Hübmaier. He founded an Anabaptist church in the city which was to grow into one of the largest in Germany. He moved on to Strasbourg but was expelled from the city on Christmas Day 1526. He was a lonely man. He spent a quiet period at Worms where he co-operated with Ludwig Hetzer (c. 1500–1529) in producing a German translation of the Old Testament prophets. As we saw, he was back in Augsburg in the summer of 1527 but had become tired of the vagaries and dissensions among his Anabaptist colleagues. He was allowed to settle at Basel but soon died there of the plague. Denck was a man of independent judgment and this is why he has been so variously estimated. His views were not typical of Anabaptism generally but he did share both its rejection of infant baptism and the conviction that Christianity is a life lived in love. He himself was a shining exemplar of this conviction in his distaste of controversy and the graciousness of his writing, not least in the most telling of his works, *Of the true love*.

Pilgram Marpeck (died December 1556) shared Denck's pacific spirit although he was the most impressive spokesman of that sober, evangelical Anabaptism which eschewed eschatological extremes and adhered to the main doctrines of Protestant orthodoxy. Marpeck came from the wealthy burgher class at Rattenberg in the Austrian Tyrol and was an engineer by profession. He exercised a widespread and influential itinerant ministry over southern Germany, the Tyrol and Moravia. Unlike many of his colleagues, he differentiated clearly between the Old and the New Testaments, partly because over-emphasis on the Old Testament led to such excesses as polygamy and the belief in a holy war. Marpeck insisted that the revelation in Jesus

Christ is unique and supreme and that he is the heart of the New Testament. The brethren should follow him, and him alone, living a life of service, love and faith.

So Anabaptism became a lively and provocative movement, including people of very different convictions in its ranks, and producing a numerous company of martyrs. But its most vigorous period was very brief and it had but a minimal influence upon the main-line Refomation. Its history in the Netherlands, however, deserves further attention.

14 Restoration, revolution and reason

Where you hear of a poor, simple, cast-off little flock which is despised and rejected by the world, join them; for where you hear of the cross, there is Christ.

From the last will and testament of Anneken Jans addressed to her infant son, Isaiah, on the eve of her execution at Rotterdam, 1539.

The years after 1530 were critical ones for radical Protestantism. It was obvious that its message appealed to thousands of people but its future was put in jeopardy, not only by the systematic opposition of secular governments, but also by the vagaries and excesses of some of its own supporters. So in these years there developed a significant contest between those who sought to ensure a continuing place for the radical testimony and those who were attracted by visionary programmes.

MELCHIOR HOFMANN

The link between southern and northern Anabaptism was Melchior Hofmann (c.1495–1543). He was a native of Schwäbisch-Hall and a furrier by trade. He became an ardent supporter of Luther and travelled widely in Livonia, Sweden and Denmark between 1523 and 1527, proving himself a preacher of quite extraordinary power. Luther became critical of him because he adopted the Zwinglian position with regard to Communion and so brought about an end to his work in Denmark. By 1530 Hofmann was at Strasbourg and in April accepted rebaptism and became a member of the Anabaptist congregation there. The city council had him arrested but he escaped to East Friesland.

It was in 1530 also that he published his *Ordinance of God*, a moving exposition of his convictions. In it he maintains that baptism is a sign of Christ's covenant with believers and should be administered only on confession of faith, while Communion is the heavenly bridegroom's ring presented to his bride, the church. His preaching at the Great Church at Emden, Germany, was so successful that some 300 people, 'burgher and peasant, lord and servant' accepted rebaptism. He made Emden the focal point of northern Anabaptism. But opposition forced him to move on. He was so gripped by the belief that the second coming was about to happen, and that the scene of Christ's appearance would be Strasbourg, that he returned there and virtually insisted on being imprisoned so that he could bear personal witness to the truth of his prophecies when Christ came in 1533. Then a world revolution would be initiated and Christ would set up a lasting kingdom of peace and justice. 1533 came and went but there was no second coming. Hofmann's hope, however, was in no way diminished and he continued to look forward to the great day until death took him in 1543. Although he was largely forgotten by then, the influence of his work remained among his followers, – the Melchiorites, – and he was the father of Dutch Anabaptism.

THE SEARCH FOR COMMUNITY

The references in the book of Acts to the Jerusalem church having all things in common fascinated the radical reformers who were especially interested in seeking to reconstitute the early church. As early as 1527 some Austrian Anabaptists were eager to see the practice revived, Wolfgang Brandhuber and his group at Linz being especially enthusiastic. But the group which has preserved this practice down to the present day are the Hutterites.

Jacob Hutter, a native of the Puster Valley in the Tyrol, a hatter by craft, became an Anabaptist preacher in 1529. The mounting repression had driven many of his fellow-believers from the Tyrol to seek peace in Moravia where some of the local rulers, in the wake of the bitter Hussite wars, had insisted on freedom of worship in their territories. That was why Hübmaier had been able to settle quietly at Nicolsburg. But in March 1528, under pressure from the Hapsburg government, Count Leonard of Liechtenstein had expelled a group of about 200, led by Jacob Wiedemann and Philip Jager. During their search for somewhere to settle, they had pooled their resources and after they had found a home at Austerlitz, they continued to practice a form of communism. The commune (or *Bruderhof*) flourished and within a couple of years had some 600 members. Unhappily there was dissension among them and it was a break-away group that Hutter joined on 11 August 1533. He saw at once that a stable organization was necessary. He displaced the men who were leading the group but continuing emigration from the Tyrol soon compensated for defections. In 1535 the Hapsburg ruler, Ferdinand of Austria, again called for more effective action against heretics. Hutter fled to the Tyrol but was captured and was burned at the stake on 25 February 1536. In honour of his memory, his followers called themselves Hutterites.

They formed a unique community. For them community of goods was as much a New Testament precept as the practice of believers' baptism. Hutter had provided them with a firm constitution. They were led by bishops, 'servants of the Word' (or elders) and 'servants of temporal needs'. They dedicated themselves to an astonishing missionary enterprise, sending out missionaries far and wide to find people who would share in their communal life. Such a mission demanded great courage for only two out of every ten missionaries escaped eventual imprisonment or martyrdom. Yet the communities increased. By 1564 there were 38 of them but the precise number of members cannot be ascertained. After Hutter's death, leadership fell to a German from Silesia, Peter Riedemann (1506–1556), a man of great dedication and ability who was the undisputed leader until his own death. So the Hutterites were able to form a community, efficient in its organization and unswerving in its faith, which united profession and practice, worship and work.

REVOLUTIONARIES

In July 1531, Bernard Rothmann (*c.* 1495–1535) returned home to Münster after studying at the University of Cologne nearby and at once began to attract attention as a preacher. By January 1532 he was publishing his Lutheran creed and by April the town council had displaced the priests nominated by the bishop and appointed evangelical preachers instead, with Rothmann becoming the Protestant pastor of St. Lambert's. Since Rothmann's views were maturing quickly in a more radical direction, dissension arose. Rothmann began to advocate believers' baptism and so attracted a growing number of Anabaptists to the town. The attempts of the authorities to expel Rothmann were unavailing and by January 1534 he was virtually in control. His influence with the poor was strengthened by his insistence that it was a Christian duty to share possessions and at a time of bad harvests and dear food, many crowded into Münster from the neighbourhood round about.

News of these developments soon reached the radicals in the Netherlands. At the beginning of 1534 they sent emissaries to Münster who rebaptized Rothmann, and he in turn rebaptized some 1,400 citizens. The fateful pair, Jan Matthys of Harlem and Jan Beukels of Leyden arrived to initiate an even more radical religious and political programme than that of Rothmann. They were intent on setting up a New Jerusalem, and there was to be a purge of all those who would not accept rebaptism. By 2 March all Lutherans and Roman Catholics had been expelled. Since the prince-bishop was preparing to besiege the town, steps were taken to strengthen the defences and to invite Anabaptists from the Netherlands and elsewhere to come to the 'holy city'. Food, property and money were declared to be common property and that meant the introduction of communism.

On 4 April Jan Matthys lost his life in a sortie against the surrounding army and John Beukels took control. The traditional government of the town was replaced by a group of twelve elders and they published a body of laws which expressed the unity of church, society, state and army in the new theocracy. It was an extremely harsh régime. Death was the penalty for a long list of offences including complaining, talking scandal and disobeying masters. But the most offensive element in the new system was felt to be the introduction of polygamy. It became an offence not to be married. Moreover, in September 1534 Beukels had himself crowned 'King of the people of God in the New Temple' and the following month Rothmann published his *Restitution* which provided an apology for the policies adopted at Münster on the basis that the Old and New Testaments must be considered a unity. Meanwhile, Beukels ruled with a rod of iron and sent messengers in every direction to seek help but none came.

Famine had made the inhabitants desperate and in the end they were betrayed from inside the town. The besieging armies broke in on 25 June and massacred almost all the citizens. King Jan and some of the other leaders were taken alive and executed on 22 January 1536.

The Münster episode was not typical of Anabaptist behaviour for the vast majority of Anabaptists took a pacifist position, but for generations 'Münster' was a word of execration. It was only by patient work and continuing sacrifice that responsible men, like the sagacious Menno Simons, could restore to the movement a measure of respect in the eyes of its critics.

INDIVIDUALS

Caspar Schwenkfeld (1489–1561), an aristocratic Silesian and a knight of the Teutonic Order, became a Lutheran in 1518. Despite playing a significant part in the development of Protestantism and being acquainted with many of the leading reformers, Schwenkfeld was a lonely man. He searched for a middle way, a 'royal road' as he called it, between Roman Catholic and Protestant. He was a searcher for peace and emphasized the significance of the role of the Holy Spirit in the Christian life. For him, the real sacraments were inward and the church should not rely too much on visible and material things. Indeed, the true church is itself a spiritual corporation. As he put it, 'To my mind, I am one with all churches in that I pray for them, in that I despise none, because I know that Christ the Lord has his own everywhere, be they ever so few'. Schwenkfeld deeply influenced Sebastian Franck (c. 1499–1542), who also sought an undogmatic spirituality and argued for complete freedom of thought, untrammelled by dogmas.

Both Michael Servetus and Sebastian Castellio were independently-minded individuals rather than the leaders of any group or party and their story is interwoven with that of the Reformation in Geneva. But Servetus's questions about the doctrine of the Trinity were raised by other thinkers too, such as the Paduan professor Matteo Gribaldi Mofa (died 1564), George Blandrata (1516–85) of Piedmont, who likes Gianpaolo Alciati (?1520–?73) was an elder of the Italian congregation at Geneva and sympathized with Servetus. But better known are the two Sozzinis, uncle and nephew. Lelio Sozzini (Socinus, 1525–62), a widely travelled scholar, had doubts about the traditional formulation of the doctrine of the Trinity but did not make them public. It was his nephew, Fausto Sozzini (1539–1604) who developed his uncle's insights into the theological system known as 'Socinianism' and so became one of the founding fathers of modern Unitarianism.

15 Reform in Denmark, Norway and Iceland

The Christian faith is free.

King Frederick I, 1527.

Ever since the Union of Kolmar (1397), Denmark, Norway and Sweden were under one crown. But it was often a turbulent relationship. Since 1513, Christian II had been king of Denmark and of Norway but had failed to consolidate his claim to the throne of Sweden despite capturing Stockholm in 1520. Christian was a perplexing character. He was an exceptionally cultured man, open to Renaissance influences; he was also genuinely concerned to improve the lot of his poorer subjects, but at the same time he was cruel and vindictive. It was the cruel streak in his character that roused the fury of the Swedes and resulted in the election of Gustavus Vasa as king of Sweden in his place in 1523.

The progress of Protestantism in Scandinavia was closely intertwined with politics and the struggles between kings, nobles and bishops. But these commotions were affected by the rapid spread of evangelical teaching under the influence of a growing body of able preachers. On the other hand, the Roman Catholic Church was unable to defend itself against the demands of the crown and the nobility, nor could it effectively counter the mounting popular enthusiasm for Protestantism. Bishops were powerful and wealthy but the provision of dedicated and learned priests in the parishes was inadequate. The condition of the church called for far-reaching reforms.

DENMARK

Christian II had a sincere desire to initiate these reforms.

He had some sympathy with the ideals of a Roman Catholic reformer like Paulus Helie (1480–1534), with his biblical and patristic emphasis, as well as his fierce criticisms of the weaknesses of the church. In order to promote improvements, the king had asked Wittenberg for its help. Martin Reinhard was sent. He was an undergraduate who knew no Danish and his services at St. Nicholas's Church proved to be a means of amusement rather than of edification. In May 1521 Andrew Carlstadt also came but he was no more successful and was back in Wittenberg within a month. Then came the Diet of Worms where Luther was declared an outlaw and the attempt to introduce Protestantism to Denmark was halted. And to add to the King's troubles, his bitter relations with the nobility led to his dethronement in 1523 and the accession of his uncle, Frederick I.

Frederick was not unsympathetic to the new evangelical ideas and several influences were pushing him in the direction of reform. There was a growing popular enthusiasm for Lutheranism, inspired not least by the exciting preaching of Hans Tausen (1494–1561), the great leader of the Danish Reformation. He returned home from Wittenberg in 1524 and his early work at Viborg in Jutland was bearing rich spiritual fruit by 1526. It was there, too, that his colleague Jorgen Jensen Sadolin founded a theological college under royal patronage. Then, again, Frederick was influenced by the enthusiasm of his son, Christian, Duke of North Schleswig, for the Reformation. Christian had already introduced Lutheran preachers into his territory and imposed a Lutheran church order.

Collapse of Roman Catholicism
The most significant developments took place in the diets held at Odense in 1526 and 1527 when the link with Rome was broken by enacting that bishops in future should seek consecration not from the pope but from the archbishop, and that the customary dues to Rome should henceforth go into the royal exchequer. When the more fervent Roman Catholics sought to persuade the King to defend the privileges of the church and halt the spread of heresy, he gave them the assurances which they sought but declined to initiate any kind of persecution. He put the point in noble

74078

words in 1527, 'The Christian faith is free. None of you desires to be forced to renounce his faith, but you must also understand that those who are devoted to the Holy Scriptures, or to the Lutheran doctrine as it is called, will no more be forced to renounce their faith . . .'. The meeting of the diet at Copenhagen in July 1530 revealed in a dramatic way both the learning and faith of the evangelical preachers. Twenty-one of them were summoned to give an account of their views. Over a number of days, acting as a team led by Tausen, they defended the forty-three articles of the confession that they had composed. Day by day the public excitement grew and the Roman Catholic defenders, despite having such able protagonists as Paulus Helie to express their convictions, soon lost heart. By then the tide of Protestantism was rising all over Denmark and the demand for a complete reformation of the church was becoming irresistible. And the spread of evangelical influence was greatly helped by the publication in 1529 of the Danish translation of the New Testament by Christian Pedersen (1480–1554).

During the remainder of Frederick's reign, the Roman Catholic Church continued to weaken, both because of the secularization of its property and because of the readiness of a Roman Catholic, like Bishop Gyldenstjerne of Funen, to encourage reformation by making the Protestant Sadolin his assistant – and Sadolin in 1537 became the first Protestant bishop of the see.

Reform completed

When Frederick died in 1533 it seemed that Denmark would dissolve in chaos. The Roman Catholics tried hard to regain lost ground and the Estates suspended all the reforms agreed upon until then. Nor did they wish to have the heir to the throne, Christian, as their king and only by taking up arms was he able to assert his claim and ascend the throne in 1536. From that moment it was clear that he intended to apply to the whole of Denmark the reforms that he had introduced in Schleswig. Christian III therefore halted the Roman Catholic reaction and the diet embraced the Protestant Reformation in October 1536. John Bugenhagen of Wittenberg was called in to supervise the erection of the new church order. In July 1537 he crowned the new king and his queen and then in September he ordained seven superintendents, the new Protestant bishops, the most distinguished of whom was Peder Plade (or Palladius, 1503–60). The same day the new church ordinance was published providing the Danish Church with its constitution. And so the way was clear for initiating those changes and improvements which would make the church life of Denmark thoroughly Protestant.

NORWAY

The story of the Protestant Reformation in Norway is not a happy one. Norway was an independent kingdom although ruled by the same king as Denmark. It followed that the policies of the kings were the same in both kingdoms. Lutheran influence in the fifteen-twenties was weak, being represented by a few preachers like Antonius, Hermann Fresze and Jens Viborg. With the connivance of King Frederick there was some destruction of churches together with the spoliation of their treasures in 1528. The leadership provided by Archbishop Olaf Engelbrektsson of Trondhjem was ineffectual and his attempt to rally the Roman Catholics in opposition to the policies of Christian III failed. He gave up the struggle, fled to the Netherlands in 1537, and died there 7 March 1538.

The victory of Charles III brought no joy to Norway. In October 1536 it lost its national liberties and became directly subject to Denmark. Spiritually, the country was in a tragic condition. There was no popular Protestant movement and no Roman Catholic vitality either. Gradually the bishops were ousted from their posts. Hans Leff (d.1545) was made Protestant bishop of Oslo and Hamar, and Geble Pedersson, who was ordained by Bugenhagen in Denmark in 1537, became bishop of Bergen and Stavanger. Elsewhere the old priests were allowed to stay in their parishes and when they died their livings were left vacant. In short, the Roman Catholic Church was just allowed to die. Since the royal policy now was to impose Danish culture on the country, no Bible or catechism or hymn-book appeared in Norwegian and Protestantism was felt to be a foreign importation. Despite the work of the occasional dedicated individual, like Bishop Jorgen Eriksson of Stavanger (1571–

1604), Protestantism took a very long time to strike roots in Norway.

ICELAND

The story of the Protestant Reformation in Iceland has a fascination all its own because it is punctuated with outrageous events, reminiscent of a much earlier age. Lutheran ideas had begun to penetrate the island thanks to the preaching of Jon Einarsson, the stern critic of the cult of the saints, and Gisli Jonsson, a future bishop. Odd Gottskalksson (d. 1556) had become acquainted with the evangelical standpoint in Norway and on his return home in 1533 began his translation of the New Testament into Icelandic. It was published in 1540, the first printed book in the language. Gissur Einarsson had been a student at Wittenberg and in 1538 was appointed assistant to Ogmund Palsson, bishop of the southern diocese of Skalholt from 1526 to 1541. In 1540 Einarsson became Protestant superintendent of the diocese and was consecrated in 1542. Iceland was a Danish dependency and Christian III was pressing for the adoption of a Protestant church order. After some shocking displays of violence, the Althing – the parliament – accepted a new order in 1541. So in the southern of the two dioceses the adoption of Protestantism was rapid and it was accompanied too by a strong evangelical spiritual movement among the people.

It was not so in Holar, the northern diocese. The swashbuckling Jon Arason, bishop there from 1524 to 1550, was as happy with a sword in his hand as he was with a chalice, and feuding with his neighbours was his constant occupation. He was determined to defend the Roman Catholic faith and led the opposition to the new church order in the Althing in 1541. The pioneer of Lutheranism in the diocese was Olaf Hjaltason and the bishop did not interfere with his work. When the Protestant Gissur Einarsson died in 1548, at only 33 years of age, Bishop Jon Arason had a mind to assume the administration of the diocese of Skalholt. By then, however, the Lutherans were in the majority and they elected Martin Einarsson as successor to Gissur. Martin had been educated in England and had learned his evangelical theology at Copenhagen from

John MacAlpine of Perth. Frustrated in his intentions at Skalholt, Jon now tried to stop the spread of Lutheranism in his own diocese and deprived Hjaltason of his orders. But the King was becoming impatient with the bishop's antics and declared him an outlaw. Jon was no coward and immediately organized a rebellion against the King's officers in Iceland and sent them packing. But he met his match in his old enemy, Dadi Gudmundsson, who caught him together with his two sons in an ambush and beheaded them on 7 November 1550. These gruesome events marked the end of Roman Catholic resistance.

Thereafter Protestantism had a free hand to make steady and solid progress under Gisli Jonsson who succeeded Gissur at Skalholt in 1558 and continued as bishop until 1587. At the same time progress was ensured in the diocese of Holar by Olaf Hjaltason, bishop from 1552 to 1569.

16 Reform in Sweden and Finland

The Gospel shall hereafter be taught in every school.

Bishops shall consecrate no priest who is incompetent to preach the Word of God.

Articles 20 and 21 of *The Ordinances of Westeras*, 1527.

Protestantism in the Scandinavian countries took two different forms. The type that carried the day in Denmark, Norway and Iceland was in many ways different from that which prevailed in Sweden and Finland, although both reformations were embodiments of Lutheranism.

SWEDEN

The Protestant Reformation in Sweden was promoted simultaneously by royal policy and by the efforts of committed Protestants of great ability. Gustavus Vasa (1496–1560) had led the national uprising against Christian II and by overthrowing him, he ended Danish rule. Vasa was elected king himself in 1523 and presided over the dissolution of Roman Catholicism and the growth of Protestantism until his death in 1560.

His chief councillor was Laurentius Andreae (Lars Anderson, 1480–1552) a man who had embraced the principle of the primary authority of the Bible and who favoured a conservative reformation in which the ultimate owner of church property should be the crown. The archbishop of Uppsala who had compromised himself by supporting Christian II had fled the country, and those bishops who were Danes had also withdrawn. Since the pope was slow to approve the King's candidates for ecclesiastical benefices, the contact with Rome was cut as early as 1524.

Lutheranism was soon making its presence felt. Olavus Petri (Olaf Peterson, 1497–1552) and his brother, Laurentius (1499–1573), were the sons of a blacksmith and both had been educated at Wittenberg. Olavus attracted the attention of the King and in 1524 was appointed clerk of the city of Stockholm. He was not only a fine scholar but a man of indefatigable energy who was to leave an indelible mark on Swedish religious life. His book, *Useful Instruction* (1526), was the first printed product of the Swedish Reformation and many more books from his pen were to follow it. He co-operated with Laurentius Andreae in producing the Swedish translation of the New Testament which appeared in 1526 and this pioneered the way for the fine Vasa Bible of 1541. The preaching of the brothers Petri was attracting increasing attention and sympathy. The chief defender of Roman Catholicism, Peder Galle, proved an ineffectual debater. On the other hand, Olavus Petri's *Answers to Twelve Questions* (1527), with its message that the church's primary duty was to preach the pure Word of God and its lucid exposition of evangelical doctrine, was deemed singularly persuasive.

Royal tactics
The meeting of the diet which the King convened at Westeras on 24 June 1527 was of crucial significance. It was symbolic of the new age that the bishops were deprived of their traditional places of honour. But they were not without influence. The King was facing a desperate crisis both politically and financially and depended upon the church to help him with some of its immense wealth. But Bishop Hans Brask persuaded his colleagues to make it clear that they would help only if the King submitted all proposed changes to the Pope for his approval, and in general defended the privileges of the church. Gustavus resigned there and then. No one doubted that without him the kingdom would collapse in disorder. So in three days the diet capitulated and the King had his way. All church possessions that were not strictly necessary to its spiritual work were confiscated. A disputation was arranged between Roman Catholics and Protestants and the outcome was an instruction that only the pure Word of God was to

be preached in the country's churches and taught in its schools. That meant granting freedom to Protestant preachers but without curtailing the freedom of Roman Catholics to continue their preaching, since they also claimed to be proclaiming the Word of God. At the same time, the church maintained its traditional episcopal government and preserved its internal freedom.

From 1527 onwards the protagonists of the Reformation worked assiduously to spread their views. Olavus Petri's books flooded the market and in 1531 his Swedish Mass was published. His brother Laurentius was appointed the first Protestant archbishop of Uppsala, yet he was consecrated with a Roman Catholic ritual. In order to secure greater conformity with Protestant practice and principle, he convened a synod at Uppsala in 1536 where all priests were admonished to preach the pure Word of God and to use the Swedish Protestant Mass in their parishes. Thus the Church of Sweden embraced the Lutheran form of the Reformation but combined its evangelical doctrine with a conservative emphasis on the value of the acceptable elements in the old tradition of worship. In addition, the succession of bishops was maintained unbroken from the mediaeval period.

Turbulence

Gustavus Vasa was apprehensive lest the new Protestant bishops should seek to concentrate too much power in their own hands. So, despite a good beginning to the work of reformation, there followed from 1539 to 1544 a period of tension, known as the 'German period'. It was so called because the King sought to emulate some of the German princes and bring the church more entirely into subjection to his own will. The instrument he used to achieve this end was a fervent disciple of Melanchthon's, George Norman. He was thorough to the point of ruthlessness. Things became more critical when Roman Catholics sought to exploit unrest in southern Sweden in order to overthrow Vasa. The reformers, and especially, Olavus Petri, showed exemplary courage in condemning the innovations and asserting that the temporal power is as much subject to God's law as any private citizen. They paid a high price for their outspokenness. Olavus Petri and Laurentius Andreae were put on trial for treason, found guilty and condemned to death on 2 January 1540. They were pardoned, however, and heavily fined instead. Olavus became a parish priest and Andreae went into retirement.

The King came to realize that the danger from Roman Catholicism was more acute than from an independent Protestant church and so there was a significant change of policy. The Diet of Westeras, 1544, now banned Roman Catholic practices and declared Sweden an 'evangelical Kingdom'. The King restored cordial relations with the reformers and they were encouraged to proceed with the task of reformation. After the deaths of Olavus Petri and Laurentius Andreae in 1552, and of Norman in the following year, Laurentius Petri became the dominating figure in church life. He had always wished to see the Church of Sweden adopt a proper evangelical constitution and, after long deliberation, that was finally achieved with the Church Ordinance of 1571. Laurentius died two years later.

The Church of Sweden occupies a unique place among Protestant churches. It adhered unflinchingly to the principle of the primacy of the Bible and yet preserved a structure and a liturgy which were reminiscent of Roman Catholicism. Moreover, despite some turbulence, the Protestant Reformation in Sweden was not a traumatic upheaval, rather was it a gradual evolution extending over half a century. And no one suffered execution for his convictions.

FINLAND

The development of the Finnish Reformation is dominated by the personality of the assiduous and devout Mikael Agricola (c. 1510–57), one of the imposing figures of early Protestantism. When 18 years of age he joined the staff of the only bishop in Finland, Martin Skytte of Abo, as a clerk. There he came under the influence of men dedicated to reforming the church. Skytte himself was a Roman Catholic reformer in the humanist tradition of Erasmus. Even more influential in Agricola's spiritual development was Peder Sarkilaks, who settled at Abo in 1523 after studying in foreign universities and eventually became archdeacon there. He was a Lutheran enthusiast and profoundly affected the younger generation before his untimely death in 1529. Since he was sympathetic to reform, Bishop Skytte sent Agricola to Wittenberg to study. He returned in 1539, became principal of the cathedral school, then in 1548 assistant to Skytte. When Bishop Skytte died in 1550, Agricola was his obvious successor but was not appointed bishop until 1554. Unhappily, he died in 1557 while on a diplomatic mission to Moscow.

Agricola was an immensely productive author and scholar, the father of Finnish literature. He undertook the translation of the Bible and published his New Testament in 1543. In 1544 he published his manual for ministers, *A Biblical Prayer Book* and five years later his two service books for conducting the liturgy of the Mass. Agricola had a deep interest in promoting spirituality and although Lutheran in his theology, he had a real respect for late mediaeval devotion and never indulged in bitter polemics against Roman Catholic practices. His generous and pious spirit, with a warm concern for pastoral care of his flock and the promotion of practical Christian living left a lasting mark on the spiritual life of his country.

17 A glorious and sweet society

> . . . he had instructed very many, as at Amersham,
> at London, at Billericay, at Chelmsford, at Stratford-
> Langthorn, at Uxbridge . . . and especially at
> Newbury, where was . . . a glorious and sweet
> society of faithful favourers . . . .
>
> From the deposition of Thomas Risby describing the
> activities of Thomas Man, burned at Smithfield in
> 1518, as reproduced in John Foxe, *Acts and
> Monuments*.

Time and again, when churches have lost their spiritual
warmth and become negligent about their pastoral work,
people have sought the consolations of Christian faith by
gathering together in private dissident groups, finding
there means of grace where the officer of the churches
claimed that none were to be had. So it was with the Lollard
movement in England. Despite all attempts to destroy it, it
had persisted and was to make a solid contribution to the
great religious revival when it came.

THE SECRET MULTITUDE

John Foxe, the martyrologist, was not writing in ignorance
when he referred in his *Acts and Monuments* to 'the secret
multitude of true professors'. In fact, that multitude was
larger than he knew. The word 'secret' must be taken
seriously for this was what would now be called an 'underground movement', consisting of people who had made it
their business to hide themselves as far as possible from
prying eyes. The information that has survived, and there
is much of it, only hints at the extent of this spiritual
movement.

It was an extensive movement, – in London, Kent, the West country, the Midlands, the Thames valley and York-shire, groups of people met together without any formal organization to read the Bible, to discuss doctrine and to pray. They had translations of portions of the Bible and religious books like *The Prick of Conscience* and the *Shepherd's Calendar*. And they could buy other books from travelling salesmen like John Hacker or Lawrence Maxwell. Socially, the groups were a mixture, mostly of ordinary people but with a sprinkling of clergy and gentry. They held many ideas in common but with differences of emphasis from place to place. They took the Bible to be the very Word of God. From their Bible reading they gathered that purgatory did not exist. They objected to images, church bells and pilgrimages. They rejected the doctrine of the sacrifice of the Mass and transubstantiation. They were intensely criti-cal of the clergy and acted on the supposition that all Christians are ministers.

The authorities took stern measures to suppress the movement, particularly William Smith (c. 1460–1514), bishop of Lincoln, and his successor, the harsh John Lang-land (1473–1547), and Richard Fitzjames (d. 1522), bishop of London. At least 60 people were burned for Lollard her-esies between 1506 and 1535 and scores of offenders were subjected to degrading penances, some even being bran-ded. Many abjured but the pertinacity of those who adhered to their convictions made an enduring impression on the public mind and deepened the hostility towards the clergy and the Roman Catholic Church. Above all, this folk – evangelical protest prepared the minds of many for the more sophisticated Protestantism of Luther, Zwingli and Calvin.

ROMAN CATHOLIC HUMANISM

Other forms of protest were emerging as well. Humanism had been an increasing influence since 1450 and found an attractive exponent in John Colet (c. 1466–1519), Dean of St Paul's from 1505. He brought to the exposition of the Bible the new humanist interest in its style, language and histori-cal content, together with a partiality for the philosophy of the Italian Neoplatonists. Despite being accused of heresy by Bishop Fitzjames, Colet remained a dutiful Roman Catholic in his theology. It was he who introduced Desiderius Erasmus to the new approach to the Bible during his first visit to England 1499–1500. Erasmus was in England again in 1506 and from 1511 to 1515, when he became Lady Margaret Professor of Greek at Cambridge. It was not merely Erasmus's prowess as a classical scholar that impressed people but also his advocacy of a simple, practical and non-dogmatic Christianity devoted to the imitation of Christ. He had no more distinguished friend than Thomas More (1478–1535), Lord Chancellor in succession to Wolsey. More was noted for his wit, but the wit concealed a heart profoundly dedicated to Roman Catholicism and his frivolity soon evaporated when confronted by the Protestantism of William Tyndale. Erasmian humanism did persuade people like John Fisher (1469–1535) and others in the circle that surrounded Queen Catherine, to devote themselves to the practice of piety and the reform of morals. But as an effective instrument to transform a nation's spiritual life, the movement was a failure because it was too superficial, and too esoteric.

LUTHERANISM

In any case, a new influence for reform began to affect English life early in 1519. Lutheran books were being smuggled from the Netherlands and King Henry VIII himself gave Luther excellent publicity by attacking him in his book, *The Assertion of the Seven Sacraments* (1521).

Lutheranism soon became a topic of interest among the intellectuals of Cambridge. According to John Foxe, 'the first framer of that university in the knowledge of Christ' was Thomas Bilney (c. 1495–1531) of Trinity Hall. He had bought Erasmus's Latin translation of the New Testament in order to enjoy its literary merits but had been converted when he read that 'Christ Jesus came into the world to save sinners' (1 Timothy 1:15). 'Immediately,' he wrote, 'I felt a marvelous comfort and quietness, insomuch that my bruised bones leaped for joy'. It was Bilney who converted Hugh Latimer, the future bishop and martyr, and Robert Barnes (1495–1540), the firmest of all the pioneers of evangelical protest in his adherence to Lutheranism. He was prior of the Augustinian monastery and that house became a centre of classical learning while Barnes chaired an influential discussion group which met at the White Horse tavern. A surprising number of later Reformation leaders were students at Cambridge at this time – Miles Coverdale, John Frith, Christopher Coleman, Thomas Cranmer, John Rogers, Matthew Parker, William Tyndale and others – but not all of them are known to have been connected with the White Horse group. Nor did the group confine itself to academic debates for some of them, like Barnes and Latimer, were vociferous critics of superstitious practices as well as being distributors of forbidden books. The group was dispersed by 1530 and Bilney suffered martyrdom at Norwich on 19 August 1531.

AN OBEDIENT CHRISTIAN MAN

In 1524 a man whose influence on English spirituality and literature was immense sailed into exile. He never returned but when he died a martyr's death twelve years later his name was a household word.

William Tyndale (c. 1494–1536) was a native of Gloucestershire who, after completing his education at both universities, became a private tutor. He was so appalled by the ignorance of lay people about the essentials of vital Christianity that he dedicated himself to the task of producing a new translation of the Bible. He failed to gain the patronage of the then bishop of London, Cuthbert Tunstall (1474–1559) but instead he found a backer in the wealthy London draper, Humphrey Monmouth. In 1524 Tyndale sailed for Hamburg and then spent several months at Wittenberg. In the summer of 1525 he was at Cologne where a start was made on printing his New Testament, only a fragment of which has survived. The opposition of the city authorities forced him to move to Worms and by about February 1526 his octavo edition of the New Testament was in circulation. Copies were distributed through the network of contacts that served the Lollard groups as well as through channels used by merchants in disposing of smuggled goods. Immediately the authorities took action to suppress it. William Warham (c. 1450–1532), Archbishop of Canterbury since 1504, and Cuthbert Tunstall were vehemently active. Copies were to be confiscated and destroyed and sharper measures were taken against known sympathizers with Lutheranism, such as Thomas Bilney and John Frith (*c.* 1503–33). And much to Tyndale's displeasure this official hostility was further inflamed by the publication of *Rede me, and be nott wrothe* (1526), a vicious satire on Wolsey produced by Tyndale's former assistant William Roye. Tyndale's next move was to Antwerp where he published *The Parable of the Wicked Mammon* (1528), *The Obedience of a Christian Man* (1528) and *Practice of Prelates* (1530). In these books, together with the Prologue to his New Testament, Tyndale expounded his evangelical theology, with the primacy of the Bible and justification by faith alone at its heart. At the same time he emphasizes that the godly prince has a contribution to make in reforming the church. A harsher tone pervades *Practice of Prelates* which gives expression to his disillusionment with the behaviour of the bishops.

Thomas More emerged as his most implacable opponent. He opened his controversy with the reformer with *A dialogue* (June 1529) aimed, as he puts it, against 'the pestilent sect of Luther and Tyndale'. The ensuing debate was a contest between two giants but neither was at his best.

Tyndale's great contribution was not so much in polemics as in his work on the Bible. In 1530 his translation of the Pentateuch appeared followed in 1531 by Jonah, and a second edition of Genesis in 1534. He was a fine linguist, excellently equipped for his work as translator. In addition he had a magical command of his mother tongue and many of his admirable idiomatic phrases became common currency in English. But for him all this was of secondary importance. The primary consideration was providing the public with Bibles. The feverish efforts of bishops to suppress his New Testament were not in the end successful because Tyndale's translation became the main constituent in the later official translations, culminating in the King James Bible.

Tyndale was a heroic figure, a man dedicated to one great mission. He was betrayed to the authorities and imprisoned at the castle of Vilvorde, north of Brussels, on 21 May 1535. Found guilty of heresy, he died a martyr's death by strangling and subsequent burning in October 1536, saying, 'Lord, open the King of England's eyes.'

So the new stream of Protestant enthusiasm mingled with the older stream of Lollard evangelical protest and borrowed something on the way from Christian humanism. Both Lollardy and Lutheranism were soon to find themselves, as a result of quite unexpected events, in a world where the future seemed suddenly brighter.

18 A royal dissenter

> . . . be it enacted by authority of this present Parliament, that the king our sovereign lord . . . shall be taken, accepted, and reputed the only supreme head in earth of the Church of England . . . .
>
> *Act of Supremacy*, 1534.

In June 1527, King Henry VIII told his wife, Catherine of Aragon (1485–1536), that he could no longer consider her to be his wife. They had been married since 11 June 1509 but of the queen's children only one, Mary, had survived. From 1520 onwards the King was becoming increasingly anxious about the lack of a male heir. In 1525 Henry became infatuated with the vivacious but calculating Anne Boleyn (*c.* 1507–36) who would form an alliance with the King only if he made her his queen. So the divorce of Queen Catherine became a political necessity.

Henry soon persuaded himself that it was also a necessity of conscience. When he married her, Catherine was the widow of his brother Arthur. Did not Leviticus 20:21 prohibit such a marriage? And was the scriptural prohibition nullified by the dispensation for the marriage issued by Pope Julius II? So the unsavoury argument which was to amuse and exasperate diplomatists and theologians all over Europe for seven years transformed a king's divorce into an opportunity to reform the church.

THE KING'S MATTER

The man upon whom the King relied to settle the matter of the divorce was Thomas Wolsey. Thomas Wolsey (*c.* 1475–1530) was the supreme English example of the magnificent mediaeval prelate. He held a large number of valuable preferments in the church and was made cardinal in 1515, the year in which the King made him his chancellor.

Indeed, next to the King, he was the most powerful man in the land. His diplomatic skills, however, were not sufficient for the task of reconciling King and Pope and he paid the price of failure. On 4 November 1530 he died at Leicester Abbey on his way to London to answer a charge of treason and was succeeded as chancellor by Thomas More.

Anne Boleyn, who was sympathetic to Protestantism, drew the King's attention to the anticlerical feeling that was exemplified by such effusions as the vicious attack on the clergy entitled *Supplication of the Beggars* (1528) by Simon Fish (d. 1531) and its predecessor, Jerome Barlow's *Burial of the Mass*. The King was in the mood to exploit such feelings.

Parliament met on 3 November 1529. No one had any ready-made plan of religious reform. There were indeed expressions of protest against the financial exactions of the clergy and against the abuses of the church courts, and bills were passed to remedy some of these abuses. But there was no consolation for the friends of reform in the fulminations of Thomas More and John Fisher against their principles, especially since these criticisms were endorsed by royal proclamations against heresy with an attendant bout of persecution which made martyrs of Frith and Bilney.

Changes however were on the way. The universities of Europe had been invited to pass judgment on the subject of the King's divorce in 1530 but the results were disappointing. Nor was the Pope amenable to persuasion because he was now under the thumb of the Emperor Charles V, who was Queen Catherine's uncle. And Thomas More would have nothing to do with divorce. By about 1530, the idea was being circulated that the King of England by ancient prescription was directly responsible to God for the government of his realm as well as being guardian of the church. In other words, he possessed an ancient autonomy that had been undermined by the popes. This concept was to be the justification for much that followed.

So the attack on papal privileges began. The opening move had already been made – the indictment of Wolsey on a charge of treason. If Wolsey could be thus attacked, what of those that served under him? In the summer of 1530 fifteen churchmen, eight of them bishops, were indicted, as Wolsey had been, under the Statute of Praemunire (1393), which forbad appeals to Rome in cases that could be settled in England under penalty of outlawry. They were subsequently pardoned but since the whole body of the clergy was in danger of being indicted in the same way, the Convocation of Canterbury resolved to offer the King a subsidy of £100,000 and to beg his pardon and by May 1531 York had followed suit with £18,000. But Archbishop Warham told the clergy that Henry would grant pardon only if they agreed to acknowledge him as 'sole protector' and 'supreme head' of the Church of England. They complied, but by insisting that the King was supreme head only 'as far as the law of Christ allows'. John Fisher (1469–1535), bishop of Rochester, and Archbishop Warham sought to ensure that the King's authority over the church did not displace that of the Pope. But in 1532 the real attack on the Pope's jurisdiction began. In March the Annates Bill was passed preventing the payment to Rome of the tax on new appointments and nullifying in advance any refusal by the pope to consecrate royal nominees to bishoprics. Next the King demanded of Convocation that all church laws should be scrutinized by a royal commission and that no new laws should be enacted without the consent of the crown. To refuse would be construed as treason, so on 15 May 1532 came the Submission of the Clergy. The following day Sir Thomas More resigned, fully realizing that the Pope had now lost his means of controlling the Church of England.

In March 1533 came the Act in Restraint of Appeals to Rome which legally severed the realm from the jurisdiction of the Pope. The way was now clear to settle the matter of the King's divorce. Thomas Cranmer, now Archbishop of Canterbury, found in his court on 28 May 1533 that the King's marriage to Catherine was invalid and that the secret marriage he had contracted with Anne Boleyn in January was legal. Anne was delivered of a daughter, the future Queen Elizabeth, on 7 September. In that month, too, the Pope excommunicated the King.

NEW MEN

Henry VIII promoted men with the wish and the ability to serve his policies. The most prominent among them were Thomas Cromwell and Thomas Cranmer. Cromwell (c.1485–1540) was the son of a general merchant at Putney. The details of his early career are hazy but he gained much experience in the world of business and Italian banking before becoming a lawyer. He became an efficient member of Wolsey's staff and entered Parliament in 1523. He survived the fall of his master but probably did not attract the attention of the King before 1530. After that his rise to power was spectacular. Within a decade he had presided over a radical change in the state and, not least, in the relationship between it and the church. He was a man of great energy, affable yet efficient, a born administrator whose pragmatic mind was not given to much theorizing in politics or theology. Nevertheless, he had a sincere desire to promote the well-being of the Church of England and to secure for the public an open Bible. He then was the man who set the stage for the Protestant Reformers.

Cranmer (1489–1556) was very different. He was born at Aslacton, Nottinghamshire, and reared as a country squire. He studied at Cambridge and later lectured there. It was while he was a private tutor at Waltham Abbey that he attracted the King's attention by suggesting that the moral and theological question of the validity of the King's proposed divorce might be put to the universities of Europe. The favour which he found with the King led to his appointment as Archbishop of Canterbury. He was consecrated on 30 March 1533. Although he was in constant danger from Henry's waywardness, Cranmer retained the King's confidence throughout his reign. Cranmer accepted high office with reluctance but his wide scholarship, his appreciation of the value of tradition and his sensitive spirituality made him a church leader of rare quality. And in his personal relationships he was gentle and magnanimous. He was to make a momentous contribution to the Anglican Reformation and his mark is upon it to this day.

Religious affairs during the remainder of Henry VIII's reign may be considered in three sections. First, the consolidation of royal influence over the church, second, the beginnings of reform and finally, the period of reaction.

ROYAL POWER

Once the matter of the divorce had been settled, it was necessary to consolidate the position of the Crown in religious affairs. All payments to Rome were made illegal by the Dispensations Act and the veto of the crown over church legislation was confirmed by the Act for the Submission of the Clergy. The Succession Act required everyone to swear to the lawfulness of Henry's second marriage and at the same time vested the royal succession in the issue of that marriage. The first-fruits of all benefices and the product of a 10% tax on clerical income were to go to the crown by the Act for First Fruits and Tenths, and that meant a revenue of some £40,000. And in order to make the necessary adjustments, Cromwell, like the efficient civil servant he was, arranged a nation-wide survey of clerical incomes the results of which appeared in the *Valor Ecclesiasticus*. Finally, the Supremacy Act of November 1534 declared that the King was to be acknowledged 'the only supreme head in earth of the Church of England'. So the King was given complete authority over the Church of England and in January 1535 he took the remarkable step of delegating the exercise of his authority to Thomas Cromwell by appointing him Vicar-General.

This severe treatment of the church aroused resistance. The two most distinguished protesters were Thomas More and John Fisher, neither of whom would take the Oath of Succession. Fisher suffered execution on 22 June 1535 and More on the 6 July. The London Carthusians were similarly treated but with added barbarities and when the Observant Franciscans resisted, their seven houses were appropriated and the friars scattered. In the main the clergy swore the Oath of Succession but disaffection was widespread as became apparent in the rebellion known as the Pilgrimage of Grace which started in Lincolnshire at the beginning of October 1536. Within a month virtually the whole of the north of England was up in arms and trouble continued until March 1537. Not all the rebels were animated by the same motives but there was a strong element of religious protest. Some 180 people suffered execution but beyond that the government refrained from wholesale butchery.

One change that had contributed towards fomenting rebellion was the dissolution of the monasteries. As Vicar-

General, Cromwell initiated a visitation of the church in
September 1535, but the visitors confined themselves to the
religious houses. They worked with breath-taking speed
and produced reports which provided Cromwell with sufficient evidence to prove that the monasteries were in a
sorry state. He had a bill ready when Parliament met in
January 1536 to force the dissolution of all houses worth
£200 a year or less – that is, some 300 houses – unless the
King granted exemption. The remaining houses were dissolved by agreement between 1538 and 1540. All monastic
property was invested in the Court of Augmentations with
power to dispose of it. So, some 800 monastic institutions
cease to exist and some 9,000 monks and nuns were pen-
sioned off. Ultimately the monastic lands passed into the
possession of the middle and higher gentry, people who
would be firmly opposed to any policy of restoring the
property to the church. It was a severe blow to the church's
finances but hardly a spiritual tragedy for the dynamic days
of monasticism were over.

HESITANT REFORM

In the Ten Articles, formulated by Convocation and issued
by Cromwell as Vicar-General in July 1536, we see the
beginning of the process of defining the faith of the Anglican Church. The articles reveal a modest leaning towards
Lutheranism. The clergy are to teach the Bible to the
people, but the references to the Communion, as well as
the article on justification, are studiously ambiguous. There
are warnings against the abuses of superstition, but images
and relics are not to be removed. These articles gave
encouragement to eager Protestants without hurting the
sensibilities of Roman Catholics. *The Institution of a Christian
Man* (or the *Bishops' Book*), while stressing that the Church
of Rome is but one member of the universal church and
insisting on the need for more Biblical preaching, is nevertheless more conservative in its theology than the Ten
Articles.

The most significant development of this period was the
official decision to bring the Bible to the people. The first
full English Bible, together with the Apocrypha, appeared
towards the end of 1535, the work of Miles Coverdale

(1488–1569), a Yorkshireman, educated at Cambridge and converted by Robert Barnes. Although he was not a master of Hebrew and Greek, his judicious use of existing versions together with the elegant style of his translation, secured for his Bible a wide circulation. Then in 1537 came 'Matthew's Bible'. 'Thomas Matthew' was the pen-name of John Rogers (c. 1500–1555), a Cambridge man, converted by William Tyndale, and the first martyr of Mary's reign. He was heavily dependent on the work of Coverdale and Tyndale, but his editorial notes made it a serviceable Bible. It was in April 1539 that a truly official Bible, under the powerful patronage of Cromwell, appeared. This was the 'Great Bible', edited by Coverdale. It earned a well-merited success. And the putting of the Bible within reach of the ordinary people of England, was, in all probability, the greatest single service of Thomas Cromwell.

REACTION

Sad to say, just a month after the publication of the Great Bible there was a change of policy. By 16 June 1539 the Act of Six Articles had become law. The King was tired of the pro-German policy that culminated in his marriage with Anne of Cleves and he was alarmed at the spread of Protestant views. The articles mark a reaction from Lutheranism. Transubstantiation, communion in bread only, celibacy of the clergy, private masses, auricular confession and the binding nature of monastic vows are all asserted. To deny any of them could lead to the death sentence. The Act was a ferocious assertion of the return of full-blooded Roman Catholicism – except, of course, for the primacy of the pope. With the collapse of the pro-German policy Cromwell fell victim to the King's petulance, was accused of treason, found guilty and executed on 28 July 1540.

Henry's reign drew to a close with ominous signs that the period of reform was over and that it was only a matter of time before the kingdom was restored to the Roman obedience. Henry VIII died on 28 January 1547, with his hand in the hand of Thomas Cranmer.

Meanwhile, dramatic changes were happening in Switzerland, changes that were to have a deep influence upon the development of religion in England.

19 A reluctant reformer

> Despite my wish always to lie in obscurity and
> retirement, God so moved and transformed me
> through a variety of experiences and never left me
> in peace anywhere until, contrary to my natural
> inclinations, he brought me towards enlightenment
> and, so to speak, forced me into the open.
>
> Calvin (1509–1564), Introduction to *Commentary
> upon the book of Psalms*, 1557.

The most vigorous propagandist of Protestantism in French
Switzerland was Guillaume Farel (1489–1565), a native of
Dauphiné in France and, until his expulsion in 1523, one of
Bishop Briçonnet's team of Roman Catholic reformers at
Meaux. In March 1528 he was appointed preacher at Bern
and was sent on a mission to Neuchâtel, where he introduced the Reformation. In 1532 he established lasting relationships with the Waldensians and on 2 October 1532 he
arrived at Geneva to open a mission there. His attacks on
Roman Catholicism, however, provoked sharp opposition
and the authorities forced him to withdraw. His fellow-
countryman, Antoine Froment (1510–84) was no more successful. This was discouraging but political developments
in Geneva were indirectly to serve the cause of the
Reformation. Geneva had been an independent city under
the jurisdiction of the Duke of Savoy and its own bishop.
Opposition to these rulers had been vigorous since 1517,
with Duke Charles III of Savoy and the luxury-loving
bishop, Pierre de la Baume, seeking to maintain their traditional authority. But thanks to the powerful patronage of
Bern and Fribourg the bishop had to withdraw in 1526 and
his jurisdiction devolved upon the city councils. With
Bern's intrusion in Genevan politics, the Protestants had a
powerful and militant patron there.

Farel returned to Geneva in January 1536 and, together

with his friends, Pierre Viret (1511–71), Pierre Olivetan (c.1506–1538) and Anthony Saulnier, instituted a vigorous evangelistic campaign, based on public disputation, preaching and house to house visitation. They gradually won over a sufficient number of council members to turn the scales in favour of Protestantism. The Mass was finally abolished on 21 May 1536 and Geneva declared an evangelical city. Although the institutions of Roman Catholicism were disintegrating quickly, the majority of the citizens had little idea what it meant to 'live by the Gospel'. And Farel knew well enough that a Reformation which came in the wake of political revolution was bound to be superficial. In July 1536 Farel was told that a promising young Frenchman was staying overnight at one of Geneva's inns and that he ought to see him. It was a momentous meeting for the young man was John Calvin.

UPBRINGING

John Calvin was born at Noyon in Picardy on 10 July 1509. His father, Gérard Cauvin, had been sufficiently educated to abandon the family's ancestral business as wine shippers on the river Oise at nearby Pont l'Evêque. He had become a legal and financial administrator on the staff of the imposing cathedral of Nôtre-Dame at Noyon. Calvin's mother was Jeanne le Franc, the daughter of an inn-keeper at Cambrai. She died when John was about five years old.

Calvin was reared therefore in the bosom of the church and he participated fully, as he later recalled, in the pilgrimages and devotional ceremonies which punctuated the life of the neighbourhood. John, like his brother Charles, attended a local school, the Collège des Capettes, and at once began to show a remarkable capacity for learning. In order to pay for his education, he was allotted a portion of the money paid to the Chapel of La Gésine, and so at twelve years of age he became a cleric and received the tonsure. He was also admitted into the household of the distinguished noble, Louis, Seigneur de Montmor, at Noyon, to learn the ways of polite society and to broaden his education in the company of Montmor's sons. To acquire the necessary proficiency in Latin to follow a university career, he was sent to Paris, to the Collège de la

Marche, and was fortunate in having the distinguished humanist (and later a convert to Protestantism), Mathurin Cordier (1479–1564), as his teacher.

UNIVERSITY TRAINING

After a year under Cordier's tuition, Calvin began his university course of arts study at the Collège de Montaigu. The real power at the college was Noël Bedier, the leading light of the Faculty of Theology at Paris and a theological bloodhound able to sniff the slightest taint of deviation from the reactionary orthodoxy of the Faculty. Gérard Cauvin, like Luther's father, wished his son to be a lawyer. So he migrated to the university of Orléans which specialized in legal studies. John's brilliance was acknowledged by the readiness of the teaching staff to use him as an assistant lecturer from time to time. He made significant friendships at Orléans, especially with his kinsman, Pierre Robert, usually known as 'Olivetan', of Noyon, Nicholas Cop of Paris and Melchior Wolmar who began to teach him Greek. Things were not happy at home. His father seems to have muddled his accounts and was excommunicated, 2 November 1528, and both John and his brother Charles were under the condemnation of the Ecclesiastical Court for absence from chapter meetings. In 1529, together with some of his fellow-students, Calvin migrated to the university at Bourges, to attend the classes of the famous jurist, Andreas Alciati. But the students' enthusiasm soon waned and so Calvin returned to Orléans to complete his studies and attain his licentiate in law. That qualified him for his doctorate but Calvin never supplicated for it. So by about 1531, he had completed his university career.

CONVERSION

Even more significant for the future of Christendom was his evangelical conversion. It is typical of his reticence about his personal life that he left no details of date and circumstance. But in the preface to his *Commentary on the Psalms* (1557) he says that his father had decided that he should study law rather than theology, then he goes on,

And so it happened that I was called away from the study
of philosophy and set to learning law. Although, in
obedience to my father's wishes, I tried my best to work
hard, yet God at last turned my course in another
direction by the secret restraint of his providence. What
happened first was that by a sudden conversion he
tamed to teachableness a mind too stubborn for its years
– for I was so strongly devoted to the superstitions of the
Papacy that nothing less could draw me from such
depths of mire.

And so 'this mere taste of true godliness', as he calls it,
turned his attention from Law to Theology, with the result
that, 'Before a year had slipped by anybody who longed for
purer doctrine kept on coming to learn from me'. According to Calvin's biographer and successor, Theodore Beza,
the human instrument of his conversion was his relation,
Pierre Robert Olivetan, and there is no sound reason for
doubting this statement.

There followed an unsettled interlude in his career. He
returned briefly to Noyon. His father's serious troubles
with the church authorities ended with his death on 26 May
1531. Then Calvin returned to Orléans, then to Paris to
continue his Greek studies where he published his first
book, a commentary on Seneca's *De Clementia*. It was a
routine scholarly exercise by a promising young humanist.
It brought him no renown and had but an incidental rele-
vance to his new faith. He went back to Orléans in the early
summer of 1533, only to return to Paris in October. And by
then he was becoming implicated in the activities of those
who sought to reform the church in France.

THE YOUNG REFORMER

These were exciting days in the history of Christianity in
France, as we shall see in a later chapter. When Calvin
joined the Protestants, he was joining a movement under
the cross. The early reform movements centred on the
diocese of Meaux had been scotched by 1525 and a period
of persecution followed. In 1533 Nicholas Cop, Calvin's
friend, had been elected rector of the university of Paris and
in his rectorial address on 1 November he had criticized the

intolerance of the Sorbonne and its theologians, and had shown his sympathy with the reformers by drawing upon both Erasmus and Luther. Proceedings were started against him on the ground of suspected heresy and since Calvin was alleged to have assisted Cop in the composition of the speech, an attempt was made to arrest him. He contrived to escape and sought refuge with Marguerite of Angoulême (1492–1549), the King's sister and later Queen of Navarre, and after that with a wealthy friend, Louis du Tillet, priest at Claix. On 4 May 1534 he resigned his benefices at Noyon and so turned his back finally on the Roman Catholic Church. When official repression of the Protestants became more intense in October 1534, Calvin and du Tillet fled to Basel and arrived there in January 1535. Calvin soon settled down to the kind of scholarly work which he most enjoyed. He helped Pierre Robert with his new translation of the Bible for the Waldensians which appeared in June 1535. More significantly, Calvin was putting the finishing touches to a book of his own. He completed it in August 1535 and the printers Thomas Platter and Balthasar Lasius published it in March 1536. It was the first edition of his *Christianae Religionis Institutio,* – the *Institutes of the Christian Religion*.

In April 1536, accompanied by du Tillet, he made a journey to Italy to visit the court of Renée of Ferrara. By June he was in Paris, making arrangements to take his brother, Antoine, and his half-sister, Marie, to the safety of Strasbourg. Because of military action between Paris and Strasbourg, they were forced to make a long detour so as to approach the city from the south. This is how Calvin came to be staying at an inn in Geneva during July 1536. It was du Tillet who told Farel of Calvin's presence. With typical energy, Farel insisted on seeing and admonishing him to stay in Geneva to help with the work of reformation. Calvin demurred and said he much preferred following his scholarly studies. Farel became incensed and said, 'God will curse your retirement and the peace which you seek from your studies, if you withdraw and refuse to help.'

The young man was struck with terror. He felt, he said, 'as if God had laid his mighty hand upon me from heaven to arrest me'. He had no choice but to stay in Geneva.

20 The Christian's service

> We are not our own . . . we are God's. To Him,
> therefore, let us live and die. We are God's. Toward
> Him, therefore, . . . let every part of our lives be
> directed.
>
> John Calvin, *Institutes*, III. 7.1.

John Calvin was just twenty-seven years old when he first
arrived at Geneva. Young as he was he had a clear vision of
the faith which he professed and a lucid perception of what
was needed to reform the city of Geneva. For him doctrine
and practice are aspects of the Christian's obedience of faith
as he seeks to serve the glory of God. There is a unity, a
consistency, a homogeneity in Calvin's thinking which is
grounded in his understanding of the Bible. And this consistency characterized his thinking throughout his career.
His biographer, Beza, held that Calvin's views remained
virtually unaltered throughout the years. They were certainly enriched and deepened, but they can hardly be said
to have changed. And because of the profound consistency
of his thinking, and its all-embracing nature, there is a very
close integration between Calvin's ideas and his actions in
Geneva.

THE WORKER

For a man who always suffered delicate health, Calvin was
extraordinarily busy. He was both an academic and an
administrator, a pastor and preacher, as well as a diligent
correspondent with a vast number of people all over
Europe. And he possessed an awesome facility for
expressing himself in an entirely suitable idiom whether as
scholar or as a teacher of children.

His great love was the Bible. In all that he did, he sought
to ensure that a place of honour was given to it. The office

of the pastor, he wrote in the *Ecclesiastical Ordinances* (1541)
'is to proclaim the Word of God'. And he himself set an
excellent example of devotion to biblical study. His first
biblical commentary appeared in 1540 and by 1555 he had
completed the series on the New Testament, except for
Revelation. His first Old Testament commentary appeared
in 1551. He was helped by Jean Budé, Charles de Jonviller
and others who carefully copied his exegetical lectures as
they were delivered and conflated their copies before sending them to be printed. This formidable series of commentaries reveal Calvin as an expositor of rare genius
whose ambition it was to make God's voice heard through
the words of Scripture.

Preaching gave him the profoundest satisfaction. He bent
all his abilities to serve the great congregation that crowded
St. Peter's Church at Geneva to hear him. Up to 1549 he
preached four or five times a week and thereafter he
preached twice on Sundays and on every weekday on
alternate weeks. He preached as he lectured, extem-
porarily, having only the Bible in the original languages
before him. Again, as with his lectures, his colleagues took
down his sermons in shorthand, a task helped by his slow,
asthmatic, delivery. Despite his physical handicaps, he
became one of the finest preachers in the history of Christianity. His preaching was vivid, lucid, passionate, persuasive,
witty – as the context and occasion demanded. And so he
opened the Bible paragraph by paragraph, working his way
through a book, seeking to bring out its wealth of meaning.
Above all, there was authority in his voice. To John Calvin,
the preacher is God's messenger, God's angel, when he is
led of the Holy Spirit rightly to interpret God's Word. At
such a time, he would tell us, when the preacher speaks,
God speaks.

He attracted international attention first of all with his
Institutes in 1536. The Latin word 'institutio' means
'instruction' or 'education'. And, as the title of the book
shows, it is meant to provide instruction in '*the whole sum of
piety and whatever it is necessary to know in the doctrine of
salvation . . .*' The impulse behind the book is plainly pastoral rather than academic. But it was also a defence and an
exposition of the Protestant faith, formally dedicated to the
persecuting Francis I, king of France. The first edition,

consisting of six chapters and extending to about three-quarters the length of the New Testament, although well received did not quite please Calvin. A second editon, extended to seventeen chapters, appeared in 1538 and was translated into French by the author in 1539. Calvin continued to work on the *Institutes* in the editions that followed and the final product was the edition that came from the press of the distinguished printer, Robert Estienne of Geneva, in August 1559. The original six chapters are now seventy-nine, divided into four 'books' dealing respectively with, 'The Knowledge of God the Creator', 'The Knowledge of God the Redeemer', 'The Way in which we receive the grace of Christ' and 'The external means or aids by which God invites us into the Society of Christ and holds us therein'.

THE KNOWLEDGE OF GOD

For Calvin, God must take the centre of the stage. Man's predicament is insoluble apart from God's intervention to save him. And by saving humanity, God enables them to acknowledge his glory and serve it. The famous opening sentence of the *Institutes* is rendered in the French edition of 1560 in the form, 'In knowing God, each of us also knows himself'. That is to say, we are entirely dependent upon God's revelation for our knowledge of him and our knowledge of ourselves. It is true that God is manifested in creation and in the human conscience but sin has so darkened the mind and poisoned the heart of man that God is only glimpsed in fitful ways in creation and conscience. For all practical purposes the knowledge of God is mediated to us through the Bible. So Bible study is a crucial pursuit. God is manifested as the Creator and as Redeemer to those readers of the Bible who regard it 'as having sprung from heaven, as if there the living words of God were heard'. That the Bible has this authority is not a proposition that can be proved by reason, nor yet is it to be believed on the authority of the church, 'For as God alone is a fit witness of himself in his Word, so also the Word will not find acceptance in men's hearts before it is sealed by the inward testimony of the Holy Spirit'.

So, enlightened by the Holy Spirit, the Christian knows

God the Creator and can appreciate both the marvels of divine wisdom in creation and the tragedy that has deformed the human nature that was so beautiful when it came from the Creator's hands.

TRAGEDY

And what a frightful tragedy sin is! Its root is disobedience to God's law. It is a rejection of God's authority and an expression of ambition and pride. The initial rebellion polluted human nature and brought a terrible curse on Adam's posterity – we are 'born infected with the contagion of sin.' Evil intentions and repulsive deeds well up from our sinful heart so that each one of us comes under God's curse, not for the sins of Adam, but for our own sins. Every part of man's personality is affected, including his will. But God has not abandoned man. The Holy Spirit has been secretly at work among sinful humanity and the fruit is seen in the achievements of science, of art, of politics, and even in humanity's religious aspirations and virtuous behaviour. This is God's 'common grace' at work, God's gratuitous curbing of the effects of sin.

THE MEDIATOR

The human race seemed condemned to utter despair. It would indeed be so were it not for God's gracious intervention. To bridge the yawning gulf between the Holy God and the miserable sinner there was need of a Mediator who is both God and man. Only through the work of such a Mediator could 'the heirs of Gehenna' be made into the 'heirs of the heavenly Kingdom'. That Mediator was Jesus Christ. He is 'true man – and yet sinless! True man – and yet eternal God!'

Christ has redeemed us through the obedience to God which he practised throughout his life and supremely in his death. He took our place. 'This is our acquittal: the guilt that held us liable for punishment has been transferred to the head of the Son of God.' And so Christ was crucified, died, was buried, descended into hell, rose from the dead, ascended into heaven and sat on God's right hand and so secured our redemption but also initiated his continuing dominion over all things. Christ, then, and Christ alone, is our whole salvation. He substituted for us and 'the effect of his shedding of blood is that our sins are not imputed to us'. And through his redemptive work, Jesus Christ has become to us, King, Priest and Prophet.

RECEIVING THE BLESSINGS

How are the inestimable blessings of the work of Jesus Christ available to sinners? Through the work of the Holy Spirit. And the 'principal work of the Holy Spirit' is faith. Faith is 'a firm and certain knowledge of God's benevolence towards us, founded upon the truth of the freely given promise of Christ.' In this way Calvin takes up Martin Luther's resounding theme, a sinner is justified by faith alone. For Calvin, to say that a person is justified is to say that 'he is both reckoned righteous in God's judgment and has been accepted on account of his righteousness.' So justification consists 'in the remission of sins and the imputation of Christ's righteousness'. And the faith that justifies is a free gift of God's grace. By faith we are united with Christ. We are regenerated so that God's image in us is restored. As far as guilt goes, the Christian is free of sin's oppression. But as to its power, remnants of it are still in us and we have a continuing battle on our hands. We can now dispense with the misleading Roman Catholic teaching about the so-called sacrament of Penance. Full satisfaction has been rendered to God on our behalf by the Redeemer and forgiveness is available to us through Christ's merits when we confess our sins to God.

SERVICE AND MYSTERY

The purpose of regeneration is to enable believers to show in their daily lives their conformity to God's righteousness. It frees believers to deny themselves, to eschew all desire for power and human glory and to concentrate on what God wills. And God wills us to extol his glory in the service of our neighbour and by subduing every aspect of human life to God's sovereignty.

But a question which haunts the mind of every Christian evangelist is why so many people reject God's rich blessings. Calvin's answer is his doctrine of predestination. This doctrine must be sought only in Scripture and must not be perverted by speculation. It was Calvin's belief that the Bible 'clearly shows' that 'God once established by his eternal and unchangeable plan those whom he long before determined once for all to receive into salvation, and those whom, on the other hand, he would devote to destruction'. The elect are chosen in Christ and their election is manifested by their being called by the gospel, their believing in Christ, their repentance, their justification and their sanctification. No one may by-pass these steps and seek 'their own or others' salvation in the labyrinth of predestination, while they move out of the way of faith set before them . . .' This is an impenetrable mystery that we cannot fathom, but it is in the Bible.

And then, Calvin treats of the church, its nature, its ministry, organization and authority, and provides a firm analysis of the biblical evidence which, he believes, pictures a church substantially different from the Roman Catholic Church, the Lutheran Churches and the various Free Churches that emerged among the radical Protestants. And Calvin ends his *Institutes* with a discussion of 'Civil Government'.

No synopsis can do justice to Calvin's *Institutes*. The work is massive but it also possesses a coherence and an architectural beauty which makes it one of the seminal works of Christian theology. A summary cannot in any way convey the remarkable dynamism of Calvin's thought. After all, his thinking was to be the motive force behind revolutionary changes in several European countries. His theology is both a programme for building up a new culture and a call to battle. That is why Calvinism left such a deep and long-lasting imprint on European society.

21 A school of Christ

This place . . . is the maist perfyt schoole of Chryst that ever was in the erth since the dayis of the Apostillis.

John Knox (c.1513–1572), writing from Geneva to Mrs Anne Locke, 9 December 1556.

Calvin's first stay in Geneva was a brief one. He arrived in the summer of 1536 and in November he was officially elected a pastor there. On the 10 November the Little Council discussed and accepted a *Confession of Faith* drawn up by Farel and Calvin. On 16 January 1537 they submitted to it *Articles on the Organization of the Church*. While the public were prepared to accept some of the suggestions about creating a new church order, as suggested in this document, they were not prepared to endorse the provision that everyone was to subscribe the Confession of Faith on pain of excommunication. Controversy followed and the city elections of February 1538 brought into office syndics (magistrates) who were opposed to the policies of Farel and Calvin. So the reformers were expelled and left the city on Easter Tuesday 1538. Farel became pastor at Neuchâtel, while Calvin eventually succumbed to the pleadings of Bucer and Capito and made his home at Strasbourg.

INTERLUDE AT STRASBOURG

The stay at Strasbourg was an enriching experience for Calvin. He arrived at the beginning of September 1538 and found employment as pastor of the French refugee congregation and as an assistant professor of Theology. He soon made the French congregation a model of a well-disciplined Reformed Church with officers and a liturgy that had much in common with the Church of Geneva in later years.

The leader of the reformers at Strasbourg was Martin Bucer and his influence on Calvin was profound, not only in theological matters but in the more delicate area of promoting reformation through pastoral work. Naturally, Calvin continued his literary work, including his impressive reply, on behalf of the people of Geneva, to the appeal made to them by Jacopo Sadoleto (1477–1547), bishop of Carpentras, to abandon Protestantism.

Calvin was less happy with the ecumenical discussions in which he was engaged as a representative of Strasbourg. He was present at the Colloquy of Frankfurt, February 1539, the Colloquy of Worms the following November and that of Regensburg, April to July 1541. Although these international gatherings gave him an opportunity to meet many leading figures in religion and politics, he felt that, on the Protestant side, Bucer's ecumenical generosity and Melanchthon's eirenical spirit tempted them to make unjustifiable concessions, while on the Roman Catholic side uprooting Protestantism was the aim of all parties, although some (like Cardinal Contarini) wished to do so by argument, while others favoured coercion.

It was at Strasbourg, too, that Calvin married in August 1540. His wife, Idelette de Bure, was a member of his congregation and the widow of the Anabaptist, Jean Stordeur of Liège. It was a happy marriage but brief, for Calvin became a widower in April 1549.

RETURN

On 21 September 1540 the Council of Geneva decided to send a deputation to Strasbourg to ask Calvin to return. By now the party that had expelled the reformers was in disgrace and there was disorder in the city. Calvin, who was away at Regensburg when the deputation arrived, was upset by the request; as he wrote to Farel, 'I dread that place'. But he was convinced, as always, that the will of God must take precedence over his own feelings. And return he did, arriving at Geneva on 13 September 1541.

CHURCH ORDER

The first task was to draw up a plan of reformation. This he did in the *Ecclesiastical Ordinances*, finally adopted, with modifications, by the city's councils on 2 January 1542. The church must have the four orders of ministry depicted in the New Testament. First, the pastors who are responsible for preaching the Word of God and administering the sacraments; second, the 'doctors' or teaching elders, responsible for Christian education; third, the elders, who are 'to supervise every person's conduct', and fourth, the deacons, who are the social workers to care for the poor and to administer the hospital. Strict rules were drawn up for the sponsoring and ordaining of ministers. The ministers were to meet once a week for theological and biblical discussions – this was the 'Venerable Company'. The Consistory, which met every Thursday, was composed of five ministers and twelve elders, the latter nominated by the Councils, and the body to be chaired at all times by a syndic.

The religious life of Geneva was to be supported by numerous public services. On Sundays, a sermon at each of the three churches at dawn, at noon the children were to be catechized, and sermons again in the three churches at 3 p.m. There were preaching services also on Monday, Tuesday and Friday, while Communion was to be administered once a month.

DISCIPLINE

For Calvin, discipline was of crucial importance because he wished the church to be as holy as possible in its morals, as well as orthodox in its beliefs. This was to be his answer to the disorder and immorality of the late mediaeval church. And the close co-operation between church and state at Geneva sustained the discipline. An offender would be first admonished privately by the elders. If that was ineffective, he was to be admonished in the presence of witnesses. If that failed, exclusion from the Lord's Table followed. Finally, excommunication was to be exercised by the whole body of elders, but restoration was possible if the offender repented. This was consonant, said Calvin, with pastoral care, for 'the severity of the Church must be tempered by a spirit of gentleness.'

The discipline exercised at Geneva has long been a matter

of severe condemnation. The Councils from time to time passed laws dealing with such topics as marriage and divorce, the theatre, public festivals, swearing, behaviour in public places and even the use of unacceptable names in baptism. Many of these regulations merely reasserted the standards set in mediaeval civic legislation. Even so, the régime tended to be a strict one and to become stricter as the years passed by. But what was striking about it at Geneva was the efficiency of its enforcement. From 1550 onwards, the ministers accompanied by an elder or deacon visited every house and examined the faith of every citizen. It was an unprecedented experiment in the control of morals and thought. No one, not even the poet Clément Marot, was exempt from the attentions of the Consistory. And the penalties were extreme. One fellow who cracked a joke about a braying ass 'singing a beautiful psalm' was banished from the city. And even more appalling was beheading a girl for striking her parents or burning 25 people as witches during the plague of 1545. In fact, capital punishment was used with surprising frequency.

LIBERTINES AND PATRIOTS

Calvin and his supporters inevitably met opposition. There were, first of all, powerful families jockeying for position; there were the Libertines, who resented the stringency of the discipline; and there were the Patriots, who feared the influence of the growing number of foreign refugees crowding into Geneva. It is not always easy to distinguish between these groups since their membership overlapped. Ami Perrin, for example, the Captain-general of the city's guard, and according to Calvin, a 'comic Caesar', was opposed to the discipline that curbed his love of pleasure. He and his wife were imprisoned in April 1546, but after his release, Perrin became Calvin's most formidable critic and during his period as Geneva's ambassador to France he seems to have had treasonable conversations with the French government. Finally, he and his supporters concocted a plan to assassinate the foreigners in Geneva, including Calvin himself. That was in 1554. He was betrayed but escaped and was condemned to death in his absence. Jacques Gruet was a true Libertine who believed

in unqualified moral freedom. His opposition to Calvin
extended to a threat upon his life. He was tried for sedition
and blasphemy and executed on 26 July 1547. Men such as
these had a fluctuating support in the city and Calvin's own
influence depended on the strength of his own supporters
in the Councils. Calvin was never a dictator of any kind.
His political ascendancy was not certainly assured until
1555, nor was he granted the privilege of citizenship until
1559.

THEOLOGICAL OPPONENTS

Hieronymus Bolsec (d.1585) was a French Carmelite friar
who turned Protestant and appeared in Geneva in 1550. He
publicly opposed Calvin's doctrine of predestination and
was put on trial. The ministers of Geneva sought the advice
of other churches before passing judgment and Bern, as
well as Heinrich Bullinger of Zürich, urged moderation and
tolerance. So Bolsec was banished but got his revenge later
by publishing an extremely libellous biography of Calvin,
and of Beza as well.

Sébastian Castellio (1515–63) was a very different man.
His origins in Savoy were humble but by hard work he
became a fine linguist. He shared Calvin's lodgings at
Strasbourg and returned with him to Geneva to be a teacher
at the school there. He soon came to disagree with Calvin
on the question of predestination and the canonicity of the
Song of Songs. Moreover, his thinking matured in the
direction of making human reason sovereign even over
divine revelation. He left Geneva for Basel in 1545 and after
suffering great privation, was appointed lecturer in Greek
at the university there. He was also a protester against the
treatment accorded to Servetus.

Michael Servetus (1511–53) was a native of Navarre,
brought up in Villenueva, Lerida, Spain, and educated at
Saragossa and Toulouse. He was a man of exceptional
ability who was at home in several branches of learning. He
was acquainted with many of his most illustrious contemporaries. There is much that is puzzling about the inner
motivations of his troubled career. His presence as a minor
official at Bologna in 1530 when Charles V was being
crowned brought disillusionment with the church and he

left the Emperor's court. By October 1530 he was at Basel
enjoying the hospitality of Oecolampadius and trying to
persuade his host that the classical definition of the doctrine of the Trinity was unscriptural. Then he migrated to
Strasbourg and had his book, *The Errors of the Trinity*,
published in nearby Hagenau in June 1531. Both Protestants and Roman Catholics were now ranged against him
and the Roman Catholic authorities issued a warrant for his
arrest on 17 June 1532 to appear at Toulouse. It was never
delivered because Servetus had disappeared. For twenty-
one years, concealed behind the assumed name, Michel
Villeneuve, he dwelt at Lyon, living the life of a gentle-
manly scholar and physician, editing Bibles and books of
learning and conforming to the discipline of the Roman
Catholic Church.

His fascination with Theology undiminished, in the mid-
forties Servetus began a lengthy interchange of letters with
Calvin on matters relating to Christology. Calvin tired of
the correspondence and broke it off in 1548 but not before
Servetus has sent him a draft of the book that was to be
published in January 1553 under the title, *The Restitution of
Christianity*. It was a statement of his long-held conviction
that the church had fallen from its original purity when it
made an alliance with Constantine the Great and embraced
the sophistries of the doctrine of the Trinity.

His real identity was made known quite by chance to the
Inquisition at Lyon and his arrest followed on 4 April 1553.
He was tried on charges of heresy but made his escape
three days later. He was found guilty in his absence and
condemned to death and burned in effigy.

He lay low for several weeks but on 13 August he moved
to the Rose d'Or hotel in Geneva. Since it was Sunday, he
attended afternoon service, was recognized and arrested.
His trial was an untidy business extending over several
weeks. Towards the end of September the other Swiss
cantons were consulted for their opinion of the case. They
were unanimous in their condemnation and Geneva had
little choice, even if it wished to act differently, but to
concur. On 26 October Servetus was found guilty and sentenced to be burned at the stake. The sentence was carried
out the following day. He had been found guilty of anabaptism and antitrinitarianism, two capital charges in the

ancient Code of Justinian. Ever since 1532 he had rejected
infant baptism and embraced believers' baptism by immer-
sion. He had modified his anti-Trinitarianism between 1531
and 1553 but not in any fundamental way. He insisted to
the end that there could be no divine Three-in-One and that
Jesus Christ could not be thought of as the eternal Son of
God, except in the sense that he was eternally present in
God's mind as a pattern or model of what true man should
be like.

Although the sentence passed on Servetus was approved
by Bullinger, Melanchthon, Peter Martyr, Farel, Beza and
many others, there was sufficient uneasiness to compel
Calvin to justify his conduct in a tract entitled, *The defence of
the orthodox faith in the Sacred Trinity*, February 1554. It is
Calvin at his most chilling. The document is as frightening
in its way as Luther's tract against the rebellious peasants.
It was left to Sebastian Castellio to open the door to the long
debate on toleration with the conviction that 'To kill a man
is not to defend a doctrine; it is simply to kill a man.'

INFLUENCE

Calvin took the international stage just at the time when
Luther's reformation was reaching a stalemate and as the
radical forms of reformation were being repressed. As Calvin's influence spread in Switzerland, the Netherlands,
France, England, Wales and Scotland, it introduced a new
militant spirit which in turn inspired a revolutionary
activism which profoundly affected the social and cultural
life of these nations.

22 War, and peace in Germany

We cannot yield, nor can we desert the truth . . . .

Melanchthon to Campeggio at the Diet of Augsburg, 1530.

The years between the Diet of Augsburg 1530 and the religious peace agreed upon at the later Diet of Augsburg 1555 were dominated by the search for unity between the churches in Germany and Switzerland, the extinguishing of the hopes for peaceful accommodation, the resort to war and final compromise. Luther from the beginning of his protest had pleaded for a universal council to consider his case and to undertake the reform of the Church, and had consistently opposed the use of violence in support of the gospel. The two men who worked hardest on the Protestant side to achieve reconciliation, mostly through councils and conferences, were Philip Melanchthon and Martin Bucer. As Bucer put it, 'Christ suffered and taught for no other purpose but that we should be one and embrace each other with the same love with which He embraced us'. But the path of the mediator was not an easy one. Luther himself was often nervous that Melanchthon would concede too much. 'I am vexed not a little,' he said in 1530, 'by this talk of compromise, which is a scandal to God.' At its final Recess, 19 November 1530, the Imperial Diet at Augsburg ordered the Protestants to conform by the following Spring and to help in the eradication of the Zwinglians and the Anabaptists. It seemed clear enough that the attempt of Melanchthon and others to effect a reconciliation was a complete failure. And since the Diet seemed intent on open war against them, the Protestant leaders formed their defensive Smalcaldic League on 27 February 1531 for 'the maintenance of Christian truth and peace in the Holy Empire.'

A UNITED FRONT?

Bucer passionately desired to create a united theological front among Protestants. The biggest difficulty was the difference of opinion about the nature of Holy Communion. Bucer himself changed his view from time to time. First of all he had accepted Luther's view, then, in 1526 under the influence of Carlstadt, Zwingli and Cornelius Hoen, the Dutch lawyer and lay theologian, he had come to believe in the symbolic role of the elements in the sacrament. But after reading Luther's *Confession* of 1528, he modified his standpoint once again and became convinced that there was no fundamental difference between Luther and Zwingli. He developed a doctrine that the material elements, the bread and wine, are conjoined with the spiritual reality, Christ's body and blood, so that the physiological consumption of the elements is in sacramental union with the spiritual ingestion of the Lord's body by faith. Melanchthon was very sceptical whether Zwingli and Oecolampadius could possibly subscribe to such a doctrine. But then, Melanchthon's own view was changing too. He was now coming to believe that Christ's presence in the sacrament was a real spiritual presence rather than a real bodily presence while the mode of that presence is a mystery apprehended only by faith. However, Luther would not budge an inch. 'The heart of our doctrine is this,' he wrote, 'that in the bread or with the bread, the body of Christ is really eaten . . . so that the body is actually torn with the teeth and eaten.'

Melanchthon and Bucer were given an opportunity to show their gifts as mediators by Landgrave Philip of Hesse. Duke Ulrich had been ejected from his duchy of Würtemberg by the Roman Catholic Swabian League and the territory made subject to Ferdinand of Austria. In May 1534 the Landgrave over-ran the duchy and restored the duke while Ferdinand by the Peace of Cadan (1534) conceded freedom to institute the Reformation in Würtemberg. But some parts favoured Luther while others were Zwinglian and therefore compromise was necessary. Philip got Bucer and Melanchthon together at the Conference at Cassel, December 1534, and they succeeded in composing a formula which was acceptable to all the parties, including Luther. So Bucer was encouraged to believe that union was possible after all.

Bucer's next triumph came with the Wittenberg Conference of May 1536. Luther was in an eirenic mood and had accepted Bucer's assurance that the Swiss, including Bullinger, were in agreement with him on the doctrine of Communion. This was not so and the Swiss demurred when they saw the final draft of the agreement that was produced by the conference. In consequence, they were not party to the final agreement. Relations between Bucer and Melanchthon were very cordial because Melanchthon was now looking for a middle road between Luther's corporal presence and Zwingli's spiritual presence. He now held that when we are offered bread and wine in the Supper, 'there is truly offered to us the body and blood of Christ, and Christ is truly there, and is powerful in us'. So he and Bucer were able to suggest a basis in the Wittenberg Concord for a wider union of Protestants in Germany, though that, of course, did not include the Swiss.

RECONCILIATION WITH ROMAN CATHOLICS?

From 1539 onwards, Bucer dedicated himself to securing unity with the Roman Catholics. No one believed reconciliation with the papacy to be possible, but many wanted to see the religious unity of Germany restored. Hopes rose in the wake of the colloquy at Leipzig in 1539 when Bucer had been able to agree on fifteen articles with the Roman Catholic representative, Witzel. A further colloquy was held at Frankfurt the following year and the discussion continued at Hagenau in June 1540 and at Worms in November. Young Calvin was present at Frankfurt, representing Strasbourg together with Capito, Sturm and Bucer, and it was at Worms that his skills as a debater won him the sobriquet, 'The Theologian'. At Worms, the Emperor engineered a private conference between the Protestants, Bucer and Capito, and the liberal Roman Catholic, John Gropper. It was from their meetings that the so-called 'Regensburg Book' emerged and it served as the basis for the resumed conversations at the Diet of Regensburg in April 1541. The participants were Bucer, Melanchthon and Pistorius for the Protestants and John Eck, John Gropper

and Julius Pflug of Mainz for the Roman Catholics. Pope
Paul III had sent Cardinal Contarini as his legate and for
him, as for the group of conciliatory Roman Catholics that
he led, this conference was of crucial importance. But the
Pope had craftily appointed the reactionary Bishop Morone
as his special nuncio. Calvin was highly critical of the
proceedings and although he was a participant, he thought
it all a waste of time. Despite the claim, based on the
Regensburg Book that there was agreement on the fall, free
will, sin, and even justification, the talks collapsed. From
Rome's point of view, Contarini was conceding too much
and from the Protestant point of view, Bucer was going
further than he had any right to do as a Protestant
spokesman. Calvin complained that Bucer and Melanchthon had 'drawn up ambiguous and varnished form-
ulas concerning transubstantiation' and Luther exploded
tartly, 'Bucer, the rascal, has absolutely lost all my confidence.' In this way the ecumenical hopes of Bucer and
Melanchthon were extinguished and when at last the long-
awaited universal council met at Trent, Luther was completely cynical about it and the Protestants, apart from a
fleeting visit by a minute delegation, took no part in it.

SCANDAL

While all this was going on, the German Protestant
movement became embroiled in serious scandal. Philip,
Landgrave of Hesse, was quite incapable of controlling his
sexual lust. Although he was married to Christina, the
daughter of Duke George of Saxony, he decided in 1539
that he would take a second wife rather than go to the
trouble of seeking a divorce. His choice was the seventeen-
year-old Margaret von der Saale. She insisted that Philip
must secure assurances that bigamy was not contrary to the
law of God. So the reformers were consulted and they gave
it as their opinion (as indeed they had done previously with
reference to Henry VIII's marital problem) that bigamy was
not specifically prohibited by divine law. But the Landgrave
was not to give publicity to their judgment. However,
after marrying Margaret on 4 March 1540, he used the
reformers' letter as a kind of public dispensation. The affair
made the theologians into objects of ridicule since they had

been only too ready to condemn the immorality of churchmen in the past. And the affair had political effects too since bigamy was punishable by death according to the laws of the Empire and Philip was driven to abject submission to the Emperor and to express a readiness to repudiate his alliance with non-German states.

WAR

On 20 July 1546 Charles V proclaimed his ban on the Protestants and hostilities started. He was now reconciled to the king of France and had allies among the Protestant princes for, in addition to Philip of Hesse, Maurice, Duke of Saxony since 1541 and Philip's nephew, was on the Imperial side. Maurice attacked Electoral Saxony and on 24 April 1547 defeated the Elector at Mühlberg. By summer the Emperor had Germany at his feet. Since he was at odds with the pope he asked a panel of theologians to draw up a statement to serve as a basis for the religious reunification of Germany. This was the 'Interim' adopted by the Diet of Augsburg, 15 May 1548. It was an extremely ambiguous document which seemed to yield on some points to the Protestants. Some theologians, feared the worst and fled, (as Bucer and Fagius did to England) since its provisions were to be imposed by military force. However, it proved impossible to compel the population at large to accept it.

The inscrutable Maurice, having betrayed his fellow-Protestants, now decided to betray the Emperor. And he, whose fortunes seemed so bright in 1548, found himself abandoned by everyone by May 1552 and he had no choice but to agree to the peace terms of the Treaty of Passau, 2 August 1552. But Maurice perished in the exceptionally bloody battle of Sievershausen, 9 July 1553. The Elector John Frederick did not long survive him. He died on 3 March 1554, a man, as Roger Ascham testified, 'reverenced of his foes, favoured of the Emperor, loved of all.'

The Emperor Charles V, worn out by the cares of state and dismayed by the failure of his German policies, transferred authority to his brother, Ferdinand, and went into retirement at a monastery. On 5 February 1555 the long-awaited Diet that was to settle once and for all the religious question met at Augsburg. It gave legal recognition to the

Augsburg Confession of 1530 and permitted each prince to decide whether his territory should be Roman Catholic or Protestant – the principle known by the Latin tag, *Cuius regio, eius religio*. It was a memorable landmark in the history of Germany and its Reformation.

A REFORMER'S LAST JOURNEY

Luther remained as busy as ever. He continued his work as professor at the University of Wittenberg. His last course of lectures was on Genesis and extended over nine years, ending on 17 November 1545. He continued to preach several times a week. His pen was never still as he busily poured out books and pamphlets. Yet he was plagued by illness and lost the sight of one eye. He could bear these troubles with his natural resilience. But spiritual and pastoral cares weighed much more heavily on him. He was deeply distressed that there was so much immorality and disorderly living in Protestant areas. And why did God permit such virulent opposition to the gospel? As the years passed by he became increasingly convinced that the end of the world was at hand and that only the second coming of Jesus Christ would herald a new era.

On 23 January 1546 he set out on a journey to Mansfeld, his childhood home. The two brothers, the counts of Mansfeld, were quarrelling bitterly and Luther hoped to reconcile them. And he succeeded in his errand. He preached his last sermon at Eisleben on 14 February 1546. But the cold German winter attacked him. He soon became too ill to continue his journey and died at Eisleben, the town where he was born. He drew his last breath on 18 February 1546 after repeating several times the words, 'God so loved the world that he gave his only begotten Son, so that whosoever believeth in him should not perish, but have everlasting life' (*see* John 3:16). His mortal remains were taken in solemn procession back to Wittenberg. There, after his minister, John Bugenhagen had preached, and his faithful colleague, Melanchthon had spoken in Latin, he was buried in the Castle Church on whose door just a little over twenty-nine years previously he had posted his Ninety-five Theses.

23 The struggle for reformation in France

No one should be obliged by force to enter the flock of Jesus Christ, but that the sword of the Word of God may be used as the only means of drawing to Him those who are called and chosen to believe.

From the bills submitted by the Huguenots at the Estates-General at Orléans, December, 1560.

Humanly speaking John Calvin was the product of French Protestantism. The reform movement in that country had developed early and was to have an epic history. The church in France was in serious need of reform, afflicted as it was by the luxury of the higher clergy, the ignorance of the lower clergy, the general spiritual debilitation and the secularizing influence of the Crown which used the 620 preferments that were under its control after the Concordat of 1516 to reward its servants.

ROMAN CATHOLIC REFORM

From December 1515 Guillaume Briçonnet (1470–1534) was bishop of Meaux. As well as taking stern measures to ensure better discipline in his diocese, he gathered around him a group eager to reform the church. His old teacher, Lefèvre d'Étaples (1455–1537) was one of them. In 1523 he published his translation of the New Testament and people began to gather together to hear it read. These were the first conventicles. In addition, on holy days, and especially on Sundays, the Epistle and Gospel set for the day were read to the congregations in the diocese in French. His Old Testament followed in 1526, while his *Commentary on the Epistles of Saint Paul* (1512) exalted faith rather than works. Other members of the Meaux group were Gérard Roussel

(1480–1550), François Vatable, who died 16 March 1547 as abbot of Bellesane, best known as the professor of Hebrew at the Collége de France, and Guillaume Farel, later Calvin's colleagues in Switzerland.

During 1519 Luther's books were beginning to cause a sensation in France and on the very day when the reformer appeared before the Diet of Worms, 15 April 1521, propositions from them were condemned by the Sorbonne. Even so, Francis I was complaining in September 1524 that for five years or so the 'Lutheran sect is swarming in the town and neighbourhood of Lyon'. Elsewhere also cases of heresy began to emerge. At Avignon the Franciscan friar, François Lambert (1486–1530), later the reformer of Hesse, was found to possess Lutheran books. The books were burnt but Lambert fled to Geneva. Michel d'Arande, a monk from Tournai and Queen Margaret's almoner was preaching during 1523–1524 at places like Bourges, Meaux, Mâçon and Lyon, while another monk from Tournai, Jean Châtelain, was preaching at Metz with marked success. He, together with Jean le Clerc, were burned at the stake as heretics in 1525. That the Roman Catholic reform was leading to something more radical is suggested by the discovery at Saumur in 1525 of a group of women who believed in the priesthood of all believers. But by then repression had begun. Even in 1522 Briçonnet had been denounced for insulting theologians and for criticizing the cult of saints. He himself enjoyed the protection of Queen Margaret, the king's sister, but his colleagues were soon scattered. By 1525 the Meaux group had ceased to be. Reaction was in the air and provincial church councils were active in condemning heresy and seeking to institute reforms. In 1533 the king, with the blessing of the pope, initiated a vigorous bout of persecution which was the cause of young Calvin's flight into exile.

RESPITE AND REPRESSION

The king was driven to fury and the Roman Catholic leaders to exasperation on 18 October 1534 when posters appeared in Paris, and even in view of the royal chamber at Amboise, bitterly attacking 'the Pope and all his vermin' and denouncing transubstantiation and the doctrine of the

sacrifice of the Mass. This bold, even foolhardy, demonstration of Protestant zeal had serious consequences. Four
hundred suspects were rounded up, representing a cross-
section of society from nobles to shoemakers, and twenty-
three were burned.

This affair of the placards suggested the theological
influence of Zwingli, but this was a time also when
Lutheran books were pouring into France through the great
book fairs at Frankfurt and Lyon as well as through the
work of clandestine printers and France itself.

Despite his bursts of persecution, Francis I was not
unsympathetic to the requests for reform, and in any case
the demands of his foreign policy and the need to secure
the support of the Lutheran princes and Henry VIII of
England, meant that the French Protestants were granted
periods of peace to disseminate their views. On 16 July
1535, the king by the Edict of Coucy suspended action
against heretics and allowed refugees to return. And there
was very little persecution between 1536 and 1538 while
Francis was at war with Charles V. But as soon as that war
was over, Francis devoted himself once again to the task of
destroying Protestantism. A series of persecuting edicts
were issued between December 1538 and June 1539 and
then came the severest of them, the Edict of Fontainebleau,
1 June 1540, making the suppression of heresy the business
of the secular courts. The Sorbonne added its support by for-
mulating twenty-six articles defining the Roman Catholic
faith, ratified by the king on 23 July 1543. By that time
Calvin's French version of the *Institutes* was circulating in
France and had been banned by the Parliament of Paris in
1542. Two years later the Sorbonne issued an *Index* of
prohibited books to limit the spread of Protestant ideas.

Even more ruthless was the policy executed by Cardinal
François de Tournon, especially towards the Waldensians,
who had continued to maintain the biblical and reforming
convictions of their mediaeval forbears. He inspired the
Parliament of Aix to produce an entirely false report that
they were in open rebellion and threatening Marseilles. The
King issued a decree that all those professing the
Waldensian faith were to be exterminated. In April 1545,
the president of that Parliament, the brutal Jean Meynier,
seigneur d'Oppède, burned down Mérindol, Cabrières and

other villages and within two months massacred over 3,000 Waldensians. Similarly, the Protestant congregation at Meaux was attacked on 8 September 1546 and sixty members were arrested and taken to Paris. On 7 October, fourteen of them were tortured and burned. And so the repression and the killings continued until the death of Francis I on 31 March 1547.

What do these feverish attempts at suppression tell us about the progress of Protestantism in France between 1527 and 1547? The impression is often given that the Protestant Reformation in France did not really begin until 1555 or even 1559. But that is to mis-read the evidence. By 1555 the soil of scores of French towns had been reddened by the blood of French Protestant martyrs but the feverish ferocity of the authorities hardly sufficed to stunt the growth of the movement.

EVANGELICAL ISLANDS

By 1547 there were evangelical groups to be found all over France. They were independent of each other and congregational in their polity. They devoted themselves to Bible reading, prayer, psalm singing and listening to sermons. Some of them preserved their anonymity to such an extent that their members continued to attend their parish churches while treasuring their real faith in the privacy of their homes and hearts, much to the consternation of Calvin who disapproved of such 'Nicodemism' – such following of the example of Nicodemus who was afraid to make public his admiration for Jesus.

The king of France from 1547 to 1559 was Henry II and during his reign the face of Europe changed dramatically. The year 1555 saw a significant pause in the struggle between the Empire and Lutheran Germany with the Peace of Augsburg. By 1557 expensive wars had brought both France and Spain to the edge of bankruptcy and within two years the two countries had agreed to bury the hatchet in the Treaty of Cateau-Cambrésis (April 1559). The Italian cities were entering a period of decline after their golden age. The tide of the Roman Catholic reformation was rising, but on the other hand Calvinistic militancy was providing a vigorous opposition in Scotland and the Netherlands, while reformed Anglicanism began a new chapter in England and Wales with the accession of Elizabeth in 1558. And in France itself the religious struggle now entered a new phase.

ORGANIZING FOR EXPANSION

Calvin was not happy with the informality of the French congregations. He believed that discipline and order were essential unless the movement was to succumb to persecution. In a constant stream of letters he provided them with the necessary guidance.

The first Reformed Church in France, organized on the pattern of Strasbourg, was that at Meaux. But it, like its sister church at Nîmes, had been extinguished by repression. The first continuing Reformed Church was the one at Paris, organized in 1555 by Jean le Maçon at the insistence of the Sieur de la Ferrière. In the same year four other churches were organized – at Angers, Loudun, Poitiers and on the Arvert peninsula. During the following years others were incorporated right across the country, from Dieppe (1557) to Toulouse (1557), and from Rennes to Montpellier. By 1559 there were 72 such churches.

They needed ministers. The chief training centre was Geneva and the first minister trained there was Philibert Hamelin who reached Saintogne on the Arvert peninsula in 1553. From 1555 to 1562 Geneva sent at least 88 men who served 65 churches. And they needed to be resourceful and courageous men for meetings had to be held in the strictest secrecy, and steps taken to guard against infiltration by spies, and meeting-places continually changed to avoid detection. Yet the movement spread with remarkable speed and Admiral Coligny was claiming in 1561 that there were no fewer than 2,150 Protestant churches in France. And Protestantism's spread was facilitated by the bold and widespread use made of the products of the printing press which were disseminated by hundreds of booksellers wandering about France disguised as beggars.

In May 1559 the first synod of the French Protestant churches convened at Paris. It was not a fully representative gathering and consisted mostly of delegates from the West and North. But it did agree to transform the informal congregationalism of the previous period into a much more structured Presbyterian form of organization. A Confession of Faith was also agreed upon, much of its substance coming from Calvin's 1557 Confession and the Genevan Catechism. The Confession is a lucid, balanced and dignified statement of the Reformed faith and before the end of the century had become the most extensively circulated of all Protestant Confessions.

TRIAL BY FIRE

The growth of Protestantism is all the more remarkable because it happened under the shadow of vicious persecution. Henry II was determined to uproot heresy in his kingdom. He confirmed his father's appointment of Mathieu Ory as Inquisitor and Protestantism had no more implacable enemy than he. In 1547 also the Parliament of Paris set up a new institution, popularly known as the *Chambre ardente* – the Tribunal of Fire – with exclusive powers in matters of heresy. In order to strengthen the campaign against heresy Henry II, by an edict of 19 November 1549, greatly extended the jurisdiction of bishops, increased the sentencing powers of the judges and insisted on closer co-operation between church and state. And the edict of Chateaubriant, 27 June 1551, further increased the powers of the authorities to persecute heretics. These draconian measures were to culminate in 1557 in the introduction of the Roman Inquisition into France and the issuing of the edict of Compiègne (24 July 1557) which imposed the death penalty, without benefit of appeal, upon all who were convicted of any heretical activity. As Henry II put it, once he had settled his foreign affairs, he would make the 'streets run with the blood . . . of the squalid Lutheran riff-raff'.

DISTINGUISHED CONVERTS

The king's insulting language betrayed his mounting frustration as he saw the highest classes in society being penetrated by Protestantism. In 1555 alone some 119 nobles and gentry had fled to Geneva. It was little wonder that the Swiss nickname for freedom fighters against Savoyard oppression, *eyguenot*, should be rendered in French as 'huguenot' and applied to the reformed Protestants of the country. Among the distinguished converts were the Bourbon brothers. Antoine (1518–62), married the remarkable Jeanne d'Albret (1528–72) who became Queen of Navarre in 1555. His brother, Louis, prince of Condé (1530–69), was one of those welcomed by Calvin at Geneva in 1555. The Montmorency family were also to play a large part in the subsequent history. Anne de Montmorency (1493-1567), the Constable of France, remained a Roman Catholic, but his sister, Louise, had three sons who became Protestant. They were Odet (1517–71), Cardinal of Châtillon, who became Protestant in 1561; Gaspard de Coligny, Admiral of France, (1519–71) who was converted in 1558, and François d'Antelot (1521–69), popular soldier and enthusiastic propagator of Protestantism. These powerful Protestant nobles were opposed by the Roman Catholic Guise family. Their native territory was Lorraine which was not at that time under the jurisdiction of the crown of France. Francis (1519–63), nicknamed 'Scarface', was the Duke of Guise and made his reputation as a warrior, while his brother, Charles (1524–74), had considerable influence at Rome as the Cardinal of Lorraine. When Henry II, king of France, was accidentally killed in June 1559 and succeeded by his son, Francis II, his accession provided the Guise brothers with the opportunity to influence royal policy. For Francis was married to Mary, Queen of Scots, and her mother, Mary of Guise, was their sister. The kings, of course, belonged to the Valois dynasty.

RELIGION, POLITICS AND SOCIETY

The conflict between Roman Catholic and Protestant was not the only factor that contributed to the outbreak of the Wars of Religion in France. Economic changes had created acute social tensions in French society. Since about 1530 the lower nobility, living on fixed incomes had suffered impoverishment through inflation and costly wars had brought the kingdom to the verge of bankruptcy by 1559. Many had left their estates and looked to the royal bounty for help. The landed gentry were becoming increasingly conscious of their independence and were glad to extend their patronage to the new Calvinist churches. The great nobles, such as the Bourbons and the Montmorencies, were jealous of the growing influence of the Guises and eager to gain greater control over the Crown. The merchant class had also been growing in influence and its critical stance towards the church's financial demands made it sympathetic to the Reformation. And finally, young soldiers of fortune, restless after the excitements of war, were only too eager to put their swords at the disposal of whichever faction chose to employ them. But the readiness of some of them to look to the Protestant churches for military support caused no little anxiety to the pastors. It was becoming obvious by 1560 that the interaction between these social forces could only lead to an explosion.

THE APPEAL TO THE SWORD

The Protestant nobles decided to make a bold bid to get the young King Francis under their control. It was the aim of the Conspiracy of Amboise (March 1560) to capture him, but the plot failed. Francis died on 5 December 1560 and his ten-year old brother succeeded him as Charles IX. Since the King was a minor, his mother, Catherine de' Medici (1519–89), became the power behind the throne. Under the influence of the Chancellor of France, Michel de l'Hôpital (1507-73), she embraced a policy designed to increase the authority of the Crown by reconciling the hostile groups. So the Huguenots were granted a generous measure of freedom to congregate for worship in places other than walled towns. The policy was not to the liking of Roman Catholic enthusiasts and the soldiers of Francis, Duke of Guise, massacred a congregation of Huguenots while they were at worship at Vassy on 1 March 1562. The following month, the first of the seven Wars of Religion started. It lasted until March 1563 and peace was restored by the Edict of Amboise, 12 March 1563. Despite the restrictions on Huguenot worship included in the Edict, the Protestant churches were able to flourish.

The peace was broken when the Prince of Condé and his associates, in the plan known as the Conspiracy of Meaux, sought to effect a coup d'état and succeeded in capturing several strongholds, notably La Rochelle. The second war followed, November 1567 to March 1568, and after a short-lived respite, the attempt of the government to arrest the Protestant leaders, Condé and Coligny, led to yet a third war. Even so, the Huguenots were able to hold their own and the Peace of Saint-Germain, 8 August 1570, extended their freedom and enhanced their legal status. By 1572 they seemed set for a stable and safe future.

A DAY OF TERROR

The revolt in the Netherlands aroused keen sympathy among the Huguenots and many of their Roman Catholic opponents were happy enough to see Philip of Spain in difficulties. Coligny, who now had considerable influence over the King, was advocating a policy of uniting France in support of William of Orange. A marriage was arranged between Henry of Navarre, the son of Antoine of Bourbon, and Marguerite of Valois, the King's sister. The Queen Mother was jealous of Coligny's influence over her royal son and conspired with Henry, Duke of Guise since the death of his father in 1563, to assassinate him. But as the assassin's shot was fired on the 22 August 1572, Coligny suddenly stooped down and escaped with an injured hand. Two days later, Catherine issued fresh instructions to kill the Admiral and so sparked off the massacre of Saint Bartholomew's Day. The Paris mob ran riot and not only was Coligny murdered but a large number of Huguenots – perhaps as many as 3,000 were massacred in Paris alone – and the killings went on in other cities for several months.

It was an event that shook Europe. Pope Gregory XIII ordered a special *Te Deum*. Philip II of Spain, so it is said, smiled for the first and last time. And Elizabeth, of England ordered her court to go into mourning. It is pleasant to report that on the four hundredth centenary of the massacre, special masses were offered all over France as an act of penitence for the atrocity, while Geneva observed its traditional annual fast.

CONFLICT AND RECONCILIATION

The massacre was a serious blow to the Huguenots. Condé and Henry of Navarre abjured their faith – but only under

duress and temporarily. The Huguenots soon regrouped
and the four wars that followed in 1573, 1574–6, 1577 and
1580 did not crush them. Meanwhile the political scene
changed significantly. The death of Charles IX in 1574
brought his brother, Henry III, to the throne, and the death
of his other brother, the Duke of Anjou, in 1584, made the
Huguenot leader, Henry of Navarre, heir to the throne.

In 1576 a Catholic League had been formed to defend the
Roman Catholic faith, led by the Duke of Guise and prepared to enter into secret arrangements with Philip of Spain
to attain their ends. They were opposed by Roman Catholics – the *politiques* –who wished to preserve the unity and
independence of France by coming to some accommodation with the Huguenots. In that way, the supporters of
Roman Catholicism were divided.

Since the League was developing anti-royalist attitudes,
Henry III put himself at its head and severely restricted the
liberties of Huguenots. But to no avail; the League's
influence in Paris and its hostility to the Crown led, by
1589, to a division that split France in half, and only by
reconciliation with Henry of Navarre was Henry able to
preserve his throne. But his death on 2 August 1589 made
Henry of Navarre the legitimate king of France. In order to
unite France Henry, not without consulting his Protestant
advisers, decided to embrace Roman Catholicism and was
received into the Roman Catholic Church on 25 July 1593.
After all, for him political considerations were always of
paramount importance. But he did not mean to betray his
co-religionists in the Protestant fold By the Edict of Nantes,
April 1598, – unique in its provisions in the sixteenth century, – he secured for the Huguenots a full measure of
freedom and virtually allowed them to become a state
within a state.

24 A young Josiah

Sir, seeing that God has brought you so far, take order . . . that He may approve you as a repairer of his temple, so that the times of the King your nephew may be compared with those of Josiah . . . .

John Calvin to Protector Somerset, 22 October 1548.

Edward VI of England was born on 12 October 1537. He was therefore nine years old when he became king in January 1547. In accordance with the will of his father, Henry VIII, government was to be exercised by a Council of Regency. On 31 January this Council appointed the King's uncle, Edward Seymour, Duke of Somerset (1506?–1552), to be Protector of the realm. He was ousted in October 1549 by John Dudley (1502?–1553), Earl of Warwick at the time, later Duke of Northumberland.

TURN OF THE TIDE

For ardent Protestants the reign of Henry VIII had been a disappointment and his last years were a time of fear. The accession of Edward VI brought intense relief as Thomas Fuller (1608–61) explained in his *Church History* (1665), 'No sooner was he come to the crown, but a peaceable dew refreshed God's inheritance in England, formerly parched with persecution.' There was turbulence enough during the reign, but for the reformers it was a time of great opportunity. Now was the time to make the kingdom truly Protestant. And under Somerset a considerable amount of freedom prevailed since all the laws against heresy, as well as the Six Articles, had been repealed and there were evangelists galore to take advantage of it. Indeed, so great was the enthusiasm that Somerset silenced all preachers on 23 September 1548. This measure lasted only a few weeks, for Protestantism was growing in vitality. The indigenous

dissenting movement, whether called Lollardy or Anabaptism, was making its clandestine contribution, while
among the religious leaders, the Lutheranism of the previous period was yielding to the influence of Calvin and
Bullinger. Calvin conveyed his own sense of urgency in his
letter to Somerset, January 1550, urging him to yet greater
efforts, for 'you know, Monseigneur, that in so great and
worthy a cause, even when we have put forth all our
strength, we come far short of what is required'. And
Bullinger was to maintain for many years a correspondence
with many of the leading figures in the English
Reformation. The influence of Calvin and Bullinger was
strengthened by the presence in England of distinguished
continental refugees, men like Martin Bucer, Peter Martyr,
Bernardino Ochino, and John à Lasco.

NEW MEN

Edward VI was the first Protestant monarch in his country's
history. His enthusiasm, young as he was, was of real help
to his uncle and his colleagues in initiating reformation.
Henry VIII's policies had ensured control of the episcopate.
Stephen Gardiner, the bishop of Winchester, was
imprisoned in September 1547 for opposing the Protestant
measures and was deprived of his bishopric on 15 February
1551. Other bishops were deprived or resigned, such as
John Vesey of Exeter, Edmund Bonner of London, Nicholas
Heath of Worcester and George Day of Chichester. So it
became possible to appoint men of evangelical convictions
to fill the vacancies. In this way Nicholas Ridley went to
London and Miles Coverdale to Exeter. John Hooper, a
close friend of Bullinger's, at first declined to go to the
diocese of Gloucester both because he objected to the
Roman Catholic form of the oath to be taken and because
he objected to the vestments. But, to the disappointment of
Bullinger, he withdrew his objections to the vestments and
went to Gloucester in March 1551.

In 1547 the work of dissolution begun by Henry VIII was
completed when an act dissolving chantries was passed.
Some 2,374 chantries, established to pray for the repose of
the souls of the dead, were involved, and their value was to
go to the Crown. The gentry and the nobility had con-

solidated their economic power by the acquisition of the church property confiscated since 1538. And Somerset himself, to the detriment of the Protestantism that he propagated, proved exceptionally greedy in his desire for wealth.

WORSHIP

For ordinary people in their parish churches, the point where theological changes touched them most intimately was in worship. Thomas Cranmer realized this and on 8 March 1548 published an *Order of Communion* containing English material for inclusion in the Latin Mass. Towards the end of the year Cranmer had a panel of 13 theologians meeting at Windsor to compose a new liturgy. The resulting volume, *The Book of Common Prayer*, was approved by Parliament in January 1549 and was to come into use on Whitsunday, 9 June 1549. The Act of Uniformity which imposed it stipulates sharp punishment for those who criticized the book or declined to use it, but the liberality of the Act is seen in its omission of any penalty for not attending church. This 1549 Prayer Book was the product of a policy that sought to retain the sympathy of Roman Catholics while satisfying the Reformers. In its office of Holy Communion it sought to appease those who believed in transubstantiation while not offending the disciples of Geneva or Zürich. It owed much to the Roman Catholic liturgies of the past, especially the Use of Sarum, but had regard also to contemporary Protestant liturgies. But if it showed evidence of compromise at several points, in one respect it was quite uncompromising. It was in the English language and no provision was made for those citizens whose only language was Welsh, Irish, Manx, Cornish or French. Indeed, this point was made by Cornishmen during the uprising in Devon and Cornwall in the summer of 1549 when they asserted that they 'utterly refuse this new English'. These disturbances expressed a vigorous conservative protest against the religious innovations. In East Anglia, however, the uprisings, whose best-known leader was Robert Ket, despite their manifest anticlericalism, were more concerned with social grievances. These revolts were put down but they were a prelude to a new struggle for power which dislodged Somerset on 11 October 1549 and made Dudley (later Duke of Northumberland) effective head of government. It was during his ascendancy that the Church of England became an unmistakeably Protestant body.

FURTHER REFORMATION

In May 1550 Cranmer's new Ordinal had quietly but significantly redefined the role of the minister. The charge said, 'Take thou authority to preach the Word of God and to minister the holy sacraments in this congregation'. He was no longer to be a sacrificing priest but a servant of the Word of God who also ministered the sacraments.

Then came a new *Book of Common Prayer*. There had been much criticism of the earlier book, not least by Martin Bucer. In March 1552 Parliament passed a new Act of Uniformity and sanctioned the use of a new Prayer Book. It was more radical than its predecessor. The word 'Mass' disappeared, as well as the theological principles that characterized it. The words of administration at Communion stress thanksgiving and commemoration but the service does not follow the usages of Geneva or Zürich. The Communion table was to be placed lengthwise with its ends east and west in order to emphasize that it was not an altar. The daily services were so phrased as to be defensible on the basis of Scripture. The mediaeval vestments were discarded, and the use of the surplice was enjoined. With very little change of substance this second Prayer Book of Edward VI was to remain the liturgy of the Church of England until the twentieth century.

The Protestant character of the Church of England was defined in the Forty-two Articles of Religion issued in June 1553. Salvation is by Christ alone and not by works and God has decreed from eternity 'to deliver from curse and damnation those whom he hath chosen out of mankind'. In a word, the Articles are Calvinistic in doctrine and they also exclude both Roman Catholicism and Anabaptism. But the reign ended before they were enforced.

The period of Northumberland's ascendancy gave eager Reformers like Hooper of Gloucester and Worcester, Robert Holgate of York, Nicholas Ridley of London, John Ponet of Rochester and Winchester, and John Scory of Rochester and Chichester, an opportunity to make Protestantism better known to the people. There was little evidence of a passionate commitment to the old religion. But, on the other hand, how strong were the roots of the New Faith? That question still remained to be answered.

Edward VI died on 6 July 1553. Northumberland sought to prolong his own ascendancy by plotting to make his daughter-in-law, Lady Jane Grey, the next monarch. The country at large, however, sided with the legitimate successor, Mary, and she became queen.

25 Reaction and settlement

The wise men of the world can find shifts to avoid the cross . . . but the simple servant of Christ doth look for no other but oppression in the world. And then is there most glory, when they be under the cross of their master Christ . . . .

Bishop Hugh Latimer (1485–1555) in an undated letter from prison addressed to another prisoner 'for the sake of the Gospel'.

Mary entered London on 3 August 1553. It was obvious at once that there would be dramatic changes in the secular and ecclesiastical government of the kingdom. Stephen Gardiner emerged from prison to become Lord Chancellor. On the other hand, Thomas Cranmer was arrested and convicted of treason. While Edmund Bonner, Cuthbert Tunstall and Nicholas Heath regained their freedom, Hugh Latimer, Nicholas Ridley, John Hooper and Miles Coverdale were imprisoned on a charge of heresy. The Duke of Northumberland paid with his life for his attempt to enthrone Lady Jane Grey and abjured his Protestantism before dying. Ardent Protestants read the signs of the times correctly and withdrew to the safety of the Continent.

PREPARING FOR CHANGE

The restoration of Roman Catholicism took time. Mary's Council and her Parliaments were disunited. And her own popularity began to decline long before persecution began. It was not so much her religious convictions as her devotion to all things Spanish that caused offence. Even the Emperor Charles V advised her to proceed cautiously and to gain the admiration, if she could, of her subjects. But that was for her an impossible task because she was quite insensitive to English public opinion. Not even the pleas of the House of

Commons could shake her resolve to marry Philip II of Spain. And that marriage intensified the ever-present fear of Spanish domination.

There was widespread discontent, with risings in Wales, Devonshire and the Midlands. Then came Sir Thomas Wyatt's much more ominous rising in Kent in January 1554. The rebels were not averse to indulging in iconoclasm and the occasional appeal to Protestant sympathy, but their main motives were not religious. The rising was suppressed and in the retribution that followed the most pathetic victim was Lady Jane Grey. She had pleaded guilty to treason at her trial in the previous November but had not been executed. Her father, the Duke of Suffolk had brought vengeance upon himself by supporting Wyatt but Lady Jane's execution was quite unjustified and served to deepen public dislike of Mary.

RESTORATION OF ROMAN CATHOLICISM

Roman Catholicism could be restored only by stages since there was a strong element in Parliament that would not co-operate to pass the necessary legislation. Thus, Parliament argued long and acrimoniously during its second session, October to December 1553, before repealing the religious legislation of Edward VI. It would not go beyond that. After all, people who had benefited by acquiring confiscated church lands did not wish to see themselves stripped of their gains. And so Mary's second Parliament in April and May 1554, although it reluctantly approved her marriage to Philip II, would not consent to the restoration of confiscated church property.

On 24 November 1554, Cardinal Pole, the papal legate, landed in England. Parliament presented a petition for reunion with Rome and on 30 November Pole solemnly absolved the Kingdom. Then the necessary legislation to give legal substance to the reconciliation was passed. All the reform legislation, with the exception of the act for the dissolution of the monasteries, was repealed. At the same time, the anti-heresy laws were revived. And so the church found itself restored to the position it held in 1529.

The way was now clear to initiate a policy of active persecution.

PERSECUTION

The first person to suffer death was the Bible translator,
John Rogers, burned at Smithfield on 4 February 1555. The
last to suffer were four men and one woman who were
burned at Canterbury on 10 November 1558. And in
between these two events, at least 276 others suffered the
same death. The vast majority of them, no less than 83%,
were executed at four places, Norwich (31), Chichester (41),
Canterbury (49) and London (112) – a total of 233. These
figures suggest that these were the places where Protestantism was most defiant. Doubtless, one needs to consider
also the enthusiasm of individual church prosecutors. This
would be relevant, for example, in the cases of Bishop
Edmund Bonner of London, Reginald Pole and Archdeacon
Nicholas Harpsfield at Canterbury and Miles Dunning,
Chancellor of Norwich, all of them men who would seek to
swell the number of sufferers.

The majority of the martyrs were ordinary people,
including many women, yet all ranks of society are represented. In the main they were Anglicans with only a few
that can be certainly identified with Anabaptist or Lollard
groups. The lengthy interrogations of scores of these
people have survived and they concentrate on such topics
as their beliefs about the Bible and its authority, transubstantiation, their attitude towards such Roman Catholic
practices as the cult of saints, prayers for the dead and
purgatory. One cannot but be impressed by the vigour and
ability with which people quite ignorant of the law and
court procedure defended themselves, as well as by the
immense courage of the sufferers in the face of unspeakable
agony.

LIGHTING CANDLES

The sufferers looked upon their trials and executions as
providentially ordained forms of public witness to the gospel. And they were diligent in communicating to their
friends outside prison accounts of their experiences. And in
those areas where the burnings occurred their appeals
touched peoples' hearts and deepened public hostility to
the Roman Catholic Church.

The great persecution had in John Foxe (1516–87) a historian who knew exactly how to etch the story indelibly on his readers' minds. When all the legitimate criticisms have been made of his *Acts and Monuments*, it still remains a fascinating and powerful study. It grew under his hand between 1559 and the great 1570 edition into a full-scale apology of the Anglican Reformation. He not only preserved a vast amount of detailed factual material, even to the point of tedium at times, but he also had a rare journalistic gift, a nose for a good story, an ear for the telling epigram, together with a stirring literary power. The sheer bulk of the work convinces the reader that he is watching a dramatic theme played out by heroic men and women. And Foxe had an instinct for the memorable saying. Hugh Latimer was the most exciting preacher of his generation. Those sermons are all but forgotten. But the shortest of them, thanks to Foxe, has reverberated down the years. In front of Balliol College, Oxford, Latimer, with wit undiminished, said to his fellow-martyr, 'Be of good comfort, master Ridley, and play the man. We shall this day light such a candle, by God's grace, in England, as I trust shall never be put out.' It was consonant with Foxe's concern to vindicate the Anglican Church that the central core of his story should be the sufferings of Latimer, Ridley, Hooper, and especially Thomas Cranmer. For modern readers there is a peculiar poignancy in Cranmer's story. He was a gentle man and the reader cannot but sympathize with his anguish, his changes of mind, his six recantations of his Protestant views under the unremitting brainwashing to which he was subjected in those last dreadful weeks. And then the defiance with which he robbed his persecutors of their choicest victory as he asserted for the last time his evangelical faith, and sealed it with the words, 'and forasmuch as my hand offended, writing contrary to my heart, my hand shall first be punished there-fore; for may I come to the fire, it shall first be burned'. And so it happened.

MAINTAINING THE CONTINUITY

The long tradition of clandestine worship continued although information about such meetings is of necessity sparse. In the face of the threat of persecution, the leaders were anxious that some should survive to maintain the testimony in future, even if that meant temporary withdrawal to the continent. As Nicholas Ridley wrote to Edmund Grindal, 'care not for us . . . ye . . . are enough through God's aid to light and set up again the lantern of his Word in England'. And so some had withdrawn into exile. Over 800 men settled in places like Zürich, Basel, Frankfurt and Strasbourg. At Frankfurt high tension developed between Richard Cox and John Knox, the former leading the party dedicated to the *Book of Common Prayer* and the latter favouring a more Calvinistic type of liturgy. Taken as a whole these refugees were a high-powered body of people both intellectually and socially and were to have a deep influence on the later history of Protestantism in England, Scotland and Wales. But their most significant literary contribution was made in the Geneva Bible of 1560, a new rendering in which William Whittingham and Anthony Gilby were the moving spirits. It was the first English Bible to have numbered verses and its scholarly notes breathed the very spirit of Reformed Protestantism. It proved immensely popular and that popularity continued for a generation or more even after the publication of the King James Version in 1611.

Queen Mary died on 17 November 1558 and as the news spread people celebrated by lighting bonfires. Her attempt to stifle Protestantism was a failure. Roman Catholicism had not the spiritual resilience to reassert itself and the fires of persecution demonstrated the vitality of the Protestant faith.

RESTORATION

The final settlement of the Protestant Reformation in England took place after the accession of Queen Elizabeth. When she became queen her preferences in religious matters were not precisely known but it soon appeared that she was Protestant in her sympathies. It was significant that three days after the death of Mary she appointed as secretary Sir William Cecil (1520–98), a firm but moderate Protestant who was to serve her for forty years. Her policy was influenced also by the returning Marian exiles. The

'Prayer Book Men', the supporters of Cox, had her ear in liturgical matters, while the vigorous Protestant faction in the House of Commons was led by Sir Francis Knollys (1514?–96), who had returned from Frankfurt, and Sir Anthony Cooke (1514–76), who had spent his exile at Strasbourg. In fact, the settlement of religion was very largely arranged by laymen and even in the House of Lords there were no more than 48 certain Roman Catholic votes.

The Act of Supremacy, April 1559, rejected the jurisdiction of the pope, repealed Mary's heresy acts, gave the Crown authority to hold visitations of the church and enacted that bishops should be nominated by the Crown and elected by dean and chapter as in the time of Henry VIII. The royal title was changed from Henry's 'Supreme Head' to 'Supreme Governor'. The Oath of Supremacy was to be tendered to all officers in church and state and those who declined to take it were to be ejected from their offices. So the new government now had the necessary legal machinery to operate its policies. All the bishops, with the exception of Anthony Kitchin of Llandaff, declined to swear the oath and were dispossessed and so the way was clear for the appointment of an entirely new bench of bishops. The key figure was the distinguished Cambridge academic, Matthew Parker (1504-75), who became Archbishop of Canterbury. He was consecrated on 17 December 1559. The new bench, although it could hardly be expected to inspire widespread spiritual revival, contained some outstanding men, like Jewel, Scory, Pilkington and Richard Davies.

WORSHIP AND THEOLOGY

For the public at large, the nature of worship in the parish churches was a matter of more immediate interest than appointments to high offices. On 27 April 1559 a new Act of Uniformity was passed. It enacted that the Prayer Book of 1552 was to be used in the churches, with a number of changes. But ambiguity in the legislation about the vestments to be used by the clergy left scope for future controversy.

As regards the theological beliefs of the church, the Forty-two Articles of 1553 were reviewed by Convocation in

1563 and issued as the Thirty-nine Articles in 1571. They rejected such Roman Catholic doctrines as purgatory and the validity of indulgences. The veneration of images and relics is rejected. Scripture is the sole basis of faith. There are but two sacraments, baptism and Communion. Infant baptism is held to be in accordance with the teaching of Christ. Holy Communion, which is not to be considered a sacrifice, is understood in the light of Calvin's teaching. In a word, the Articles were positively Protestant and Calvinistic as to the main points of theology, but too moderate in the view of the more radical reformers.

The intellectual vindication of the settlement was provided by Bishop John Jewel (1522–71) in his *Apologia* (1562) which argued that the reformed Church of England was not a new church but the ancient Church of Christ purged of the innovations introduced by the papacy. And another apologetic work, as has already been mentioned, was John Foxe's *Acts and Monuments*.

It was one thing to pass laws making Protestantism the state religion, but it was a very different thing to ensure the flowering of spirituality. The more learned and enthusiastic Protestants were given positions of responsibility in the new order but the great difficulty was finding men of similar calibre to work in the parishes. The vast majority of parish priests had accepted the changes with little or no enthusiasm and their spiritual condition was low. As Fuller tartly put it, 'A rush-candle seemed a torch where no brighter light was seen before', but even rush candles were hard to come by. And yet there was a growing demand for preaching, especially in those areas where Lollardy had been tilling the soil for generations. Thus Thomas Lever (1521–77), friend of Bullinger and Calvin and one of the most powerful preachers of his generation says of Coventry, 'that vast numbers in this place (are) in the habit of frequenting the preaching of the gospel'. Town and city 'lectureships' were springing up in London, and places like Colchester, Yarmouth, Ipswich, Warwick and elsewhere. They were evidences of a burgeoning spirituality. After all, the state by its legislation could only provide the opportunity for Protestantism to flourish. The spiritual vitality that could take advantage of that opportunity could only come from sources beyond the command of the state.

26 Anglican reformation in Wales

> Inasmuch as I know well . . . that every country
> from here to Rome, such as great Germany, Poland,
> England, France . . . and other places are eagerly
> and warmly welcoming the word of God through
> the second blossoming of the Gospel of our Lord
> Jesus Christ . . . wake up, good Welshman, my dear
> and loving brother in Christ . . . and receive the
> heavenly gift that the Lord's grace sends you today.
>
> Bishop Richard Davies (1501?–1581) in his "Epistol
> at y Cembru" (Epistle to the Welsh People), pre-
> faced to the 1567 Welsh translation of the New
> Testament.

By 1530 the Roman Catholic Church in Wales was in a
critical condition. Roman Catholicism had degenerated into
a collection of superstitious beliefs and magical practices
while the prophetic call for reform was scarcely heard.
Monasticism was in decline and there was bitterness and
dissatisfaction among the clergy. Since the age of Glyn Dŵr,
at the beginning of the fifteenth century, Welshmen were
excluded from the highest offices in the church. No Welshman was bishop of Bangor from 1408 to 1500, nor of St
David's from 1389 to 1496, nor of Llandaff from 1323 to
1566. And the foreigners who held these offices were
bureaucrats and diplomatists who had earned the gratitude
of the Crown. They were absentees and not resident pastors. This meant, of course, that the everyday business of
the diocese was discharged mainly by local Welsh officials.
But these again were little concerned with spiritual matters.
They enjoyed the comfortable style of life characteristic of
the gentry to whom they were closely related.

WALES: DIOCESES AND TOWNS

ANGLESEY

Rhuddlan
St. Asaph
Conwy
Llansannan
Chester
Bangor
Llanrwst
Denbigh
Caernarfon
Ruthin
Wrexham

BANGOR

ST. ASAPH

Bala

Shrewsbury

Newtown

Aberystwyth

Leominster

Cardigan

ST. DAVID'S

Brecon
Hereford

St. David's

Carmarthen

Monmouth

LLANDAFF
Chepstow
Swansea
Llandaff
Cardiff

0   25
Miles

S O M E R S E T

HINTS OF AWAKENING

The lower clergy were, for the most part, poor and uneducated. Even when it is recalled that the learning associated with Welsh culture was very largely transmitted orally, the lack of education among clergymen was widespread. And even those who were educated were not trained in theology with the result that they had only a vague appreciation of the significance of the Protestant Reformation when it came. There had been signs of revival from about 1450 onwards. One artistic sign of this was the fine work done on the rood lofts erected at that time in churches like Llaneleu and Llanfilo. And another, and more significant proof, was the composing of religious texts, especially in Glamorgan, to meet the devotional needs of the period. But this revival was not in any way strengthened by the accession of Henry VII to the throne of England. His interest in the church in Wales was fitful and motivated by political considerations rather than religious concern.

All in all, the Roman Catholic Church in Wales on the threshold of the Reformation was in need of a thorough awakening.

ROYAL CHANGES

The legislation passed by the Reformation Parliament from 1529 to 1534 was applied to Wales before the Act of Union (1536) brought Welsh members into the House of Commons. Both the religious legislation and the incorporation of Wales into England stemmed from the Tudor policy of seeking to create a united, uniform and centralized kingdom that would at some future time include the whole of the British Isles.

Nevertheless, Wales accepted the religious changes without protest. It is true that William ap Llywelyn, a Caernarfonshire priest, expressed his disgust at the king's divorce proceedings by saying on 4 July 1533 that he would like to have Henry VIII on Snowdon to 'souse the King about the ears till he had made his head soft enough.' He was not only a bold protester but a lonely one. Certainly the bishop of Llandaff refused to accept the royal divorce and the

Royal Supremacy, but then he was George de Athequa, the
Spanish confessor of Queen Catherine of Aragon and he
remained utterly faithful to her until her death on 7 January
1536. And in the following December he left for Spain.
There were individual Welsh Roman Catholic martyrs outside Wales, like John Davies, the Carthusian, and John
Eynon, the secular priest executed at Reading in 1538. But
in Wales itself there were none.

THE END OF THE MONASTERIES

There were 47 religious houses in Wales, and they were
occupied by some 246 inmates. Their combined value in
1535 was no more than £3,178. In order to facilitate the
process of dissolving them, visitors were appointed to
inspect them and produce reports on their condition. The
men appointed to visit the Welsh monasteries were Dr
Adam Becansaw, canon of St Asaph, Dr John Vaughan,
and the notorious 'Red Doctor', Ellis Price (Elis Prys, ?1512–
95?), whose grandfather had been standard-bearer to
Henry VII at Bosworth.

Their visitation lasted from 6 August 1535 until April
1536. The reports of this have disappeared but some of their
letters have survived. By the time they had finished their
inspection, the law to dissolve houses with an income of
less than £200 a year had been passed and since all the
houses in Wales came into that class, they were all due to
disappear. Three of them, however, were able to prolong
their existence for a couple of years, namely Strata Florida,
Neath and Whitland. Tintern also prolonged its existence
until 1539. The friaries were treated separately. Between 17
August and 6 September 1538 they were visited by Richard
Ingworth, bishop of Dover, and he accepted the submission of all ten houses. So, by 1540 all the monasteries of
Wales had been dissolved. Their possessions passed to the
Crown and thence into the hands of the gentry by pur-
chase. And there was little sentimentality about the ext-
inguishing of monasticism. A loyal Roman Catholic like Sir
Edward Carne (c. 1500–61), Mary Tudor's ambassador at
Rome, was as avid an acquirer of monastic lands as the
devoted Protestant, Sir John Price (c. 1502–55).

LIGHT AND SHADE

The monasteries had outlived their usefulness. Most of them had too few inmates to sustain the discipline and round of duties demanded by their own rules. Hospitality was more a matter of providing a rest home for distressed gentlefolk (like the poets Guto'r and Lewis Môn at Vale Crucis) than helping the destitute. There were able heads of houses, like Leyshon Thomas, the distinguished abbot of the Cistercian Abbey at Neath and Griffin Williams, prior of the Franciscan Friary at Carmarthen. But there were rascals too like Robert Salisbury, the last abbot of Vale Crucis who was imprisoned in the Tower of London after perpetrating highway robbery in May 1535. There was immorality, but far more significant was the sloth, the carelessness, the loss of ideals which afflicted almost all the houses. Few mourned the dissolution and the monks and nuns were granted pensions that kept them above the breadline.

More bitterness was caused by Cromwell's campaign against pilgrimages, shrines and images. The destruction of the great statue of the Virgin at Pen-rhys in the Rhondda, or of the image of Derfel Gadarn which was ignominiously carted away from Llandderfel to be burned in London, touched the fondest superstitions of ordinary people and created resentment.

PROTESTANT ENTHUSIASTS

It is regrettable that we know nothing of Wales's first Protestant martyr. His name was Thomas Capper. He would not profess belief in transubstantiation as demanded by the Six Articles of 1539. Capper was brought to the stake at Cardiff in the year 1541–2 and it cost Cardiff four shillings and four pence to execute him.

The first vociferous preacher of Protestantism in Wales was William Barlow (1499?–1568), an Essex man, whose career as an Augustinian canon and diplomat brought him in 1534 to Haverfordwest priory. He was out of Wales for some months before being elected bishop of St Asaph in January 1536 and translated in April to St David's. There is no denying Barlow's Protestant enthusiasm and his persistence in proclaiming his views. But there is no denying either the rashness which pitched him into an acrimonious quarrel with the cathedral chapter which had more to do with questions about his jurisdiction than about the nature of his theology. He did little to commend Protestantism to Welsh people before he was translated to Bath and Wells in 1548.

Barlow was succeeded by Robert Ferrar (c. 1505–55), a native of Halifax, Yorkshire, and bishop of St David's from July 1548. He seems to have inherited Barlow's quarrel with the chapter and made enemies of Protestants as well as Roman Catholics. But Ferrar is honoured for his heroic death. He was tried as a heretic by his Roman Catholic successor, Henry Morgan, and suffered death by burning in Carmarthen market square on 30 March 1555.

Two other martyrs of Mary's reign were William Nichol of Haverfordwest, of whom nothing further is known, and Rawlins White, an illiterate Cardiff fisherman who had been preaching for five years before the accession of Mary. These were the only martyrdoms in Wales during the Roman Catholic reaction. Many were dispossessed because of their Protestant sympathies or because they were married priests, but in the main the change to Roman Catholicism was accepted with little incident, and possibly with a sense of relief, in Wales.

MEN OF THE FUTURE

By the Act of Union (1536) the Welsh language had been banned from legal and official use. The 'one nation policy' that was being pursued by Henry VIII and his successors was a serious threat to Wales and its national culture. Would the religious change to Protestantism be part of the process of weaning the people from their language and traditional values? One of the most remarkable aspects of these years was the emergence of a succession of scholars and literary patrons who appreciated the danger and made bold to meet it. And in so doing they gave to Anglicanism in Wales a flavour that distinguishes it from Anglicanism in England or Ireland.

In the basins of the two rivers, Clwyd and Conwy, within the area bounded by the four ancient towns of Conwy, Llanrwst, Ruthin and Rhuddlan, the Renaissance fused with the classical culture of Wales to produce a splendid flowering in the sixteenth century. In the numerous mansions that dotted this neighbourhood there was a highly civilized gentry ready to patronize poets and craftsmen. And there emerged in this same area a flock of superb poets. Here, where people were sensitive to the value of their historic culture and conscious of the achievements of both commercial and Renaissance Europe, there emerged men who were to combine an ardent Protestantism with their Welsh Humanism.

Two of them demand particular attention. William Salesbury (c. 1520–c. 1594), born at Llansannan, scion of one of the most influential of Denbighshire families, educated at Oxford and the Inns of Court, was possibly the most learned Welshmen of the age. He had understood the crisis, both moral and cultural, that faced Wales. In the preface to his book, *Oll Synnwyr pen Kembero ygyd* (All the Welshman's wisdom, 1547), he had warned his compatriots:-

Unless you desire to be worse than animals . . . get scholarship in your language; unless you wish to be less natural than any nation under the sun, love your language and those who love it . . . With unshod feet make pilgrimage to his grace the King and his Council and beseech him to grant you the Scriptures in your language.

And Salesbury devoted his energies for twenty years to providing Wales with the Bible in Welsh. He translated the lessons of the Book of Common Prayer in *Kynniver llith a ban* (1551) – 'All the lessons and articles' – while he demonstrated his humanism and his wide erudition, as well as his glowing Protestant faith, in other books. Nothing could be done in the reign of Mary. But with the accession of Elizabeth a new opportunity came. The new bishop of St. Asaph was a native of the Conwy Valley, – Richard Davies (?1506-81), son of Dafydd ap Gronw, Roman Catholic curate of Gyffin, educated at Oxford and an exile at Frankfurt during the Marian persecution. He and Salesbury now began their epoch-making co-operation.

PREPARING THE WAY

Salesbury addressed a petition to the Privy Council begging them to order 'learned men to translate the book of the Lord's Testament into the vulgar Welsh tongue'. Meanwhile, Thomas Davies, who followed Richard Davies at St Asaph, had commanded his clergy in November 1561 to read the epistle and the gospel in Welsh as well as English in their services. Although we know nothing of the details, it is obvious that a considerable amount of work was being done behind the scenes to persuade Parliament to legislate in this matter. The result was the Act of 1563 commanding the four Welsh bishops, together with the bishop of Hereford, to produce Welsh translations of the Book of Common Prayer and the whole Bible for use in the churches by 1 March 1567. It is likely that the measure was steered through the Lords by Bishop Richard Davies and through the Commons by Humphrey Llwyd (1527–68), physician and antiquary and a native of Denbigh, – again the Vale of Clwyd. The Book of Common Prayer was published in May 1567, the work mainly of Salesbury but revised by Richard Davies.

THE 1567 NEW TESTAMENT

The New Testament, the first instalment of the Welsh Bible, appeared 7 October 1567. The bulk of the translating was done by Salesbury with Richard Davies doing I Timothy, Hebrews, James and I and II Peter and Thomas Huet (d.1591), the precentor of St David's, translating Revelation. It was a first-rate piece of work, unswervingly faithful to the original but showing on every page how conversant Salesbury was with the methods and materials of the best biblical scholarship of the day.

Not only so, but Bishop Richard Davies prefaced the Testament with an 'Epistle to the Welsh people' in which he elaborated carefully the Protestant and Anglican understanding of the history of Britain. Christianity was brought here by Joseph of Arimathea and the purity of the early church was preserved by the British until the monk Augustine brought the errors of Rome to sully the beauty of the Celtic church. But now those errors have been rejected and so the Anglican Reformation is to be seen as the resurrection of the Celtic church. And for Welsh people, so Davies implies, the Church of England is no foreign imposition but the reappearance of the church of their own forefathers. The history is hardly convincing but the legend commended Anglicanism to the Welsh people and gave them a dramatic historical role. So despite the churlish treatment of the Welsh language by the Act of Union, parliament had quite surprisingly ordered the church to adopt a bilingual policy in Wales. The influence of Richard Davies and William Salesbury (not to mention their successors as Bible translators) upon the future of Welsh Christianity was immense, but despite good intentions, the Welsh Elizabethan bishops found it a daunting task to provide the parishes with an effective and learned ministry. Nevertheless, the process of transforming Wales into a Protestant country had been set in motion.

27 Conflict in Ireland

The King of England and his successors 'shall be accepted, taken, and reputed the only supreme head in earth of the whole Church of Ireland'.

The Irish Supremacy Act.

The attempt to introduce the Protestant Reformation to Ireland provides a poignant counterpoint to the story of the Anglican Reformation in England and an instructive variation on its development in Wales.

BACKGROUND

The period from 1534 to 1603 saw crucial developments in the long struggle between English and Irish culture and in that struggle the conflict between Roman Catholicism and Protestantism was of the highest significance. The conquest of Ireland had begun with the Anglo-Irish invasion in 1169. Its most immediate result was the creation of the English mediaeval colony, known as The Pale, occupying the area along the coast between Dublin and Dundalk and extending inland some 40 miles. Beyond the Pale were two groups of interlocking independent states, the Anglo-Irish, led by the great Kildare family, and the Gaelic lordships, still maintaining the Irish language and culture. By the agreement made with the High King of Ireland in 1175, Henry II of England and his successors became bearers of the title 'Lord of Ireland', but outside the Pale and a few royal strongholds, it was a purely nominal lordship. It was in 1541 that the Irish parliament conferred upon Henry VIII the title 'King of Ireland' and that monarch did not look upon it as a merely formal title.

THE CHURCH

The church in Ireland was divided along cultural lines into the 'Church amongst the Irish' and the 'Church amongst the English'. The latter had but incidental formal links with the former. Important sees, like Dublin, Armagh, Kildare and Meath, were usually occupied by Englishmen who were, however, papal appointments rather than royal nominees. The lower clergy were recruited from the local population and were not of high quality either spiritually or intellectually. Beyond the Pale, the papacy controlled a large proportion of appointments and this put a curb on state intervention. Even so, many benefices did suffer by becoming the possessions of laymen who had no thought of taking holy orders. But Rome was seen, in the main, as a benefactor and Ireland did not share the feeling, so powerful on the Continent, that the Papacy was rapacious, nor was there any widespread anticlericalism. In the religious life of the country generally the monastic orders were of greater significance than the secular clergy, and the most vigorous and dedicated section of the church was the mendicant orders and particularly the Franciscans. In addition, the church among the Irish had developed a complex system of land and office tenure which brought lay people into close association with the administration and organization of the church's life in a way which was unique in Europe.

Nevertheless, the church and the spiritual life of Ireland stood in need of both revival and reform. Although there was no hint of heresy in the land and no vociferous demand for reform, the spiritual life in many parishes was at a low ebb and wars and commotions had left much devastation.

ROYAL AIMS

Henry VIII's actions in Ireland were rooted in the same convictions as those which governed his policies towards Wales, the Kingdom of Scotland and the realm of England itself. He wished to elevate his own royal dignity, to assert his unchallenged sovereignty in his kingdom, to improve and centralize administration and generally to prepare the way for creating in the British Isles, including Ireland, one homogeneous 'empire', having one king, one language, one legal system, one culture and professing one common form of Christianity. So religion had an essential part to play in the dream. At the same time, Irish challenges to his authority provoked him into introducing a more aggressive policy there.

The royal lordship of Ireland was exercised nominally through the Lieutenant, usually a member of the royal family, but the executive functions were discharged by his representative, the Lord Deputy, a post rarely held by an Englishman before 1534. When the Lord Deputy, the ninth earl of Kildare, was in London in 1534 answering the allegations of his critics, his son, Thomas Fitzgerald, Lord Offaly (1513–37) renounced his allegiance to the King on 11 June and raised the banner of rebellion. The new Lord Deputy, Sir William Skeffington, took Offaly's castle at Maynooth in March 1535 and the insurrection collapsed. The executions which followed created an atmosphere of dread which eased the passage of Reformation legislation through the Irish parliament.

REFORMATION BY LAW

The Irish parliament, although it consisted nominally of the temporal and spiritual lords, proctors to represent the lower clergy, and representatives of towns and shires, in fact drew few representatives from without the Pale. And it had little scope for independent action since all legislation had first of all to be approved by the Crown.

The Reformation Parliament met at Dublin on May Day, 1536. It was prorogued several times and did not complete its work until the autumn of 1537. The legislation eventually passed, echoed that already passed in the English parliament. The Supremacy Act made Henry and his heirs 'supreme head' of the church in Ireland. Complementary to it was an act against the authority of the Bishop of Rome which had an Oath of Supremacy attached to it. An Act of Subsidy allotted some church revenues to the Crown while the Act of Slander made it a treasonable action to call Henry a heretic, schismatic or usurper. All appeals to Rome were prohibited by the Act of Appeals and parliament also agreed to the dissolution of thirteen monasteries. A large number of bills were passed dealing with social and economic matters, the Irish language was proscribed, and everyone, on pain of fines, was to speak and dress like Englishmen.

The wishes of parliament were to be implemented by a special commission led by Sir Anthony St Leger (1496?– 1559). This had authority to suppress monasteries or to receive their voluntary submission and to transfer their properties to the Crown. The house at Grane was the first to suffer, in 1535, and by 1540 monastic life in the Pale was at an end. If the dissolution was meant to benefit the exchequer, it was a disappointment since their combined revenues did not amount to more than £400. But the process continued and by the end of Henry's reign some 130 monasteries had been suppressed. If the dissolution was motivated by the desire to curtail the influence of the monks, it misfired because by dispersing them the King only compelled them to work at large among the people and so increased their influence on behalf of the papal cause.

COMMENDING THE NEW ORDER

The main instrument in promoting Henry's Reformation in Ireland was George Browne (d.1556), archbishop of Dublin since March 1535. He was an Englishman who had been provincial of the Austin Friars. Together with Sir John Alen, the Chancellor, and Sir William Brabazon, the Vice-treasurer, Browne was appointed to the commission named to exercise the powers of the Vicar-general, Thomas Cromwell, on 3 February 1539. One duty discharged by the commission was to destroy images and shrines. Over a year and a half some thirty shrines were destroyed, much to the disgust of pious Irish Catholics. Browne was also the publisher of the first book issued by the Anglican Church in Ireland. It was *The Form of the Beads* (May, 1538), intended to make the people acquainted with the new order. It was Browne's intention to preach wherever English was understood, while Dr. Richard Nangle, bishop of Clonfert, was to preach in Irish. But it was no help that the Irish language was proscribed and that there was no one near him 'to preach the Word of God', as he complained with bitterness.

Indeed, the other active reformer, Edward Staples (1490?-1560?), bishop of Meath until 1554, had no wish to co-operate with the archbishop. Nor were the efforts of Lord Deputy Leonard Gray (d.1541) to foster enthusiasm for the new order any more successful. Certainly, he had little difficulty in persuading leading figures to take the Oath of Supremacy but this had little religious significance. In any case, there was no question yet of imposing any specifically Protestant theology upon Ireland. Browne found it all debilitating work. There was probably not a single Protestant in the whole of Ireland and the bulk of the people were quite untouched by the legal changes.

At the same time, it was proving quite impossible to exercise the royal supremacy in such a key matter as the appointment of bishops. The King had rejected papal jurisdiction and the pope continued to make appointments. The result was the failure of the King to extend his ecclesiastical royal authority over the 32 Irish dioceses. By the time of Henry's death, 24 January 1547, the Reformation had made virtually no mark on Irish religious life.

IMPOSED PROTESTANTISM

A high-handed policy was adopted during the reign of Edward VI. Parliament was not summoned and the changes which affected the church in England were imposed on Ireland on the sole authority of Archbishop Browne. The conciliatory policy pursued by Lord Deputy St. Leger yielded to a policy of coercion when he was replaced by Sir Edward Bellingham in April 1548. But that was no help to the Reformation. Edward Staples, the bishop of Meath, preached against the Mass in 1547 and provoked general opposition from the people and from the Primate, George Dowdall of Armagh (1487-1558), and he had to withdraw for safety's sake to Dublin. Bellingham was removed and St Leger recalled but his attempts to encourage the use of the 1549 Prayer Book were quite unavailing. It was in English, of course, and incomprehensible to the vast majority of Irish people. The clergy took no notice of a proclamation banning the Mass. All in all, no progress was being made.

Even the appearance of an enthusiastic Protestant bishop

was of no help. John Bale (1495-1563) was consecrated bishop of Ossory at Dublin on 2 February 1553. Quite typically, there was uproar at the service for Bale would not suffer a Roman Catholic service and insisted on an Anglican one. He was a man of great learning and a prolific author. He was also a master of invective and it was the bitterness of his polemical writing that earned him the nickname, 'Bilious Bale'. His sharp tongue gained him more enemies than friends in Ireland and he had to confess, 'Helpers I found none among my prebendaries and clergy, but adversaries a great number.' As Archbishop Browne soon realized, there was need of suitable men to evangelize in the country and it was one of the foremost weaknesses of the new order that none were forthcoming.

When Mary Tudor ascended the throne, she set to it immediately to restore Roman Catholicism. Naturally, those who favoured Protestantism, Browne, Bale, Staples, Lancaster of Kildare and Travers of Leighlin, were deprived and the English establishment in Ireland became Roman Catholic with little difficulty. Nor were there any burnings in Ireland under Mary.

TIGHTENING HOLD

The accession of Elizabeth led to the return of Protestantism. The religious legislation which was applied to England and Wales was extended to Ireland also, but with the consent of the Irish Parliament. It was one thing to pass laws, but it was a very difficult task indeed to apply them. In the Pale there was a real danger that the traditional loyalty of the inhabitants to the Crown would be undermined by imposing an alien faith upon them. But that loyalty led them to acquiesce in a formal acceptance of the Prayer Book while adhering privately to their Roman Catholicism. And that practice set a pattern that was to spread all over the country in the wake of English expansion. Then the vast majority of the bishops declined to take the Oath of Supremacy. Outside the Pale, the Queen could not apply sanctions to them and even if she could dispossess them, where could she get men prepared to serve in the Church of Ireland?

The man who led the Church of Ireland for over forty

years was Adam Lofthouse (1533?–1605), a Yorkshireman who was consecrated archbishop of Armagh on 2 March 1563 and translated to Dublin on 8 August 1567. Despite his long residence in the country, and the important offices that he held, he never learnt Irish and he had little real understanding of Irish life beyond the Pale. His ability and dedication were not sufficient to make a great spiritual reformer of him.

Throughout Elizabeth's reign, Irish uneasiness rumbled on, and occasionally exploded into armed conflict. And despite the complexity of the motives that inspired the wars, religion was not far from men's minds. For religion was closely intertwined with the life and culture of the Irish nation. This was crystal clear to Hugh, who succeeded to the title of O'Neill in 1595. He was one of the towering figures of the age. He saw the expansion of English power as a threat to both Roman Catholicism and Irish civilization and so took up arms against Elizabeth in September 1595. The substantial help that he expected from the Continent did not come and the issue was settled at the Battle of Kinsale, 24 December 1601. The consequences were serious. Ulster's resistance to English expansionism ended. Gaelic Ireland suffered the most serious blow in its history. The Tudor conquest was completed. So now the Anglican Church was in a position to extend its influence over the whole island and that influence was to be strengthened in the future by extending the plantations and settlements of English and Scottish colonists on lands confiscated from the Irish.

But all this was hardly conducive to creating a sympathetic attitude towards the Protestant faith in Irish minds. In the main, the story of the campaign to establish Protestantism in Ireland by government policy and by military conquest is a dismal one.

28 Blasts on the trumpet

'. . . we do promise that we . . . shall with all diligence continually apply our whole power, substance, and our very lives, to maintain, set forward,
and establish the most blessed word of God and his
Congregation . . .'.

The Common Bond of the Lords of the Congregation, 3 December 1557.

The Protestant Reformation in Scotland has a fascination all
its own, partly because its first historian was also a central
figure in it. John Knox in his *History of the Reformation of
Religion within the Realm of Scotland* succeeds in capturing
both the excitement of the period and the momentous
character of the principles at the heart of the struggle.

THE OLD ORDER

At a Provincial Council held in Edinburgh in November
1549, Roman Catholic churchmen attributed the growth of
heresy and the religious unrest to the profane immorality
and the gross ignorance of the clergy. But there was more
to be said. Monastic life varied in quality. Monasteries had
lost their ascetic enthusiasm and their abbots were often
wealthy laymen, but there was little evidence of flagrant
immorality. That was certainly not so in the nunneries
which had a shocking reputation. The friaries were in a
much better condition and, like the canons regular, they
contributed some remarkable men to the ranks of the
reformers.

The most striking weakness of the church was the neglect
of effective pastoral care in the parishes. The vast majority
of them, perhaps as many as 85%, had been appropriated,
that is, their revenues diverted to support bishops, abbeys
and the more central churches, leaving only a pittance for

the poor vicar whose ignorance only too frequently inhibited him from providing an effective ministry. And the constant demands of vicars for 'offerings' in payment for their services became a harassment which greatly irked the laity.

There were sporadic demands for reform, the most insistent of which came in the Provincial Councils of 1549, 1552 and 1559, under the leadership of John Hamilton (1511?–71), the formidable archbishop of St Andrews since 1546. The programme was thorough enough and aimed at securing an effective supervision of church life, the better instruction of the laity and the raising of the standards of education for the priesthood. But the vested interests of leading clergy in the system as it was, together with the constant bestowal of church revenues upon laymen, particularly by the Crown, nullified all attempts at reform.

LOLLARDS AND LUTHER

Voices were being raised in favour of more radical reform. Lollardy had some influence in preparing the ground, especially in Ayrshire. And in July 1525 Parliament passed an act prohibiting the importing of heretical books, a reaction to the flood of Lutheran literature flowing into the country from the Continent. And after 1526 Tyndale's New Testament was in circulation in the diocese of Glasgow. So it was little wonder that the first Protestant martyr was a Lutheran. Patrick Hamilton (1504?-1528) was the great grandson of James II (1430-60) and had been educated at St Andrews, Paris and Wittenberg. It was his eagerness to preach the gospel to his fellow-countrymen that brought him back to Scotland. But James Beaton (d.1539), archbishop of St Andrews, lured Hamilton into a conference only to detain him. He was tried and condemned to death. He was burned at the stake on 29 February 1528.

ROYALTY AND MARTYRS

The outlook for reformers was bleak in the following years. The young king, James V (1512–42) was under the influence of David Beaton (1494–1546), who worked hard to maintain cordial relations with France and to counter the threat from the King's uncle, Henry VIII of England. It was he who arranged the King's marriage with Mary of Guise. Beaton was eager to extirpate Protestantism and several were sent to the stake. The act of 1543 permitting people to possess Bibles, and the death of James V in 1542, did not mean a relaxation in the campaign against dissent. James was followed by his infant daughter, Mary, and James Hamilton (d.1575), Earl of Arran, became regent. In 1544 George Wishart (1513?-46) returned to Scotland. He had made many contacts with the men of the Reformed faith on the Continent and had taught at Cambridge. Beaton soon put a stop to Wishart's successful preaching tours in Kyle, Dundee, Edinburgh, Leith and Perth. He suffered martyrdom by fire at St Andrews on 1 March 1546. According to Knox, distinguished men 'at open tables avowed, that the blood of Master George should be avenged'. And retribution came on 29 May 1546 when admirers of Wishart broke into the castle at St Andrews and assassinated Beaton.

THE BLOWER OF TRUMPETS

Wishart had no more fervent admirer than John Knox (1513–72), who had followed the reformer as a self-appointed bodyguard, armed with a two-handed sword. Wishart made a Calvinist of him. Much of Knox's early career is hidden in obscurity. He was born at Haddington, 17 miles from Edinburgh, attended a university but did not graduate and then became a private tutor. His first sermon, delivered at the castle of St Andrews at Easter 1547 at the request of John Rough, later to die at the stake at Smithfield, made an immediate impact. Knox was taken prisoner when the French took the castle and spent 19 months in the French galleys before being released early in 1549 after representations by the government of Edward VI. From April 1549 until March 1554 he was in England and participated in the work of the Edwardian reformers but migrated to the Continent to escape Mary's persecution, staying first of all with Calvin at Geneva, then with Bullinger at Zürich, before finally becoming minister to the English exiled congregation at Frankfurt. There was soon considerable turmoil there, with Knox and William Whittingham (1524?–79) advocating forms of worship similar to those at Geneva and Thomas Lever, and later Richard Cox (1500?–81) and John Jewel (1522–71), pleading for the *Book of Common Prayer*. Knox and his friends withdrew to Geneva in April 1555 and, apart from a year's stay in Scotland from August 1555, he was there until 7 January 1559. So he had been at Geneva during the years of Calvin's greatest influence. Despite his close links with most of the leading supporters of Protestantism in Scotland and the notoriety he had gained as a vigorous pamphleteer, particularly with his ill-timed tract against female monarchs, *First Blast of the Trumpet against the Monstrous Regiment of Women* (1558), he had as yet played but an incidental part in the development of the Reformation in Scotland.

SETTING THE STAGE

Repression had not cooled the ardour of the Protestants. From 1555 onwards Protestant congregations – the 'privy kirks' – being formed in the Lowlands, and in such places as St Andrews, Stirling, Dundee, Edinburgh and Perth and their organization, with elders, deacons and kirk sessions, matured quickly. It was John Knox who, during his 1555–6 visit, first administered Communion among them in a Reformed manner. Moreover, some of these congregations were intruding into church buildings, often with the connivance of the town councils. Popular support was manifested in such outbursts of iconoclasm as the destruction of the image of St Giles, burned by the people of Edinburgh.

Then the 'Lords of the Congregation', the leaders of the 'Congregation of the Lord', the Protestant party in Scotland, began to take concerted action. On 10 March 1557 they wrote to John Knox pressing him to return from Geneva. On 3 December 1557, five of these great leaders signed the first Common Bond, or Covenant, to 'establish the most blessed word of God and his Congregation', as well as to renounce 'all the superstitions abominations and idolatry' of the Roman Church. In October 1558 John Willock (d.1585) returned from exile at Emden to put his talents at the disposal of the reformers. He was deeply impressed by what he saw and especially by the work of Paul Methven, as a result of which 'the town of Dundee began to erect the face of a public church reformed' as Knox put it. And Willock became the means of transferring the 'weekly exercise', from Emden, held by ministers to expound the Bible in Germany, to both the Church of Scotland and English Puritanism, where it became better known as 'prophesying'.

So the stage was set for the revolution.

POLITICAL STRUGGLE

On 1 January 1559 a placard was put up at the entrances of religious buildings all over the country. This was the *Beggars' Summons* and it demanded that unless the friars yielded wealth to the widows, the orphans and the poor, these oppressed people would take possession of it. This remarkable document shows the concern for the downtrodden which runs like a silver thread through the history of the Scottish Reformation. It also shows that the poor had a real stake in the Reformation.

At the other end of the social scale, the lairds came into sharp conflict with the Queen Regent, Mary of Guise. She hoped to overcome their mounting opposition by a mixture of threats and deceit. This only served to strengthen their resolve. Under the leadership of James Stewart (1513?–70), earl of Moray from 1562, and Archibald Campbell (1530–73), the fifth earl of Argyll, the Lords of the Congregation occupied Dundee, Perth, St Andrews and Edinburgh by the end of July 1559. And Knox was appointed minister of the Tolbooth, Edinburgh. It was a short-lived success, however, for Mary, with French help, was able to regain Edinburgh. Still defiant, the Lords of the Congregation, meeting at the Tolbooth on 21 October 1559 declared, in the name of the absent sovereigns, Mary and Francis, that Mary of Guise was deposed from the regency. In October the redoubtable William Maitland (1528?–73) left the service of the Queen Regent and sided with the reformers, bringing with him his invaluable diplomatic experience and inside knowledge of the royal court. And it was he who secured the intervention of England in support of the Lords of the Congregation. Events moved swiftly in the summer of 1560. On 10 June Mary of Guise died. The Treaty of Edinburgh, 6 July 1560, not only secured the withdrawal of the French and English armed forces from Scotland, but left the Lords of the Congregation masters of the country. The main part of the struggle was over but harvesting the fruit of the victory was to take several anxious years.

THE REFORMATION PROPER

Those concerned with the transformation of the church and the revival of biblical Christianity quickly produced the necessary blueprints. Parliament met on 1 August 1560 and asked the ministers to produce a statement of their doctrine. The *Scots Confession* takes a place of honour among the influential documents of Protestantism. It is a lively and warm document, thoroughly biblical in its phraseology and expressing clearly a Calvinistic theology which impressively emphasizes the centrality of the Lord Jesus Christ.

On 5 December 1560, Francis II, king of France and husband of Mary Queen of Scots, died and the absent queen was now ready to return home. She arrived in August 1561. This was not good news to the reformers and they realized that they had to hurry with their work. Parliament abolished the jurisdiction of the pope and prohibited Roman Catholic practices in August 1560 and in the January following considered the *Book of Discipline*. It is a long and fascinating document. Scotland was the first nation to base a national discipline on Reformed principles. The church was to have elders and deacons, annually elected, as well as readers and superintendents. The spiritual life of the people was to be nourished by frequent preaching, by weekly exercises or 'prophesyings' for Bible study and by a strict but not vindictive system of correction for those guilty of moral lapses. The *Book of Discipline* is noteworthy also because of the arrangements which it suggests for poor relief and national education. The debate about it in Parliament, which began in January 1561, was long and inconclusive but many of the most distinguished leaders subscribed to it.

A generous accommodation of the old system to the new developed in Scotland. Knox might fulminate against the iniquities of the Church of Rome, but in the Scotland of 1560 it was impossible to tear it down and build a new church. For one thing, Parliament did not impose the

Confession of 1560 on anyone. Again, the Reformed Church developed alongside the existing Roman Catholic structure and a good proportion of the men who had served the old church, – perhaps as many as half of them, – gradually adopted Protestantism and continued to work in the new system. The new wine filled the old wineskins and Scotland enjoyed profound religious changes which involved virtually none of that appeal to faggot and stake which caused anguish in other countries.

QUEEN AND REFORMER

Mary's tragic drama unfolded inexorably. On 29 July 1565 she married the disreputable Henry Stewart, Lord Darnley (1545–67), who connived at the murder of Mary's secretary, David Rizzio (1533?–66), and was himself murdered in mysterious circumstances at Kirk o' Fields on 10 February 1567. Meanwhile, there was high tension between her and the reformers, particularly Knox. Her charm and vivacity won her the admiration of her Scottish councillors but her ardent Roman Catholicism and wayward sexual life made her an object of distrust to ardent Protestants. John Knox, all but exhausted through his immense labours, was prematurely old at forty-five and was in no mood to sacrifice the gains of 1560 and 1561. And his influence was given a new boost when he was triumphantly acquitted on a charge of treason on 21 December 1563. His four famous interviews with Queen Mary merely revealed that he was completely impervious to what he called the 'enchantment whereof men are bewitched'.

To marry James Hepburn (1536?–78), 4th Earl of Bothwell and the chief organizer of Darnley's murder, was a fatal mistake on Mary's part. Public opinion swung against her and on 25 June 1567 the General Assembly declared that she had forfeited the crown and on 29 July her infant son was crowned James VI. The sermon on the occasion was preached by John Knox. So once again the Reformation was saved after a very turbulent period. The Earl of Moray became regent but his career was cut short by his assassination on 23 January 1570. It was a serious blow for he had played a key role in the events of the previous twelve years. He takes his place fittingly as one of the outstanding lay architects of the Reformation, along with Coligny of France, Elector John Frederick of Saxony, William of Orange and Somerset of England.

John Knox struggled on in increasing weakness and died on 24 November 1572. Despite his extremism and faith in violence, he was one of the great preachers in the history of Christianity, a dedicated Protestant and patriot, and a man of iron resolution. One report has it that Regent Morton said above Knox's open grave, 'Here lies a man who neither flattered nor feared any flesh'. It was a fitting epitaph.

The good work went on without him. There would be changes, developments and crises in plenty, but there would be no going back on the achievements of the decade between 1560 and 1570.

29 Water and blood

> . . . the blood of these people, although they were
> misled, fell hot on my heart.
>
> Menno Simons (1496–1561), describing the effect
> upon him of the killing of Anabaptists on 7 April
> 1535.

The Burgundian state extended from south eastern France
to the North Sea. Our main interest now concentrates on
the northern part of this area, the Low Countries or Netherlands, the countries we know as Holland and Belgium. By
1500 Burgundy was part of the vast Habsburg territories
and so in 1519 came under the rule of Charles V, the Holy
Roman Emperor. Ecclesiastically, the six dioceses of the
Low Countries, from Utrecht in the north to Cambrai in the
south, were included in the archdioceses of Reims and
Cologne.

ROMAN CATHOLICISM

The church in the Low Countries was no stranger to the ills
that afflicted it in other countries. The majority of its priests
were poorly educated. Celibacy was observed by no more
than perhaps two-fifths of the clergy. The financial oppression of the church was a constant cause of complaint while
the luxury enjoyed by leading clerics contrasted with the
poverty of the deputy pastors who performed the duties of
absentee priests. The criticism of the church and its clergy
found mordant expression in the plays composed for com-
petitions in those unique Dutch institutions, the Chambers
of Rhetoric.

The monasteries were still powerful institutions, but not
mainly because of their spiritual influence. In 1517 there
were in the diocese of Utrecht, for example, 3,100 monks
and 10,000 nuns in 477 monasteries and priories. But that

all was not well with monasticism is made clear in the biting criticism of Erasmus who knew Dutch monasticism as an insider. It suffered from moral lassitude and had become intellectually sterile. Yet some monasteries administered their extensive territories with such business acumen that merchants and the craft guilds found it difficult to compete with them.

SPIRITUAL VIGOUR

There is another side, however, to the story. The Netherlands has a notable place in the religious history of the late mediaeval period because it was the home of a vigorous spiritual revival. It was the land of Geert Groote (1340–84) who, together with his follower Florentius Radewijns (1350–1400), founded the influential Brethren of the Common Life. It was the land also of Thomas à Kempis (c. 1380–1471) whose study of the soul's communion with God, *The Imitation of Christ*, has appeared in over 2,000 editions. Men like the scholar Rudolf Agricola (1444–85), and his pupil Alexander Hegius (d.1475), Johannes Pupper of Goch (d.1475) and Wessel Gansfort (1419–89), helped to awaken a spirit of reform and to generate a love of scholarship, both of which reached a brilliant expression in the work of the prince of humanists, Desiderius Erasmus. The Netherlands was also influenced by the observantine movement which sought to revive ancient ideals of discipline and spirituality in the monasteries. A well-known example of this revived monasticism is the Congregation of Windesheim, a considerable force for disseminating concepts of reform. It has been argued that this evidence justifies the assertion that there was a reform movement of substantial proportions in the Netherlands before Luther began his work. But this is to claim too much. It was a restricted movement and can hardly compare with the power and extent of the Protestant movement that eventually emerged.

LUTHERANISM

The vigorous commercial life of the Dutch cities ensured the rapid transmission of ideas as well as goods. By early 1518 Luther's books were finding a ready sale at Antwerp.

Students were also transmitters of Lutheran ideas. Jacob Praepositus and Henry van Zutphen were Wittenberg students who became evangelical pioneers at Antwerp. And among the early pioneers, none was bolder or more successful than Wouter, 'the Lutheran monk', who worked at Delft and numbered among his converts such influential leaders as Cornelius Hoen, Johannes Sartorius and Willem Gnaphaeus. It was an advantage too that Protestantism had powerful patrons in such men as Werner von Palant of Wassenberg and Hermann von Wied (1477–1552), the reforming archbishop of Cologne from 1515 to 1546 a prelate who eventually became a Protestant himself. So Lutheranism gained a foothold at quite an early date in the Netherlands and became especially influential in East Friesland where the teaching of Wessel Gansfort had prepared the way and the sympathy of the ruler, Edzard I, secured toleration for the reformers. But Lutheran societies and groups were formed also in many places in other parts of the country such as Bruges and Brussels.

SACRAMENTARIANS

Quite soon Protestantism in the Netherlands entered a new phase. Almost from the beginning the adjective 'sacramentarian' was used to describe it, but it is important to realize the specialized meaning which the word has in this context. Negatively it meant denying the doctrine of the corporal presence of Jesus Christ under the forms of bread and wine on the altar, and positively it meant an emphasis on the rich symbolic significance of the elements in the spiritual communion which Christians have with their Lord. In other words, this was a rejection of both the Roman Catholic doctrine of the Mass and of Luther's doctrine of Communion. What were its roots? Doubtless it owed something to the teaching of Gansfort and Erasmus, as well as to the emphasis of the Modern Devotion upon the supreme value of spiritual communion with Christ, but most of all it stemmed from close study of the Bible itself. The two men who gave literary expression to sacramentarian convictions were Cornelius Hoen (d.1523) and Johannes Sartorius. The manuscript of Hoen's book, *Epistula Christiana* (1521), although condemned by Luther,

gained the approval of Oecolampadius of Basel and Capito
of Strasbourg, and was warmly applauded by Zwingli. In
this way the Netherlands influenced the emergence of convictions about Holy Communion that were to remain a part
of the broad evangelical tradition ever afterwards. Sartorius
(1500–57), the editor of the Dutch edition of Erasmus's
Adagia, set forth his views on Communion in his book, *The
Holy Eucharist* (1525). He was a Christian humanist and a
close friend of Wouter Deelen, who became librarian to
Henry VIII and died in London in 1563.

Despite the exile imposed upon the leaders, the movement spread. At Utrecht the early Lutheranism of Hinne
Rode, exiled in 1523, yielded to the sacramentarianism of
Herman Gerrits and Willem Dirks, whose burning made
him the first Protestant martyr of the province. At Utrecht
too his courage was emulated by Jan Cornelisz Winter, the
vicar of Hoorn, who was beheaded as a heretic, 24 June
1533. In Gelderland, the pioneer was Gerard Geldenhauer
at Tiel, just as Willem Frederiks was at Groningen. In
Amsterdam, an old Wittenberg student, Claes van der Elst,
was one of six priests who conducted frequent clandestine
meetings. And there was similar activity in the southern
part of the Netherlands.

The authorities were compelled to take action as the
evangelicals made their views increasingly known by
means of plays, posters, printed books and popular hymns.
Repression had started in November 1519 when the University of Louvain condemned Luther's books and it continued with increasing severity after the appointment of
Frans van der Hulst as Inquisitor-general by the emperor in
1523. And an edict of 14 October 1529 made the dissem-
ination of Lutheranism a crime punishable by death. But
imperial repression did not prevent the growth of Protestantism. Indeed sacramentarianism soon began to produce a
yet more radical form of Protestantism – Anabaptism.

ANABAPTISM

The father of Dutch Anabaptism was Melchior Hofmann
(1495–1543), whose career has already been outlined. Hofmann's followers – the Melchiorites – were men of peace
who believed that the heavenly kingdom would be initiated

by direct divine intervention. But there were others, like Jan Matthys and Jan of Leyden, who hoped to initiate the kingdom by political action and become embroiled in the tragedy of Münster. The spread of Anabaptism, particularly in the north of the Netherlands led to persecution. Sicke Freerks, the first of many Dutch Anabaptist martyrs, was beheaded at Leeuwarden, 20 March 1531. The harsh treatment of the Anabaptists culminated in the vicious persecution of early 1534. In desperation, thousands, possibly as many as sixteen thousand, made for Münster only to be intercepted by the authorities and sent back home penniless. Under such provocation, men like Jan van Geelen, a Munsterite, found it easy to persuade some groups to consider direct military action. It was indeed at his instigation that the Old Cloister monastery in Friesland was occupied by his armed followers on 30 March 1535, and the similar occupation of Amsterdam Town Hall followed on 10 May 1535. The reprisals were harsh and there was a real possibility that the whole movement would be drowned in blood.

MENNO SIMONS

One man who had been moved to the root of his being by these events was Menno Simons (1496–1561), the greatest and most attractive of the Dutch Anabaptist leaders. The blood of the men who had occupied the Old Cloister, he wrote, 'fell hot on my heart'. He had begun his career as parish priest at Pingjum, Frisia, in 1524, had learnt the principle of the unique authority of Scripture from Luther, adopted sacramentarianism as a result of his Bible study and had been intellectually influenced by the teaching of Melchior Hofmann. In 1536 he submitted to believers' baptism and was ordained an Anabaptist elder by Obbe Philips in 1537. Obbe and Dirk Philips were the sons of a priest at Leeuwarden. Obbe left the Anabaptists and died at Lubeck 1568, probably as a Lutheran. Dirk was influenced by Hofmann and the sacramentarians and became an Anabaptist in 1533. From 1536 to 1544 he worked as a travelling evangelist in East Frisia and then ministered to the congregation of Dutch Anabaptists at Danzig until 1567. He died at Emden in 1568. His *Enchiridion* (1568) provides the fullest exposition of Anabaptist theology and enjoyed a well-deserved popularity.

To return to Simons. He was soon a hunted man and was constantly on the move for fear of arrest. His ministry took him to Amsterdam, Cologne, Holstein, then the Baltic coast where he worked between 1546 until his death, 31 January 1561.

Although he adhered to the millenarian hope of Christ's second coming, he was implacably opposed to the militant Anabaptists. His views were set forth in a series of books, the most popular of which was his *Foundation of Christian Doctrine* (1540). In his theology, Simons was a firm Trinitarian, but his view of the incarnation was peculiar. It had already been propounded by Hofmann and it grew out of a desire to safeguard Jesus's sinlessness by asserting that Mary's own sinful human nature did not contribute anything to our Lord's body. So Simons taught that Jesus's body was a new creation by the Holy Spirit in the Virgin's womb and was not therefore derived from her humanity.

Simons was firmly committed, at least in intention, to the biblical revelation and that is why he so vigorously disapproved of both the views and actions of his old colleague, David Joris. Joris claimed prophetic inspiration equal to that of the Scriptures and held that outward conformity to both the world and other churches was permissible as long as Anabaptists were loyal in their hearts to the true faith. He left the Netherlands, appeared in Basel in 1544, concealed his true identity and lived and died there in honour, only to have his body disinterred and burned when the truth about him became known.

Simons had a formidable task to hold the Anabaptist movement together, especially since the name itself had become odious after the Münster affair. But he succeeded and when he died in 1561, the reins of leadership fell into the hands of Dirk Philips who had already made such a distinguished contribution to the movement. So evangelical Anabaptism began to make its unique contribution to Protestant witness and to enrich Dutch Christianity with its gentle and practical spirituality.

30 Militant Calvinism

> I see nothing else to propose but that it be permitted
> to practise the Reformed religion according to the
> word of God, and that this whole country and state
> return to its ancient privileges and liberty.

> William of Orange ('the Silent' 1533–1584), in a letter
> to his brother stating his aims, 5 February 1573.

The Protestant life of the Netherlands was further diver-
sified and enriched by the emergence of Calvinism. But
important as the direct influence of Geneva was, Dutch
Calvinism owed much also to Erasmian humanism, sacramentarianism and Anabaptism. Then again there was the
contribution of Heinrich Bullinger of Zürich, who had himself when a schoolboy at Emmerich in Cleves been
influenced by the piety of the Brethren of the Common
Life. The Dutch version of his books, especially the sermons distilled into the *Huysboek* and the extracts from his
Decades contained in the *Summa* (1562), proved popular
both as manuals of practical devotion and as guides to
Reformed theology. In other words, Dutch Calvinism
developed a flavour all its own.

BEGINNINGS

In 1540 the Pole, John à Lasco (1499–1560), started work as
pastor at Emden in East Friesland. Three years later he
became superintendent of the churches in the territory of
Countess Anna of Oldenburg, the patroness of Anabaptists
and other radicals, and introduced a form of organization
which had affinities with the Reformed pattern. This
impressed the many refugees who had sought a haven in
East Friesland. Calvin soon showed a highly personal
interest in these developments. His wife was from Liège
and he himself had once claimed, 'I too am a Belgian'. His

THE NETHERLANDS

North Sea

Leeuwarden
Franeker
Gröningen
FRIESLAND
GRÖNINGEN

Alkmaar
Zuider Zee
Kampen
Zwolle
Haarlem
Amsterdam
OVERYSSEL
Leyden
HOLLAND
UTRECHT
ZUTPHEN
Hague
Delft
Utrecht
GELDER
LAND
Duisburg
Brill
Rotterdam
Dort
Nymegen
Cleves
ZEELAND
Breda
Bergen
Middelburg
Bruges
Antwerp
BRABANT
GERMANY
Nieuport
Ghent
Dunkirk
Louvain
LIÈGE
FLANDERS
Brussels
ARTOIS
Namur
Liège
to Artois
Douay
Arras
HAINAULT
Cateau-
Cambrésis
LUXEMBOURG
CAMBRÉSIS
to Liège

FRANCE

Luxembourg

0   50
Miles

successor at Strasbourg, Pierre Brully, migrated to Valenciennes and Tournai and exercised a fruitful ministry which
culminated in his martyrdom on 19 February 1545. Streams
of young men flowed to Geneva to be instructed in the new
theology with the result that Calvinism began to spread
with remarkable speed in the fifteen-fifties. Flanders and
Hainault were the chief centres, with strong congregations
appearing in Ghent, Bruges, Ypres, Valenciennes and
Tournai, as well as Antwerp. But Calvinism was spreading
also in the northern provinces of Utrecht, Zeeland and
Holland.

CONSOLIDATION

As yet, the movement, while bubbling with evangelical
enthusiasm, lacked the cohesiveness that comes from a
strong commitment to a clear theology and an effective
organization. Both these were provided by Guy de Bres
(1522–67), the outstanding pioneer of Dutch Calvinism. He
was a native of Mons and spent the years between 1548 and
1552 as a refugee in England. He spent some time in France
before having to flee from persecution to Geneva and
returned to the Low Countries in 1560 to organize the
congregations in the neighbourhood of Tournai. He had
published, Le baton, his statement of faith at Antwerp in
1555 and became the prime mover in preparing the Belgic
Confession of 1561, being assisted by Hermann van Strijker,
Gottfried Wingen and Adrien (or, Hadrian) de Saravia, –
later one of the translators of the English King James version of the Bible. Although the earlier articles of the confession follow closely the wording of the French Confession of
1559, it is more than twice the length of its predecessor
since it elaborates more fully on several points of doctrine,
partly to counteract the teaching of the Anabaptists on the
incarnation and infant baptism. The Belgic Confession fittingly takes its place as a noble expression of the evangelical
faith; its authority was acknowledged at a synod at Emden
in 1571, as well as at the Synod of Dort on 29 April 1619.
Together with the canons of that synod and the beautiful
Heidelberg Catechism, it became an authoritative statement of Dutch Calvinistic orthodoxy. Guy de Bres, in the
face of renewed persecution, had withdrawn to Metz,

where his ministry proved exceptionally fruitful and he had high hopes of bringing the various Protestant groups into closer unity with each other. By 1564 he was back in Brussels and when the Antwerp consistory met in July 1565, he persuaded it to accept the Belgic Confession as a doctrinal basis for Calvinists but hoped also, by commending the *Wittenberg Concord*, to secure a yet wider unity. But events were unfolding which were to draw the Calvinists of the Netherlands into one of the great struggles of European history.

SPANISH OPPRESSION

By 1548 Charles V had completed the legal changes which gave the Netherlands a special position as an identifiable unit in the Empire. He was to be represented by a Governor-general and his authority in the provinces was to be exercised through lieutenants known as stadholders. He allowed the representative assemblies of the individual provinces, – the States, – to function freely and even strengthened the central assembly, the States General, at Brussels. And the country was flourishing economically at mid-century. Charles retired to his monastery in 1555 and his brother Ferdinand became Emperor. But the Netherlands, together with Spain and Sicily, went to Philip, Charles's son. Philip II was a singularly unattractive monarch, cruel, vindictive and given to duplicity. He ruled the Netherlands personally from 1555 to 1559 and then left his half-sister, Margaret of Parma, as Governor-general, with the Frenchman, Antoine Perronet de Granvelle (1517–86), bishop of Arras, as chief minister. Spaniards and foreigners were promoted to key positions, the native nobles disparaged. The traditional jurisdiction of the archbishops of Reims and Cologne was transferred to new bishoprics, funded by depriving the nobility of their patronage of rich abbeys. So the nobles were discontented, the Protestants were apprehensive, the merchants feared for the future of their influence in the cities, and the poor suffered hardship and famine as prices rose in the mid-sixties. The Netherlands was ripe for insurrection.

NOBLES AND PREACHERS

By 1565 some of the leading nobles were convinced that a public declaration was necessary. Early in the following year, the 'Compromise' was drawn up, probably by the Calvinist, Philippe Marnix, Seigneur de Sainte-Aldegonde (1540–98). The original copy was signed, not only by distinguished Protestant and Roman Catholic leaders but also by some 400 supporters. On 5 April 1566 two hundred of the signatories rode in cavalcade to present a petition against the Inquisition to the Governor-general. Indeed, the oath that the members of the party took spoke of the Inquisition as 'iniquitous and contrary to all laws of God and man, in its barbarity exceeding the worst of tyrants'. Little came from this demonstration except that the Roman Catholic baron Berlaymont referred to the deputation as 'beggars' (in French, gueux) and the protesters immediately adopted it as a proud nickname.

Later in 1566, events took a serious turn. The Calvinist preachers were now attracting huge and enthusiastic congregations. People congregated in their thousands to listen to the sermons. Thus Ambrose Wille had a congregation of some 15,000 at Amsterdam, Hermann Strijker had 7,000 at Ghent and Peregrine de la Grange had 10,000 at Tournai. Camp-meetings (as a later age was to call them) multiplied and soon no city of any consequence was without its field preaching. It was a striking manifestation of the power of the preached word, and all the more striking for its spontaneity and the way it brought all social classes together. Then on 10 August 1566 rioting began and from 11 August to 6 September, the great 'Iconoclasm' swept the country as the statues, ornaments and stained glass of some 400 religious buildings were destroyed. And yet a remarkable feature of the disturbance was that, despite the extensive damage to property, no personal injuries were inflicted on anyone. The authorities, including the Protestant nobles, were alarmed and Philip II decided on a change of régime. He replaced Margaret with his able general, Fernando Alvarez de Toledo. He was a ruthless sadist, devoid of any diplomatic acumen. He arrived on 22 August 1567 and set to it immediately to reduce the Netherlands by terror. He instituted the Council of Troubles, soon to be popularly known as the Council of Blood, and its most energetic officer, the terrible Juan de Vargas, secured the execution of 12,000 in a matter of weeks and some 100,000 refugees left the country. On 5 June 1568 the Council's most distinguished victims, Count Egmont and Admiral Hoorn, were executed at Brussels. The whole country was paralyzed by fear.

THE STRUGGLE FOR FREEDOM

It was now that William, Prince of Orange, emerged as one of the most striking princely patrons of the Protestant Reformation and the hero of his nation's struggle for freedom. His sobriquet, 'the Silent', meant that he was a man who kept his counsel to himself, for his jolly, spendthrift days in the court of the Emperor lay in the past. By 1568 he was convinced that the Spaniard could only be ousted by force and on 6 April 1568 he issued a solemn commission to his brother, Louis of Nassau, to open a military campaign against the Spaniards. Campaigning on land was difficult and William's own attempt at invasion in 1568 failed. Not so the war at sea. The Sea Beggars, using Dover as their base for a time, harried Spanish shipping in the Channel. Nor were other means of resistance forgotten. In 1569 Aldegonde published the brilliant French satire, *The Bee Hive of the Roman Church*, in Dutch translation. Thus it teases the Pope, the 'King Bee' (according to George Gilpin's translation, 1623),

> He goeth seldome abroad, but when hee doth determine to goe forth any whither, it may bee perceived long before, by the swarming and the humming of the forerunners. For whensoever he goeth out, the whole swarme followeth round about him, and oftentimes they carrie him on their shoulders . . .

And much more to the same effect.

On 1 April 1572 the Sea Beggars captured the port of Brill and they went on to capture the towns of the provinces of Holland and Zeeland one after the other. On 14 April 1572 William called upon the inhabitants of the Low Countries to rise against Spain and in July at Dordrecht the revolutionary States of Holland, meeting for the first time on the initiative of its members, acknowledged William as its Stadholder. Gradually, William built up his reputation as a wise and impressive leader of the resistance. He set out his policy in a letter dated 5 February 1573. He wished the country to be free in matters of religious conscience and government. He had embraced a generous vision for the future of the Netherlands. In his own spiritual pilgrimage he had started life under Lutheran influences, then been instructed as a Roman Catholic and finally embraced the Reformed faith, but without yielding the Erasmian ideal of toleration for all loyal citizens. The Calvinists, however, were not sympathetic to his hopes of creating a new Netherlands where Catholic, Lutheran, Calvinist, Mennonite and Socinian could dwell in peace, and William, for his part, admitted that in view of their great contribution to the national struggle, the state should have a special relationship with them.

DIVISIONS

The armed struggle continued with William and his supporters eventually becoming powerful enough to unite the representatives of the provinces in support of the 'Pacification of Ghent', 8 November 1576. This demanded the withdrawal of the Spanish troops, an amnesty for those implicated in the resistance, the convening of the States General, peace between Roman Catholic and Protestant and freedom for all citizens. But the struggle was not over. Further resistance to Spanish policies led to the 'Peace of Religion', 22 July 1578, a bold assertion of religious toleration supported by all parties. But it was a fragile peace and William had to intervene to prevent the persecution of Mennonites by Calvinists.

In any case, Spain still had hopes of subduing the country. When Alexander Farnese, Duke of Parma, became Governor-general in October 1578 he proceeded to reconquer the southern provinces. Within seven years he had succeeded. William's authority thereafter was confined to Holland and Zeeland. On 6 January 1579 the Roman Catholic southern provinces formed the Union of Arras while the northern provinces on 23 January 1579 formed the Union of

Utrecht. So the Netherlands became divided. The northern United Provinces on 26 July 1581 repudiated Spanish sovereignty and declared William of Orange head of government. But the great patriot was assassinated on 10 July 1584 and the struggle was continued by his son Maurice.

So the seven provinces of the north became a Calvinist stronghold while in the south Protestantism, which had met with such success there, was completely eradicated.

31 Dissent in Italy

Think what grace you have received from God through being led from the deepest shadows to his marvellous light, and love one another with a pure heart, with all sincerity and fullness of heart, without pretence.

From the last letter of Francis della Sega, the Italian Hutterite, to his fellow-countrymen in Moravia. He was executed by drowning at Venice, 26 February 1565.

One of the more obvious characteristics of the reform movements in Italy was their variety. They covered a wide spectrum from Roman Catholics seeking spiritual renewal to rationalists who were equally opposed to both Roman Catholicism and main-line Protestantism. In consequence it is no easy matter to draw hard and fast lines of demarcation between the various groups. It is appropriate, however, to start with the oldest of the dissenting movements.

THE WALDENSIANS

It was in the twelfth century as we saw in chapter 2, that Valdés of Lyons launched an evangelistic movement which sought to recapture the simplicity of the gospel. With his condemnation by the Council of Verona in 1184 the movement became a schismatic sect. It spread in southern France, Spain, the Low Countries, Germany and Bohemia but severe repression destroyed it in many places. Yet those remnants who inhabited the remote valleys of the Cottian Alps had sufficient vitality to extend their missionary activity to Apulia and Calabria and to bring upon themselves the wrath of the French king around 1500.

In September 1526 a synod at Vallon du Laux, 140 Waldensian 'barbes' (as they called their ministers) met to consider their relationship with other reform movements, in Bohemia, Germany and Switzerland. They decided to send two of their number, Martin Gonin and Guido of Calabria, to visit Luther and report on his views. At a subsequent synod held at Mérindol in Provence in 1530, it was resolved to send two other barbes, George Morel and Peter Masson, to confer with Farel, Haller and Oecolampadius in Switzerland, and Bucer at Strasbourg. Masson was arrested at Dijon and executed as a heretic but Morel escaped to make his report on the conversations. Morel had become an enthusiast for closer alliance with the Swiss and in the synod of Cianforan, 22 September 1532, he was supported by the presence of Farel, Anthony Saulnier and Robert Olivetan, Calvin's cousin. The delegates, although by no means unanimously, resolved to embrace the principles of the Swiss Reformation while maintaining some of their own distinctive practices as well as their pacifism. A valuable consequence of the synod was that Olivetan was persuaded to translate the Bible into French and the version was duly published in 1535. It was unfortunate, however, that French was not the language of the Waldensians and that the translation was a disservice to their traditional culture.

The Waldensians continued to be a church under the cross. True enough, they enjoyed a period of peace in Piedmont from 1537 to 1559 but in Calabria in southern Italy the vicious crusade begun in 1561 utterly destroyed the movement.

As it happened, Waldensianism had nothing to do with the beginnings of Protestantism in Italy. On the contrary, this was almost entirely an import from Germany and Switzerland.

SMUGGLERS OF THE GOSPEL

In 1528 Luther exclaimed that 'the Venetians receive the word of God. Thanks and glory be to the Lord.' For some years German and Swiss merchants had been smuggling Protestant books and pamphlets over the Alps. Indeed, as early as 1519 Francesco Calvi of Pavia was distributing Luther's books. And about the same time Aldo Manuzio's printing house was publishing Luther's books under false names, and the pope in September 1520 forbade people to read them. In Rome itself Protestant books were circulating in the papal court in 1519. Similarly, the books of Melanchthon, Zwingli and Bucer also found a ready market, not least in the universities of Turin, Padua and Bologna. The church and the rulers of the various cities affected were deeply disturbed by all this and issued injunctions to stem the tide. But for several years these prohibitions were of little avail.

Protestant influences were felt in cities like Venice, Turin and Aosta from an early date and by 1530 Lutheranism had penetrated such cities as Lucca, Brescia and Cremona. Even Rome itself was affected by Lutheranism, not least after the terrible sack of Rome on 6 May 1527 when thousands of Lutherans in the German armies marched through the streets shouting, 'Long live Pope Luther' and causing fearful destruction.

Much of the enthusiasm for buying and reading Lutheran books was due to the desire to reform the church or to revive a flagging spirituality rather than a wish to embrace fundamental theological changes. So the authorities were slow to execute the papal and civic condemnations of Lutheranism, at least in the period up to 1535. Even in 1539 it was claimed, doubtless with some exaggeration, that there was 'scarcely a city in Italy' that was not affected by heresy and Modena was the worst affected of all. At Castelmaggiore virtually everyone was a Protestant and large gains were made at Cremona, Pavia and Milan. And what was particularly alarming to the authorities was the way in which Protestantism was attracting support from all classes in the community.

'EVANGELISM'

'Evangelism' is a term adopted (rather confusingly) by contemporary historians to describe a movement within the Roman Catholic Church which was sympathetic to certain aspects of Protestantism, and therefore more conciliatory towards it than the Roman Catholicism of the Counter-Reformation. It flourished first of all in Venice and consisted of young humanists, former students of the University of Padua, who were eager to recapture the spirit of Paul, to exalt the authority of the Bible, to emphasize the role of faith in justification and to reform the church. The most prominent of them was Gasparo Contarini (1483–1542) who underwent a spiritual agony not unlike that of Luther which brought him by 1523 to the conclusion that 'no one can at any time justify himself through his works'; on the contrary, 'we must justify ourselves through the right-eousness of another, that is, of Christ'. So the thinking of this group was maturing before the beginning of Luther's protest but it is hard to resist the conclusion that its later development was influenced by Protestant writings.

But Contarini and his friends were troubled by the Lutheran schism and dedicated themselves to maintaining the unity of the church while respecting what they believed to be true and valuable in Luther's teaching. The leading lights of the movement were Gregorio Cortese (1483–1548), Giovanni Morone (1509–80), Reginald Pole, Bernardino Ochino (1487–1564), Peter Martyr Vermigli (1500–62), the Spaniard, Juan de Valdés (1500–41).

A ROMAN CATHOLIC REFORMER

Valdés settled in Naples in 1529. He was a man of deep spirituality and a skilful pastor of souls and gathered around him a group of disciples and admirers. It included persons of influence like Vittoria Colonna (1492–1547), the friend of Michelangelo; Caterina Cibo (1501–57), grand-daughter of Pope Innocent VIII; Marc Antonio Flaminio (1485–1550), the humanist scholar; as well as churchmen like Pole, Pietro Carnesecchi (d.1567), Ochino and Peter Martyr. Valdés was eclectic in his teaching owing a debt to Spanish mysticism, humanism, Luther and Zwingli. Although an object of distrust to church leaders, Valdés was a faithful Roman Catholic dedicated to the promotion of piety and moral improvement. Only a minority of his intimates – among them Ochino, Martyr and Carnesecchi, – eventually left the Roman communion.

DASHED HOPES

This large group of reformers reached its highest point of influence in the late 30s but its hopes were dashed by the

failure of the Diet of Regensburg in 1541 to achieve reconciliation with the Lutherans. Contarini led the Roman
Catholic deputation and agreement was reached on the
crucial matter of justification but the discussion of the
church's status and sacraments ended in a complete
stalemate. Soon after 'Evangelism' began to disintegrate.
Contarini broke his heart and died in 1542; Valdés died in
1541; Ochino,the greatest preacher in Italy, defected to the
Protestants, as did Martyr and in 1542 Caraffa reorganized
the Roman Inquisition.

GATHERING CLOUDS

Round about 1543 the most popular book produced by
Italian Protestantism was published at Venice. It was *The
Benefits of Christ's Death* and was the joint product, so it is
believed, of Benedetto Fontanino, a Benedictine monk of
Mantua, and Marc Antonio Flaminio. Although the
opening chapters echo the teaching of Valdés, the later
chapters owe much to Calvin as they emphasize that good
works make no contribution to salvation and yet Christians
must arm themselves by prayer, awareness of predestination and frequent communion for the great combat that
awaits them.

Such a warning was salutary at the time because the
authorities were taking more ruthless action against heresy.
The promoters of 'Evangelism', even when entrusted with
the responsibility for checking heresy, clung to the hope
that preaching and persuasion would be sufficient to do
that. But in general a much harsher policy prevailed. In
1542 one of the leaders of Venetian Protestantism, Baldass-
are Altieri (d.1550), wrote to Luther beseeching his help
because 'Antichrist was beginning to rage' against his
fellow-believers. In 1541 Ercole Gonzaga, the cardinal and
regent of Mantua, ordained vicious punishments for all
who professed agreement with evangelical doctrines. And
with the coming of Caraffa's Inquisition, persecution
became more systematic and extensive.

DISPERSION

The consequences were grave for Italian Protestantism.

Many of the leaders fled. In 1542 Celio Secondo Curione (1503–69), the most distinguished of Piedmontese Protestants, left Italy to become Professor of Rhetoric at Lausanne. No finer character was produced by Italian Protestantism than Pietro Carnesecchi, one time secretary to Clement VII, a member of Valdés's circle, and close friend of Cardinal Pole. In 1546 he withdrew to France since his Lutheranism had led to a citation to Rome on suspicion of heresy. He, however, returned in 1553 only to suffer a martyr's death by burning at Rome on 21 September 1567.

Peter Paul Vergerio (1498–1565) had a remarkable career. An enthusiastic supporter of Rome at the Colloquies of Worms and Ratisbon, and bishop of Capodistria from 1536, he became a Protestant after a prolonged and painful spiritual pilgrimage and renounced his allegiance to Rome on 13 December 1548 before migrating first to the Grisons and then to Germany. He died at Heidelberg.

Peter Martyr is a better-known figure. He had gained widespread notice as a preacher and reformer before leaving Italy in 1542. After spending some time in Strasbourg, he migrated to England at the invitation of Cranmer, returned to Strasbourg in 1554, and died at Zürich, 12 November 1562.

In some ways Bernardino Ochino was the most remarkable of the Italian leaders. He was born at Siena and became an enthusiastic monk. He was a preacher of astonishing popularity, in constant demand by church leaders, including the pope. When he was summoned to Rome, 15 July 1542, his friends suspected the worst and on their advice, he fled with Peter Martyr over the Alps. From then on he led a wanderer's life and held many posts, including that of prebendary at Canterbury, before ending his days in Silesia, lonely and rejected because of his doubts about the divinity of Christ and the atonement.

So the growing enthusiasm and efficiency of the Roman Catholic reaction caused immense havoc among the Protestants of Italy.

THE RADICALS

The case was no different with those whose sympathies were with the radical reformers.

Protestantism appeared in several radical forms. Thus,

Camillo Renato (c.1500–c.1572), one of the influential pioneers, advocated a high doctrine of divine election coupled with an insistence on the bondage of the will, asserted that the soul died at the same time as the body and that therefore belief in purgatory, in requiem masses and prayers for the dead, was groundless superstition. Tiziano, the man who did most to spread Camillo's ideas, linked them with Anabaptism and joined with Peter Manelfi and others to organize Anabaptist conventicles in Venice. The movement met with considerable success and in September 1550 was able to hold a secret synod at Venice, attended by sixty representatives from some thirty widely scattered congregations. Its resolutions showed that the majority (but not all) of these churches had adopted views that could be considered heretical by Lutherans and Calvinists. They denied the divinity of Christ and his virgin birth, asserted that justification was by God's eternal mercy not by the merits of the Saviour. Jesus was to be seen as an outstanding prophet who exemplified love in his life and death. And they held also that there were no angels or devils; that hell did not exist and that the soul expires with the body.

In October 1551 Manelfi returned to the Roman Catholic fold and provided the Inquisition with all the information necessary to destroy the Italian Anabaptist movement. Some survived, however, and made contact with the Hutterites of Moravia who provided them with an asylum. But three of their staunchest leaders suffered martyrdom, Julius Gherlandi in October 1562, Francis della Sega and Anthony Rizzetto on 26 February 1565. All three died by drowning in the waters of Venice.

THE GRISONS

Rhaetia (or the Grisons or Graubunden), at that time an independent republic of three covenanting confederacies with a common Diet, proved to be a haven for representatives of all the religious parties then working in Europe. John Comander (d.1557) began to preach evangelical doctrine at Coire as early as 1524 and by June 1526 the Diet had extended toleration to orthodox Protestantism. Among the Romansch-speaking people of the Engadine, Philip Saluz (1504–66), a powerful preacher of striking character, and

Ulrich Campell (1510–82) introduced evangelical Christianity, as did Augustine Mainardi (d.1563) at Chiavenna. The tolerant attitude of the authorities attracted to Rhaetia a large number of the radical reformers, people like Tiziano, Renato, Laelius Socinus and many others.

COLLAPSE

Despite the brilliance and courage of many individuals, Protestantism did not flourish in Italy. The radicals did not strike deep roots nor did the Lutherans or Calvinists succeed in winning the patronage of any of the numerous Italian states. Calvin himself was unhappy with the tendency of so many Italians to embrace 'Nicodemism' and so to cultivate their Protestantism as a clandestine and private profession. On the other hand, many of the serious and devout promoters of reform found satisfaction in the improvements that came in the wake of the Counter-Reformation.

It is perhaps significant that the one Protestant church to survive was the Waldensian Church, precisely the body that had had the longest experience of facing persecution. Under God it had been granted the grace of survival.

32 Brief harvest in a golden age

At the Emperor's court, in the churches, in the convents, in the inns and on the highways, everyone has the *Enchiridion* of Erasmus in Spanish.

Alonso Fernandez (*fl.*1516–20) the Spanish translator.

In 1500 Spain was not only beginning her so-called 'Golden Century' but giving signs of developing a new liberal age. But the signs appeared against a sinister background.

A MELTING-POT

Mediaeval Spain was a country where Christian, Jew and Moslem had found ways of tolerating one another, though not always in peace. With the linking of the two kingdoms of Aragon and Castile through the marriage of Ferdinand and Isabella in 1469 and their accessions to their respective thrones, the policy of creating one pure Spanish nation was adopted with dour determination. After centuries of Christian advance, the Islamic kingdom of Granada fell in 1492 and the Moors became a minority in a Christian state. In the same year, the Jews were expelled from Spain, the culmination of a long series of pogroms extending back to the thirteenth century. Over the centuries these atrocities had produced a large number of 'conversos', Jews forcibly converted. And by expelling those of Jewish faith, the sovereigns at a stroke doubled the number of *conversos*.

Already preachers like Alonso de Hojeda of Seville had impressed upon Isabella the dangers that might be posed by large numbers of insincere converts. A judicial body was necessary to guard against the peril and so, on 27 September 1480, a new Inquisition was established. The 'old Christians' in Spain welcomed its establishment because they had now developed a passionate commitment to both Roman Catholic orthodoxy and racial purity. It was a very formidable institution. Its proceedings were shrouded in secrecy at the time, but the efficiency with which its officials kept their accounts has enabled modern historians to make a close study of its methods and procedures. That its procedures were governed by strict rules, that its prisons were more comfortable than secular ones and that it was less likely to have its victims executed than similar tribunals in other countries, does nothing to mitigate the terror aroused by its secrecy, its use of informers and its automatic confiscation of the property of accused persons. Its efficiency was to be revealed in its struggle with Protestantism.

RENAISSANCE

It was the remarkable spread of humanism that raised hopes that a new liberal age was dawning. Inspired by Italy, humanists like Antonio de Nebrija brought new distinction to an old university like Salamanca which by 1552 was to have over 6,000 students. Nine new universities were founded between 1472 and 1526 and women as well as men were given the opportunity to enjoy their facilities. And it was one of these new foundations, Alacalá University, that produced the beautiful six-volume Polyglot Bible.

The first printing press in Spain was set up at Valencia in 1474 and during the next twenty-five years 720 books were printed on 25 presses in the country. And foreign books had a duty-free passage into Spain. The welcome given to the new learning is best shown in the immense popularity of Erasmus. His witty criticisms of laxity and obscurantism in church life were read with appreciation. He was read everywhere and Erasmianism won its most signal victory when some Dominicans as part of their campaign to prove Erasmus a heretic insisted on a public debate at Valladolid in March 1527. They completely failed to impress the audience and Erasmus was triumphantly vindicated.

Even the great Cardinal Ximénez had pressed Erasmus to visit Spain. Francisco Ximénez de Cisneros (1436–1517) was Archbishop of Toledo, the most prestigious diocese in Christendom after Rome. He was also High Chancellor of Castile and a sagacious statesman. Yet despite holding high

office, he lived the life of an austere friar. In 1507 he became
Inquisitor-General. He is a good example of the pre-
Reformation reformer and he succeeded where so many
failed. He overhauled the monasteries of Spain and they
became among the best disciplined in Europe. In all aspects
of church life the highest standards were demanded. The
preaching of indulgences was banned before Luther had
been heard of. And, ironically, in no country did the pope
have less direct influence than in Spain. To crown it all,
Ximénez had a reverence for learning. He founded the
University of Alcalá and was the patron of the Polyglot
Bible. It was quite in keeping with his character that he
should wish to see Erasmus coming to Spain.

When all these various influences are considered, it will
be obvious why Spain was to prove such infertile soil for
evangelical teaching.

BEGINNING OF REACTION

It was not long before the Inquisition began to detain such
supporters of Erasmus as the distinguished humanist and
secretary to Ximénez, Juan de Vergera. To express the
slightest doubt about the existence of purgatory, the
offence of Mateo Pascual, professor at Alcalá University,
was to invite a summons to appear before the Inquisition.
The same threat faced anyone who doubted the value of
monasticism or who sympathized with the doctrine of justification by faith alone. It was just such a threat that drove
Juan de Valdés into exile in Italy in 1530. It was the growing
hostility to humanism that provoked the authorities to ask
such a distinguished scholar as Pedro de Larma, once the
dean of the Faculty of Theology at Paris, to abjure a series of
Erasmian propositions in 1537. Larma was no Protestant,
but his nephews were. Jáime de Enzinas, a Spanish
Lutheran and a correspondent of Calvin's, was the first to
suffer martydom for the Protestant faith in Italy. He was
burned at Rome on 16 March 1547. His brother, Francisco
de Enzinas (1520–70), better known to Protestants as
Dryander, had studied at Wittenberg and lodged with Melanchthon. He offended the authorities with his Spanish
translation of the New Testament, which he was permitted
to present to the Emperor in person on 23 November 1543,

and found himself in prison as a result. He escaped and wandered around Europe holding a number of positions, one of which was the chair of Greek at Cambridge. He died at Augsburg on 30 December 1550. There were other men too, such as Mateo Adriano, the professor of Hebrew at Wittenberg, and Juan Diaz who accompanied Bucer at the Colloquy of Ratisbon, who were of Spanish origin. But the authorities were resolved to eliminate Erasmianism and they were successful. And if Erasmianism was unacceptable, Lutheranism was considered a horrid plague. Up to 1558 thirty-nine people had been cited by the Inquisition as 'Lutherans' although the majority of them were very far indeed from holding any Protestant convictions.

EVANGELICALS AT SEVILLE

Despite the efficient repression, evangelicalism was not without its proponents. A group was gathered at Seville primarily through the work of Juan Gil, or Egidio, who died in 1556. He, like so many Spanish reformers, had been educated at Alacalá and had been canon of Seville from 1537. He had been converted by a nobleman, Rodrigo de Valer, an evangelist whose boldness in preaching in public places convinced the authorities that he was mad, with the result that he was imprisoned for life. Gil acquired a more systematic knowledge of justification by faith alone from Constantino de la Fuente, an excellent Greek and Hebrew scholar who was educated at Alcalá. Both men were helped by Vargas whose strength was in biblical exposition. This was very much an underground movement, as is shown by the surprising fact that Constantino was the Emperor's confessor from 1548 to 1551 and was later sent to England after the marriage of Philip II to Mary Tudor. At its largest the group consisted of some 127 members including the prior and some of the monks in the monastery of San Isidro, as well as nuns from Santa Paula. The secrecy of the meetings ensured peace for the members but eventually Gil and Vargas were indicted by the Inquisition. Vargas died almost immediately but Gil was tricked into making a public recantation on 21 July 1552. He was subjected to strict penance and prohibited from discharging any priestly functions. He died in 1556. Constantino, however, was able to carry on his clandestine Bible classes.

EVANGELICALS IN VALLADOLID

The prime mover of the second group of evangelicals was Agustin Cazalla, a man who had enjoyed a distinguished career in the Emperor's service since 1532 and had been drawn towards Protestantism by his brother, Pedro, and the Italian Carlos de Seso, who had brought his Protestant convictions with him when he settled in Spain. In the neighbourhood of Toro he had influenced many well-to-do people, including Domingo de Rojas and the Cazalla family. The group, numbering some 55 people, met at Valladolid and held their services, which included Holy Communion, at the house of Leonor de Vibera, Agustin Cazalla's mother.

SUPPRESSION

Neither group enjoyed peace for long. Gradually the Inquisition pieced together sufficient evidence to proceed against them. Fourteen persons were burned on 24 September 1559 at Seville and the group's meeting-place, Isabel de Baena's house, was destroyed. A second auto-da-fé on 22 December 1560 led to a further eight martyrdoms and the survivors, which included Constantino and Juan Perez, the translator of the 1556 Spanish New Testament, ensured their safety by leaving Spain. At Valladolid members of the Protestant group suffered arrest in June 1558 and the Inquisition's proceedings against them culminated in the auto-da-fé of 21 May 1559 when fourteen of them were burned, including Agustin Cazalla. Later his mother's house was destroyed and thirteen other Protestants burned in the presence of the king on 8 October 1559. Other evangelicals at both Seville and Valladolid were sentenced to lesser punishments.

By 1560 the ruthless efficiency of the Spanish Inquisition, faithfully supported by the Crown, had effectively silenced the evangelical testimony.

33 The clash of convictions in Poland

Our Polish brethren are very wondrous and burdensome.

Heinrich Bullinger (1504–1575).

Poland became the home of many different theological parties and the centre of vigorous controversy. At the time of the Reformation it was a very large country. It had close connections with Lithuania, itself an extensive territory, even before that Duchy was brought into federal union with the Kingdom of Poland in 1569. The Kingdom itself under Sigismund I (1506–48) consisted of Great Poland, Little Poland, Ducal (or East) Prussia and Royal Prussia. So we are talking about a territory which extended from Livonia in the north to the river Dniester in the south, and from Cracow in the west to Smolensk in the east. Orthodox believers, Roman Catholics, Hussites, Waldensians and Bogomiles (the mediaeval sect originating in Bulgaria which rejected the Old Testament and the Catholic doctrine of the sacraments), were to be found in the territory before Martin Luther was heard of. The substantial independence enjoyed by local lords made them impatient of centralized control and that, on the one hand, provided a generous measure of liberty of which Protestant refugees were glad to avail themselves, and on the other, it made a magisterial Reformation impossible.

HUMANISM

Sigismund I had married Bona Sforza of Milan who was a fervent patroness of Renaissance art and ideas. And humanism was warmly welcomed at the University of Cracow. Such influences strengthened the demand for church reform. Reform was needed because the weaknesses that afflicted the church elsewhere in Europe were evident also in Poland. Worldliness, lack of spirituality and ignorance were rife among the lower clergy and the moral life of the church was put in jeopardy by the fact that so many of the key offices in the hierarchy and the religious orders were limited, by agreement with the pope in 1515, to members of the nobility. And yet it was the resistance of the nobility to a strong central monarchy which gave Protestantism a golden opportunity to spread during the reign of Sigismund II Augustus (1548–72).

LUTHERANISM

The proximity of Poland to Germany and the fact that a proportion of the country's population was German speaking, ensured an early circulation for Luther's writings. The first striking evidence of Protestant sympathy was in 1518 when the port of Danzig began to welcome Lutheran preaching. Disturbances followed and these culminated in the supplanting of the old town council by a new one which virtually abolished Roman Catholicism. That was on 22 January 1525. King Sigismund, however, intervened viciously, executed the leaders and restored Roman Catholicism. At the time he hoped to absorb the Duchy of East Prussia, the stronghold of the new moribund Teutonic knights, into his kingdom. He was thwarted in his intention when the Grand Master, Albert, was converted to Protestantism and converted the duchy into a secular and hereditary territory which became a fief of the King but without forfeiting its independence. So from 1525 the duchy under Albert became a centre of Protestant activity. Lutheran refugees were granted asylum and Lutheran preachers, like Adrzej Samuel and Jan Seklucjan were patronized, as were the printers who issued Polish versions of Luther's books. Not less influential was the University of Königsberg, founded in 1544, which soon became a vital centre for Protestant studies.

All this proved irksome to Sigismund I, despite the partiality of his queen for such radical preachers as Francis Lismanino. The Roman Catholic hierarchy pressed the King for action against heresy and he promised draconian penalties such as death at the stake for smuggling Luther's books into the country. But, with one exception, no one suffered as a result of the King's threats.

PROTESTANT GROWTH

The reign of Sigismund II, one of the most brilliant in Polish history, provided Protestantism with an opportunity to spread the gospel. The concept of a Polish national church with a liturgy of its own and released from the control of Rome – rather on the lines of the Anglican Church under Henry VIII – inspired many Poles. It motivated Peter Paul Vergerio, the former bishop of Capodistria, in his attempt to form a national Lutheran church in Poland and Lithuania under Sigismund. Despite Vergerio's enthusiasm, the plan had failed by the end of 1556. But if a general and uniform Reformation was out of the question, a vigorous Protestantism was emerging. The expulsion of the Bohemian Brethren from their homeland in 1548 meant an influx of many of them into Poland and they found supporters in such places as Poznan, Leszno and Torun (Thorn).

Vergerio was by no means the first pioneer of thorough reform. Some notable figures who contributed to developments in Poland were George Blandrata who was a physician at the royal court from 1540, Francis Stancaro, professor of Hebrew at Cracow from 1549 and Laelius Socinus who arrived in 1551. It was of great help to the reformers that the powerful and rich Chancellor of Lithuania, Prince Nicholas Radziwill, patronized them.

CALVINISM

From 1544 onwards Calvinism became more influential than the other forms of Protestantism in Poland. It was not only that its central Christian message was congenial, but its presbyterian polity and the opportunity it provided for lay people to contribute directly to the government of the church proved attractive as well. The books of Calvin, Beza and Bullinger were circulated freely. The consequence of this vitality was a resolution passed by the Diet in 1555 permitting every nobleman to patronize the religion of his choice in his territory until a national council should be convened to discuss the matter further. It was in March 1555 also that the pastors in Little Poland felt sufficiently strong to elect Felix Cruciger as their first superintendent. Later in the year this group formed a federal union with the Bohemian Brethren and later in the same month of September Francis Lismanino was elected co-superintendent with Cruciger, an indication of the close links now established between the united movement and the Calvinists of Geneva.

It was the ambition of the saintly and irenic John à Lasco (Jan Laski, 1499–1560), a man of distinguished Polish antecedents, to bring Lutherans and Calvinists, as well as the Bohemian Brethren, into a united body. He was respected by many of the leading Protestants of Europe and had made his own contribution to Protestantism in England, Emden and elsewhere. When he returned to his homeland in 1556 he tried hard to create a united movement but his plans were unacceptable and he died in 1560 without having realized his ambition.

ANABAPTISM

In 1549 the Anabaptist leader Menno Simons arrived in royal Prussia to compose the differences that had caused dissension among his followers there. By that time Anabaptism had been strengthened by the accession of Silesian refugees in the previous year. Dirk Philips, Simon's close colleague, settled in the neighbourhood of Danzig round about 1551 and met with sufficient success to cause anxiety in nearby towns. By 1556 King Sigismund was complaining to the Prussian diet about the tardiness of many towns to obey his specific request that Anabaptists should not be tolerated. Even the Reformed churches were being affected by the movement for at the synod of Secymin, January 1556, Peter Gonesius, declared publicly his adherence to Anabaptist principles. It was little wonder that the orthodox Simon Zacius, superintendent of the Calvinists at Vilnius (now in the U.S.S.R.), should write anxiously in 1557 that 'the spirit of many pious and virtuous Christians' was being depressed by the 'Evil One' through the multiplication of Anabaptists, followers of Schwenkfeld, Servetus, Gonesius and Arius.

Other Calvinists who were moving in the direction of Anabaptism in the early sixties were Martin Czechowic, teacher
at the Reformed school at Vilnius, and Simon Budny of
Kleck. So by 1565 Vilnius had become an Anabaptist centre.
But the death of Prince Radziwill on 28 May 1565 and the
effects of George Wetzel's pointed attacks on the pacifism
and social teaching of the radicals, with the consequent
alarm among the authorities, brought a halt to the development of Anabaptism in Lithuania.

In addition, Protestantism in general in Poland was con-
vulsed by theological controversy.

THE DOCTRINE OF THE TRINITY

When he proclaimed his adherence to Anabaptist principles at the synod of Secymin in January 1556, Peter Gonesius also, and for the first time in the Polish language,
expressed his disagreement with the orthodox doctrine of
the Trinity. After his views had been condemned by the
synod, he visited Wittenberg, only to find himself condemned by Melanchthon as an Arian. His views were
indeed reminiscent of those of Arius, for he held that there
was only one God, the Father, that Jesus Christ was created
out of nothing but he existed before the remainder of
creation. Gonesius also held that the Holy Spirit is not God.
The Reformed synod, under the leadership of Francis Lismanino, once the close confident of King Sigismund and
Queen Bona, rejected his views.

The questions raised by Gonesius became major points of
controversy when Francis Stancaro (d.1570) took them up.
Stancaro was a rude man with a pathological delight in
controversy. He had been professor of Hebrew at Cracow
in 1548 but lost his chair and was imprisoned. After
escaping, he wandered about Europe before returning to
Poland in 1559. He became the self-appointed defender of
the doctrine of the unity of the divine Persons in the godhead and found virtually everybody – not excluding Melanchthon – guilty of asserting belief in three gods. His
behaviour convinced John à Lasco, Lismanino and Cruciger
that he had to be opposed and his views were duly condemned by the Reformed synod in 1560. Another theologian against whose views Calvin had uttered warnings

was George Blandrata. He sought to overcome the difficulties posed by Stancaro by insisting that discussions of the doctrine of the Trinity should be conducted using only the language of the Bible and eschewing the technical language of the creeds. His personal preference was for an ethical and rational Christianity with but a light emphasis on abstruse points of theology. Although his orthodoxy was vindicated by the Reformed synod in 1561 and 1562, his solution to the controversies helped the more radical theologians.

Among these, Gregory Paul of Cracow stirred the determined opposition of the orthodox Stanislas Sarnicki who decided to form a new congregation in opposition to Paul's. It was the beginning of the final rift. The arguments became more intense with the arrival of Gianpaolo Alciati in 1562 and of Giovanni Gentile in 1563, for both were open critics of the Athanasian doctrine of the Trinity. Despite the attempt of the church to maintain peace under the leadership of Lismanino, Sarnicki's campaign, supported by the equally orthodox Christopher Tretius, continued to gather strength. The main battle between Sarnicki and Paul occurred at the General synod of Pinczow, August 1562, and the truce arranged there with its agreement to limit theological discussion to the language of Scripture provided a brief respite. But a synod of ministers who supported Calvinist orthodoxy, which was held at Cracow on 16 October 1562, vigorously reaffirmed the validity of the standards of orthodoxy used at Zürich, London and Geneva and condemned the views of Servetus, Gonesius, Stancaro, Gribaldi, Gentile and Alciati.

Changes of circumstances weakened the radicals. In 1563 Blandrata had left for Transylvania and Lismanino had retired to Königsberg. Prince Radziwill had died on 28 May 1565 and the Edict of Parczow, 7 August 1564 had expelled the Roman Catholic apostate refugees from Poland, and so Alciati, Gentile, Negri and Ochino had to leave. The two sides in dispute, the orthodox Calvinists and the radical antitrinitarians, faced each other in debate at Piotrkow in March 1565. The orthodox were led by Sarnicki and Tretius and their opponents by superintendent Stanislas Lutomirski, Gregory Paul of Cracow and

George Schomann of Lublin. But agreement was impossible and the antitrinitarians became the Minor Reformed Church of Poland.

We may take 1565 and the splitting of the Protestant movement as the end of the formative period of the Reformation in Poland, although the churches were to maintain their considerable vitality for years before the movement was finally destroyed by the militancy of a revived Roman Catholic Church.

34 Argument and liberty in Hungary

> Our Lord Jesus Christ orders us to seek first the Kingdom of God and its righteousness; therefore it was resolved in the matter of the preaching and hearing of the word of God, that . . . the word of God shall be preached freely everywhere; no one shall be harmed for any creed, neither preachers nor listeners . . . .
>
> Law of religious freedom endorsed by King John II Sigismund of Transylvania in January 1571.

During the sixteenth century Hungary presented a scene of disintegration and social strife. The crown had the greatest difficulty in preserving any independence over against the rapacity of the nobles who in their turn oppressed the peasantry with pitiless efficiency. The Roman Catholic Church was in a parlous condition with virtually every benefice in the land in the gift of the crown or the nobles. Hungary was a spiritual desert.

On 29 August 1526 came the tragedy of the Battle of Mohacs when the Hungarian army was annihilated by Sultan Suleiman I, the Magnificent, and his Turks. Louis II of Hungary was killed and the kingdom divided into two. John Zapolyai and Ferdinand of Habsburg initiated a civil war but in 1528 Zapolyai was defeated and became a Turkish vassal. Zapolyai died in 1540 and his infant son, John II Sigismund, was elected king and the Turks acknowledged the election. Ferdinand tried to frustrate the arrangement by an appeal to arms but was defeated and the central part of the country was absorbed into the Turkish empire. So north-western Hungary remained under Ferdinand, Transylvania was a vassal kingdom and the remainder of the country, Turkish Hungary, was under direct Turkish rule.

As for Transylvania, it was divided into 'nations', namely, the indigenous Huns or Szeklers, the Magyars, and the Saxons, each of these three ethnic groups having a constitutional voice in the Diet. The Wallachs or Romanians had no such privilege.

THE COMING OF PROTESTANTISM

Lutheranism spread rapidly through travelling merchants, students and the inhabitants of the German towns in the north. The earliest proceedings against heretics took place in 1524. By 1529 Hermannstadt was Lutheran and within six years Lutheranism had taken a firm hold upon the German burghers in Habsburg Hungary as well as the Saxon nation in Transylvania. The spread of Lutheranism was helped by the demands in some circles for reform along Erasmian lines. This was the kind of reform desired by people like János Sylvester, the translator of the New Testament into Magyar. Another helpful influence was that of the University of Wittenberg which was attended by many Hungarians over the years. Indeed the apostle of Lutheranism among the Magyars was an old Wittenberg student, Mátyás Dévai Bíró (d.1545). Although arrested as a heretic and sent to Vienna for interrogation in 1533, he escaped to resume his work. István Magyari Kiss was a doctor of Theology of Wittenberg and broke new ground by working directly as an evangelist among the people of the Tisza valley rather than seeking a benefice. And by 1547 the town of Debreczen in the upper Tisza had become the foremost centre of Magyar Lutheranism. And similarly in Transylvania the three nations were united in one Lutheran church while the Roman Catholic diocese of Transylvania was secularized in 1542.

THE REFORMED TRADITION

Within fifteen years, Debreczen was to become an equally strong centre of Calvinism, since both Biro and Kiss adopted the Reformed theology. As in Poland, the Calvinistic doctrines about the nature of the church and its relation to the state proved more attractive to the lower nobility than the Lutheran ones. Moreover, the inevitable German flavour of Lutheranism was unacceptable to patriotic Magyars. Presbyterian polity was an added attraction because it provided laymen with a greater opportunity to influence church affairs. The result was that by 1550 the Lutheran congregations in Turkish Hungary were adopting the Reformed position, while in Transylvania Calvinism also soon carried the day among the Hungarian-speaking Magyars. This develoment in Translyvania was helped by political changes. From 1551 to 1556 Ferdinand had usurped the throne and John Sigismund and his mother, Queen Isabelle, were in exile. The assassination of the oppressive Roman Catholic bishop of Nagyvárad in 1551 had signalled the beginning of a new period of opportunity for Calvinism and Protestant preaching soon gained large numbers of converts. And just as Johannes Honterus was the most influential preacher among the Transylvanian Lutherans, so Peter Melius (d.1572), bishop of Debreczen, emerged as the outstanding exponent of the Reformed positon. It was Melius's *Catholic Confession* (1561) which ensured the allegiance of the Magyar Protestants to a full Calvinistic theology.

This militant activity shook the Roman Catholic Church to its foundations. Monasticism disappeared and the extensive secularization of church property was completed by the Diet in 1557, after declining in the previous year to restore Roman Catholicism. At the same time Queen Isabelle granted, on the advice of the Diet, full freedom of worship to all religious groups.

GROWING DIFFERENCES

Soon the Protestant churches of Hungary, and especially the Refomed churches, began to develop a radical wing. Thus Francis David (1510–79), who was a student at Wittenberg from 1545 to 1548, became superintendent of the Hungarian Lutherans and was converted to Calvinism by Peter Melius. But this was not to be the end of his spiritual pilgrimage. From 1554 to 1558 Francis Stancaro was in Transylvania pressing his favourite theory that the orthodox doctrine of the unity of the three divine Persons in the Holy Trinity involved the exclusion of Jesus Christ's divine nature from any participation in the work of

salvation. His doctrine was countered with a flurry of condemnations and he had to leave the country, but not without stirring questions in people's minds about the Trinity.

In 1560 David was excommunicated by a Lutheran synod
at Medgyes because he denied Luther's version of the doctrine of the real presence, but he still kept his place as a leader
in the church. The following year saw the first open avowal
of antitrinitarian views at Debreczen by Thomas Aran of
Korospeterd, who moved quite soon to Transylvania. Far
more influential in the development of Unitarianism was
George Blandrata who became court physician to John Sigismund in 1563. He was to convert David to that view. By
1565 David was publicly criticizing the orthodox doctrine of
the Trinity, to the great alarm of Peter Karoli, the rector of
the Kolozsvar school, and Peter Melius, and they immediately drew the attention of the king to the heresy espoused
by both David and Blandrata. But it was in February 1566
that the Unitarian controversy opened in the church courts
when David convened a synod at Gyulafehervar, the capital of Translyvania, and propounded his particular teaching
about the nature of the godhead. A synod convened by the
king at the same place two months later secured a temporary truce between the orthodox and the Davidians
when all parties agreed that in discussing the doctrine
appeal should be made to Scripture alone.

Peace did not last long. At the synod of Torda in February 1567 David and Blandrata presented an Arian creed
which professed belief in one God, the Father, making the
Son subservient to the Father and defining the Holy Spirit
as the power of God. And it was accepted. A week later
Melius held a synod at Debreczen which adhered to the
Nicene doctrine of the Trinity. David saw himself now as
the leader of a campaign to bring the Reformation to its
eschatological climax. Luther, Zwingli and Calvin had
indeed pioneered the way but the culmination of their
work, he argued, could only be the rejection of Roman
Catholic trinitarianism as a final preparation for the second
coming in 1570. Obviously, he was echoing the views of
Servetus.

The climax of the debate was rather different from
David's expectations. The king summoned the two sides to
a debate to begin at the royal palace at Gyulafehervar on 3

March 1568 which was to last for ten days. Peter Melius led
the orthodox side and Blandrata and David led the
Unitarians. It was generally agreed that the Unitarians had
had the best of the argument but Melius and his supporters
were by no means convinced that they should change their
convictions. On the contrary, they were resolved to maintain their beliefs at all costs. So when a six-day debate,
beginning on 20 October 1569, was held at Nagyvarad the
final rift came. The Reformed Church in Transylvania divided and the side which enjoyed most public support as
well as the patronage of the king was the Unitarian section.
Nevertheless, in January 1571 the king gave the royal
assent to the Diet's request for full freedom of preaching
and worship to all the churches. In this way Transylvania
takes a significant place as one of the pioneers of religious
toleration in Europe.

We can take this division in the Transylvanian church as
a convenient terminus for our study of the formative period
of Protestantism in Hungary, with a mixed pattern emerging, consisting of Greek Orthodox believers among the
Romanians, Lutheranism continuing among the German
element in the population, and the Reformed Church now
divided into Calvinists and Unitarians.

35 In the steps of John Hus

Without being aware of it, I have till now taught and
held the whole doctrine of John Hus . . .

Martin Luther (1483–1546), in 1520.

Bohemia and Moravia during the fifteenth century demonstrated how potent an influence John Hus had been.
Powerful reform movements had been set in motion and in
many ways they anticipated the principles of the Protestant
Reformers.

CURRENTS OF REFORM

Communion in both elements was the most prominent
symbol of Czech reform by 1417. Its protagonists were
called Utraquists from the Latin formula, *sub utraque specie*,
meaning 'in both elements', wine as well as bread. They
divided into two wings, a moderate one led by John
Rokycana (*c.* 1390–1471) and a radical one led by John
Zelivsky in the formulation of its ideas, and by the redoubtable one-eyed noble, John Ziska who died in 1424 on the
field of battle. The latter were known as Taborites, from
their stronghold on Mount Tabor, south of Prague. They
rejected the Roman Catholic doctrines about the saints,
purgatory, relics, the distinction between priests and laity,
as well as transubstantiation. For a time they were able to
form a united front with the main body of Utraquists to
withstand the crusading armies sent against them by the
Roman Catholic authorities. Thanks to the diplomatic acumen of Rokycana the Roman Church accepted the *Compac-
tata* of Prague which conceded Communion in both
elements and provided a legal basis for a partly autonom-
ous Czech Church. This remained the established church of
Bohemia until 1620 when Roman Catholicism was fully
restored. However, many of the Taborites could not accept

this arrangement but they were shattered by the combined forces of the Utraquists and the Roman Catholics at the Battle of Lipany, 1434.

THE BRETHREN

One man who was sorely distressed by the bloodshed and protested against it was Peter Chelcicky (1380–1467). Inspired by the writings of Wyclif, he vigorously criticized the church and its priests in a series of tracts. The church, by its close identification with the state since the time of Constantine, was guilty of transgressing the express teaching of Jesus Christ by using force in spiritual matters as well as by the luxury and greed of the priests. Peter formed no movement but his pleas for closer adherence to the New Testament standards impressed many people. And his views were endorsed by John Rokycana. Rokycana's nephew, Gregory (d.1474) 'the Patriarch', founded a new protest movement based on Peter's views. With the accession of the Hussite king, George Podebrady, to the throne of Bohemia in 1457, Gregory's followers were granted permission to settle in the almost deserted neighbourhood of Kunvald in north-eastern Bohemia. Here they constituted themselves into the *Unitas Fratrum*, the Unity of the Brethren, a body that was to make an outstanding contribution to evangelicalism in later years.

Life was not easy for the Brethren. They had formed themselves into a community in which both secular and religious activities were governed by an agreed system of discipline, but even so they still thought of themselves as a reform movement within the Utraquist church. Persecution from 1461 to 1463 compelled them to reconsider their status. They gradually became convinced that they must think of themselves as separatists. At their first synod at Reichenau in 1464 they asserted their resolve to maintain peace with all, but by the following year they had become convinced that it was God's will that they should separate and institute a ministerial order of their own. So at the synod of Lhota in 1467 three brethren were chosen by lot to be their first priests. It was also resolved that they should be ordained by bishops. But where could they find bishops prepared to ordain their priests? One of their leaders,

Michael Bradacius, parish priest at Kunvald, was sent in search of a church with a 'godly ministry' and he found it in the south of Moravia among the Waldensians. So Bradacius was consecrated bishop by Stephen, a Waldensian bishop, and he returned to Kunvald to ordain the chosen brethren. So the Unity of the Brethren became an independent church.

After the death of Gregory the Patriarch on 13 September 1473 the next notable leader was Luke of Prague (c.1460–1528). He was a prodigious worker who published a substantial body of literature. He also introduced changes into the views and convictions of the Brethren. He persuaded them to abandon their former absolute pacifism and their refusal to accept offices under the state. He also persuaded them to introduce more elaborate forms of liturgy and he expressed his passion for congregational singing by publishing the very first European collection of hymns in 1501.

Even more striking was the maturing of the Brethren's views on justification. In 1495 the Council of Elders, the ruling body of the community, was asked the question, 'By what is a man justified?' And the answer they gave was, 'By the merits of Jesus Christ'. So in theology the Brethren had embraced the central evangelical affirmation by the time Martin Luther was no more than twelve years old. Not only so, but the Brethren by 1500 had recruited some 100,000 members organized in over 300 churches and over the next thirty years the membership doubled. Their growth had been facilitated by the peace which they enjoyed after 1475 but after the turn of the century they were subject to persecution and troubled by the emergence of a radical movement under the leadership of Jacob Stekensky and Brother Amos. The result was that a party of Minor Brethren had been formed by 1500 with a later Amosite schism from that group.

The religious position in Bohemia was a peculiar one. The majority of the population were communicants in the national Utraquist Church which was itself schismatical. However, this had introduced extensive reforms and had all but extinguished monasticism. But in essence this was still a Roman Catholic church. Then there was the main

body of the Unity of Brethren, together with the Minor
Unity as well as the schismatic Amosites.

THE REFORMATION

Bohemia and Moravia had enjoyed a substantial measure of
reform before 1517 and the population, despite vicious
wars and outbursts of repression, had enjoyed more
religious freedom than in many places. When news of
Luther's protest reached Bohemia in 1517, the Brethren
were overjoyed. But the joy was a little premature. Luke,
the Brethren's leader, at first disliked Luther's teaching on
Christ's presence in the Communion elements as well as
his rejection of five of the seven Roman Catholic sacraments and his emphasis on Christian freedom. Luther for
his part was impatient with the Brethren's lack of perception in matters of doctrine and their obsession, as he saw it,
with outward observances. He expressed his impatience in
harsh words, describing the Brethren as 'sour-faced hypo-
crites and self-grown saints'. But more cordial feelings soon
prevailed. Luke died in 1528 and in 1532 the young and
forceful John Augusta (1500–75) was consecrated bishop
and became the Brethren's leader. By this time several of
the Brethren had been educated at Wittenberg and bishop
Augusta shared their enthusiasm for the Protestant doctrines. In 1532 a confession, which the Brethren had first of
all presented to Margrave George of Brandenburg, was
printed at Wittenberg with a commendatory preface by
Luther. By 1540 the Brethren had extended their circle of
fraternal intercourse to include Bucer, Capito and Calvin.
For Calvin their order of discipline was an especially pleasing aspect of their discipleship. This reaching out to other
Christians was to remain one of the striking characteristics
of the Brethren throughout the years. For Luther, however,
it was their emphasis on the primacy of the Word of God
and the evangelical content of their faith which most commended the Brethren to him.

RADICAL REFORM

Since Bohemia and Moravia were developing a modestly
tolerant attitude towards differing beliefs, and since the

feudal social structure (as in Poland and Hungary) secured for the gentry a measure of independence and freedom within their individual estates, refugees with radical religious views found a haven, even if only for brief periods, in the two territories.

It was to Nicolsburg in Moravia, as we have seen, that Balthasar Hübmaier travelled after leaving Waldshut. This was in 1526. He soon set himself the task of changing the Lutheran parish of Nicolsburg into an Anabaptist one with the connivance of the local lord, Leonard of Liechtenstein. But the parish had drawn a variety of refugees to it, and it was almost impossible to weld them into a united congregation. There were conservative Anabaptists, led by Hübmaier, John Spittelmeier together with Leonard of Liechtenstein himself. On the other hand, just outside the town, was the refugee camp of the radical Anabaptists led by Jacob Wiedemann and Philip Jager. The tension between the two groups was intensified by the advent of Hans Hut in 1527. He anticipated the second coming of Jesus Christ in 1528, preached that there was therefore no need for a magistracy and believed that Christians should commit themselves to evangelical communism on the pattern of the Jerusalem church in its earliest days. In May 1527, at Nicolsburg Castle, a disputation was held between the two parties. The most significant points of debate concerned the role of the prince or magistrate and the legitimacy of war. Hut's enthusiastic pacifism perturbed Leonard because it sounded like sedition and the fiery preacher was imprisoned. He made his escape but it was a sore disappointment to the refugees that an Anabaptist lord should behave in this way and the disappointment turned to foreboding when it became clear that Leonard could not save Hübmaier from the persecuting Ferdinand of Austria.

Hübmaier was martyred at Vienna on 10 March 1528. His radical opponents at Nicolsburg were expelled by Lord Leonard and some 200 of them sought refuge elsewhere. They got permission to settle at Austerlitz under the patronage of the four brothers Kaunitz, and by 1529 they had adopted a twelve-point programme in which a communal life was envisaged including the sharing of temporal goods, an earnest of the discipline that was to be the distinguishing characteristic of their lineal descendants, the Hutterites.

HARD TIMES

Because the Unity of the Brethren refused to take up arms against their fellow Protestants in Germany during the Smalcaldic War, King Ferdinand banished them from his realm in 1548. John Augusta began seventeen years of imprisonment in 1547 and the leadership devolved upon George Israel who led many of the Brethren to Poland where they were able to join the Calvinists and the Lutherans in 1570. In Bohemia itself, the reign of Maximilian II, 1564 to 1576, brought peace and freedom to the Brethren and they too were able to form a united front with other Protestants in 1575.

36 The revival of Roman Catholicism

The Church is an army drawn up for battle. She cannot proceed to the attack until her equipment is complete. We have first to prepare our weapons, and then to engage the enemy.

Cardinal Reginald Pole (1500–1558), speaking at the Council of Trent, 26 February 1546.

Roman Catholic leaders had long pondered measures of reform but with little success in implementing them. Then came the most powerful of all the reform movements, the Protestant Reformation, and this provided those who sought to mend mediaeval ills by applying mediaeval remedies with a grave challenge. They met the challenge with enthusiasm and the result was a mighty revival of Roman Catholicism. There were three aspects to the revival: the correction of abuses, the refurbishing of doctrine and the revivifying of spirituality.

THE PAPACY

The papacy itself had long been a source of scandal. Leo X, a lover of luxury, died on 1 December 1521. His successor was the Dutchman, Adrian VI, a scholarly ascetic, who reigned but twenty months. He was followed by the irresolute Medici, Clement VII. The pope from 1534 to 1549 was Paul III who had given up the immoralities of his youth and was the first pope to show real sympathy for the men who advocated reform. Between 1536 and 1542 he made cardinals of men like Gasparo Contarini, Jacopo Sadoleto, Reginald Pole and Giovanni Pietro Caraffa, later Paul IV.

These men, together with others, had ever since 1517 met together to deepen their own devotional life and to seek reform in the church in the group known as the Oratory of Divine Love. Similar groups sprang up in several Italian cities. And it was from among this group that a working party was formed, under the chairmanship of Contarini, to report on the need for reform. This they did in 1538 in their *Advice on reforming the Church*. This report did not mince words. It called for the abolition of practices that merely served the greed and ambition of churchmen rather than the welfare of believers. Bishops should stay at home and do their pastoral work. Cardinals should be at Rome to advise the pope. Religious houses should be properly inspected and heresy should be excluded from schools and colleges. The exploitation of people through indulgences should end and those who wished to be priests should be effectively screened and tested before ordination.

The report made it clear that drastic changes were necessary.

THE COUNCIL

The papacy and its supporters were suspicious of the demand for a general council to initiate reforms. They remembered how in the previous century the authority of the pope had been threatened by councils. Nevertheless, after several announcements and false starts, Paul III summoned a council to meet on 15 March 1545 at Trent, a north Italian town on imperial territory, 'for the exaltation of the Christian faith and religion; for the extirpation of heresies and 'for the reformation of the Christian clergy and people', as the opening decree put it. The first session opened on 13 December 1545 with only thirty-one church leaders in attendance. And no time was it as representative a gathering as its supporters had hoped for. After heated debates about the agenda, it was decided that the two central themes of the council, discipline and definition of doctrine, should be discussed concurrently. The council did its work in three series of sessions, December 1545 to February 1548, then April 1551 to April 1552 and finally from April 1561 to 4 December 1563.

DOCTRINE

The council was clear in its mind that the primary matter at issue between Roman Catholics and Protestants was theology. On every point of controversy in doctrine, the council rejected the standpoint of the main line Reformers. In opposition to the Protestant emphasis on the supreme authority of Scripture under God, the council asserted that the 'truth and discipline' of the church 'are contained in the written books, and the unwritten traditions which, received by the apostles from the mouth of Christ Himself, or from the apostles themselves, the Holy Ghost dictating'. The canon of Scripture includes the Apocrypha and the books of the Bible are to be received 'as they are contained in the old Latin vulgate edition.' So the 'Decree on the Canonical Scriptures', 8 April 1546, opened the way for the reassertion of the validity of a large number of beliefs and practices which were sanctioned by tradition but hardly justifiable from Scripture.

On justification, the council, with the help of a plethora of scholastic distinctions, declared that salvation comes to a sinner through both an inherent and an imputed righteousness, the inherent righteousness being the fruit of faith adorned by works of love and not, as Luther had maintained, the fruit of Christ's atoning sacrifice. For Trent a sinner is saved because of what he is, not, as the Reformers held, because of what the Saviour has done. And so human merit was still an essential element in the Roman Catholic doctrine of salvation as expounded at Trent.

The seven sacraments remained intact and the Mass was held to be a 'truly propitiatory' sacrifice, repeating the sacrifice of Calvary, 'the manner of offering alone being different'. This conviction rested on the assumption that 'the whole substance' of the bread and wine on the altar are converted at consecration into the very substance of Christ's body. And since the whole Christ is present in either element, it continued to be unnecessary for lay people to receive the cup; eating the bread at Communion was sufficient.

Purgatory was declared to exist and the souls of the dead there 'are relieved by the prayers of the faithful, but chiefly by the acceptable sacrifice of the altar'.

In doctrinal matters, then, Trent decisively rejected Protestantism. The Roman Catholic Church made it quite clear
that it was not prepared to reform itself according to the
Word of God in Scripture, only according to the Bible and
Tradition. In short, by carefully defining the points at issue,
Trent ensured that Protestantism was no longer merely a
schism but a heresy.

DISCIPLINE

The council did not issue any decrees on the papacy as
such, but it greatly strengthened the position of the pope
by centralizing authority in his hands. But it also restored to
bishops the power that they had lost. No longer could a
pope condone slackness among bishops and grant them
dispensations from their duties. From now on, the pope,
while remaining the final court of appeal, would expect
bishops to carry on with their work and introduce reforms,
in conformity with the spirit of Trent, without any hind-
rance from Rome. These changes enabled ardent bishops,
such as Charles Borromeo, archbishop of Milan from 1560
until his death in 1584, to introduce extensive reforms in
their dioceses.

Although such practices as the use of images, the invo-
cation of saints, pilgrimages, prayers for the dead and the
provision of indulgences were approved by the council,
strict directions were issued to ensure that they did not
strengthen superstition or provide means for illicit gain.
The concern for the enlightenment of the laity is shown in
the declaration that preaching is 'the chief duty of bishops',
as well as in the prescription that bishops should see to it
that there is an adequate supply of preachers in their
dioceses. Ordinands should be carefully examined and
properly trained while pastoral oversight of clergy, laity
and religious houses should be faithfully undertaken. The
time and care taken at Trent to remove all kinds of abuses
show that the bitter complaints of thousands of critics had
not gone unheeded.

THOUGHT CONTROL

It was one thing to define orthodox doctrine, it was a

different matter to uproot heresy. The church, of course, had its elaborate system of courts for maintaining discipline but it was felt that the suppression of heresy demanded the services of specialists. The Inquisition was a tribunal that could use such people. It had been founded in the thirteenth century, had then become dormant and was revived in Spain in 1473. Its successes there so impressed Cardinal Caraffa that he persuaded Pope Paul III to establish a central and permanent tribunal of the same kind at Rome by the bull *Licet ab initio*, 21 July 1542. Caraffa instructed the Inquisitors to punish on suspicion, to show no favour to the great and to eschew mildness, especially when dealing with Calvinists. Caraffa became pope in 1555 and reigned as Paul IV until his death in August 1559. He made Michael Ghislieri head of the Inquisition, and he was even more ruthless than Caraffa. He became Pope Pius V (1566–72) and so during this crucial period the tribunal was assured of the highest possible support. It proved remarkably successful. When all is said to correct exaggerated tales about its methods, it still remains one of the most sinister institutions ever devised by any Christian church.

The Inquisition was not the only instrument for controlling people's thoughts. A list of forbidden books, the 'Index' was issued in 1559 by Paul IV. It prohibited the reading of a wide variety of books. Erasmus's books were proscribed. All vernacular translations of the Bible were banned, as were all Protestant books. In this way Rome was able to inhibit Christian humanism as well as the finest biblical scholarship of the age.

SPIRITUALITY

These negative activities, however, would not of themselves have produced a Roman Catholic revival. For that zeal, commitment and a burning vision was necessary. So it is in the new spirituality that we discern the motivating force that powered the revival of Roman Catholicism.

First of all, new religious orders appeared. The influential Oratory of Divine Love has already been mentioned. In 1524 the Order of Clerks Regular – the Theatines – was founded by Gaetano da Thieni (1480–1547). In 1525 Matteo da Bassi (1495–1552) seeking to return to the strictness of the rule of St Francis, founded the Order of Friars Minor Capuchin. They produced no greater preacher than their third Vicar-general, Bernardino Ochino, who became a radical Protestant. No less enthusiastic were the Oratorians, founded by Philip Neri (1515–95) and authorized by Gregory XIII in 1575, who did so much to promote devotion and who made use of Palestrina's music in their beautiful liturgical services. Similarly among women, the first teaching and nursing order was founded in 1535 by Angela Merici (1474–1540) of Brescia.

But the militant propagator of the Roman Catholic Revival was the Order of Jesus, the Jesuits. Its founder was the Basque, Ignatius Loyola (1491–1556). After suffering wounds in battle in 1521 he abandoned romantic ambitions of military glory in favour of the pursuit of spiritual distinction as a soldier of the church. He subjected himself to severe fasting and hammered out the principles that were embodied in his *Spiritual Exercises* (1548). In order to equip himself for his life's mission he went back to school at Barcelona and climbed up the educational ladder to the universities. It was in Paris that he recruited his first followers, most notably Francis Xavier (1506–52), Diego Lainez (1512–65) and Alfonso Salmeron (1515–85). The group took the vows of chastity and poverty and resolved, should the pope approve, to go on a mission to the Holy Land. The mission proved impossible and so they lived and worked in Rome. The Society of Jesus was formally instituted by the pope on 27 September 1540. Loyola became its first general. The aims of the Order were sharply militant, – to advance souls in the Christian life, to propagate the faith, to preach and to educate. Their parish was the world. Their most enterprising missionary was Xavier who propagated Catholicism successfully in Goa, southwest India and Japan. But the Jesuits also were very effective educationists in many countries, as well as the most vigorous intellectual opponents of Protestants. They combined high ideas with an accommodating pragmatism which gained them immense influence but also made them objects of increasing suspicion in many countries. But Loyola and his Jesuits were the spearhead of the Roman Catholic counter-attack against Protestantism.

MYSTICISM

Loyola was no stranger to mystical experiences but he was not alone in this. The combination of mysticism and practicality was an outstanding characteristic of Teresa of Avila (1515–82). She had vivid visions of God's love culminating in the so-called 'Transverberation', the ecstasy in which she felt an angel plunging a fiery spear into her heart and experienced the pain and joy of being transfixed by divine love. Starting in 1562 she founded new monasteries in Spain and subjected them to a strict rule. She died on 15 October 1582. She described her pilgrimage in her autobiography while in her other works she analysed the complexities and refinements of the life of prayer. Above all, her constant wonder at the mystery of divine love gives to her work a moving beauty.

She was assisted in her work by another great mystic, Juan de Yepes, better known as St John of the Cross (1542–91). His picture of the spiritual pilgrimage is more tragic than that of Teresa, for he held that the pilgrim must nurture a profound humility in which a state of utter emptiness is achieved. When God starts to do what man cannot do, the dark night of the soul descends and all consolation disappears. Only then will the pilgrim begin to know something of the burning fire of divine love. Often John is extremely obscure but, at other times, he shows himself a great master of words, especially so in the haunting beauty of his finest poems.

There was, then, an intense piety at the heart of the Roman Catholic Revival. Although at many points it is not easily reconciled with the teaching of the New Testament, particularly in its passion for schematizing the spiritual life and for emphasizing techniques of meditation and ways of inducing ecstasies, yet its power and fascination can be appreciated by those who are familiar with very different patterns of piety.

THE NATURE OF THE REFORM OF PRACTICE

The Roman Catholic Reformation was such a massive movement, and so full of variety, that it is no easy matter to analyse its general characteristics. But an attempt must be made to do so.

It transfomed the administration as well as the moral tone of the church. At last the church had listened to the complaints about corruption, inefficiency and graft which had been voiced over several generations by many critics. Practices which encouraged financial rapacity and greed were very largely abolished. Indeed the abolition of the traffic in indulgences, which was only one of these unacceptable practices, was a tacit admission of the validity of Luther's original protest.

Again, moral laxity among clergy and laity had long been a source of embarrassment. It was no easy matter to counter-act the moral confusion that followed in the wake of war, economic distress and social upheaval. Yet Roman Catholic reformers (no less than Calvinist puritans) were dedicated to the task of restoring ethical discipline in private and public life. Thus, Pope Pius V (1565–72) was a complete contrast to the pleasure-loving Renaissance popes, not only in the fierce asceticism of his private life, but in the stern measures he adopted in Rome to curb public immorality. His critics there complained that he was trying to turn the city into a mon-astery!

For the Council of Trent, the clergy were the key to successful reform. So measures were now recommended to ensure that the parishes were served by enlightened and dedicated priests. The single most significant recommenda-tion was that every bishop was to see to it that there was a suitable seminary or university within reach of his ordinands. And he was to be discriminating in his choice of men for training. Young men were to be imbued with a commitment to high ideals of excellence. And these recom-mendations were soon implemented in many places and brought a new enthusiasm into the work of the parishes in many countries.

Even more crucial was a strong episcopate. From now on bishops were to reside in their dioceses, to conduct visi-tations and to ensure that the prescriptions of the council were applied. Above all, priests and bishops were to be diligent preachers. No one proved to be a more dedicated exemplar of the new kind of pastoral bishop than Charles Borromeo (1538–84), the Archbishop of Milan, with his new seminaries, his numerous day schools and Sunday Schools, his frequent sermons and tireless application to his duties.

THE SIGNIFICANCE OF DOCTRINAL DEFINITION

Luther had said that whereas others had attacked the scandals of the papacy, he had attacked its doctrine. He never ceased to hope for a council of Christians to consider the theological reformation which he had demanded. It was a grievous disappointment to him that Rome should show no sign of desiring to help build a reformed, biblical, catholic and united church. He was not alone. John Calvin had written that he would 'not be afraid to cross ten seas' if that would restore unity to a church whose 'body . . . lies wounded and bleeding'. And Thomas Cranmer, too, had advised Henry VIII to support the convening of 'a synod of the most learned and excellent persons, in which provision might be made for the purity of Church doctrine.' Martin Bucer of Strasbourg was animated by the same ideal as well.

The council that met at Trent, however, was not the kind of synod envisaged by these men. It was far too restricted in its personnel and exclusive in its spirit. When it came to defining doctrine – Luther's foremost concern, – Trent's answer to the Reformation was 'No!'. Cardinal Pole believed that the most important debate at Trent was the first one, the debate upon the relationship of the Bible to tradition. Once that point had been settled, the other decisions on doctrine would follow inevitably. Trent did indeed embrace a high doctrine of Scripture but it went on to say that it 'receives and venerates . . . those traditions, pertaining both to faith and morals, as having been uttered either by the lips of Christ or by the Holy Spirit, and preserved in unbroken continuity in the Catholic Church'. True enough, the bishops argued warmly in the council about the precise meaning of the word 'tradition'. But once the decree was accepted in its final form, with no clear definition of the term, there was no knowing what usages, beliefs and institutions might be considered part of the sacred tradition. And how could Protestants criticize them by reference to Scripture?

THEOLOGY AND SPIRITUALITY

The Council of Trent was no more than an aspect of the Roman Catholic Reformation. But it was a formative aspect. It gave a decisive direction to the spirituality of the following

years. The new devotion to the Eucharist was greatly
encouraged by the strong reassertion of transubstantiation.
Again, the intenser pursuit of sanctity, as well as the
activism and application to works of love, which contributed
so much to later piety, were indebted in some measure to the
attention that the council gave to free will, the role of good
works and of divine grace in the order of salvation. Men's
efforts were not unavailing, as the Protestants seemed to
say. Not to mention the larger place given in contemplation
to the humanity and sufferings of the Saviour.

So it was that the discipline of methodical prayer,
advocated by the new religious orders and mystical writers,
interfused with the theology of Trent to produce a vigorous
spirituality that was sacramentarian, individualistic, disciplined, often intense in its emotion, but rarely extreme in its
asceticism.

A SUCCESS?

The Roman Catholic Revival was a success in that it transformed the Roman Catholic Church. It was a success too in
that it regained perhaps one third of the territory lost to
Protestantism. And it succeeded also through its missionary
outreach in opening up new and extensive territories.

On the other hand, the decrees of the Council of Trent met
with a mixed reception even in Roman Catholic countries,
such as France and Spain. Kings and princes had political
and social reasons for opposing reform.

If Trent be thought of as an attempt to re-unite Christian
Europe, it was a failure. And for those who worked and
prayed for the church to submit itself to the scrutiny of
Scripture, Trent was a disaster. The church defined itself in
such an exclusive way as to imperil its right to call itself
Catholic. Its character as an ecclesiastical institution centred
upon Rome and the papacy seemed to overshadow its
catholicity. And that meant the extinguishing of any fruitful
interchange of theological views between Roman Catholic
and Protestant.

37 The heart of the Reformation

Thus I planted. Matthew, Luke, Paul and Peter watered, but God in a wonderful manner gave the increase.

Zwingli (1484–1531) in 1522.

For the people who participated in the sixteenth century Reformation, the religious awakening was the fruit of God's powerful and gracious intervention in human history. When Matthias Flacius Illyricus (1520–75) and his colleagues came to compose their encyclopaedic survey of church history, the *Magdeburg Centuries*, which was published between 1559 and 1574, they depicted Luther as the man who had released the pure Word of God from the oppression of the papal Antichrist. Luther himself had taken this view when he said of the Reformation, 'I did nothing. The Word of God did it all.' And Melanchthon also, when announcing Luther's death to his students, echoed the same conviction: 'It was not through human wisdom that the teaching of the remission of sins and the faith of the Son of God was perceived; but it was disclosed by God through this man.' These declarations were an application to contemporary history of the principle 'to God alone be glory', itself one of the foundation stones of Protestantism.

THE WONDER OF FAITH

It has long been the custom to condense the characteristic doctrines of the Protestant Reformation under three headings, – by faith alone (*sola fide*), by grace alone (*sola gratia*) and by Scripture alone (*sola Scriptura*). The sinner is justified by faith in Jesus Christ and in his saving work, without any reliance whatsoever on his own good deeds. So the basis of his justification is quite extraneous to the sinner; it lies in the Saviour. Justification is by trusting implicitly in the Saviour. So 'by grace alone' means that justification is God's free gift, not in any way a reward for human merit. All this we know through the Bible, God's divine Word addressed to us. And we know it through the Bible as the Bible is interpreted in its own light and not in the light of any human or churchly authority. For as the Word of God inscripturated, the Bible has a unique and overriding authority which is revealed to the believing heart by the internal testimony of the Holy Spirit.

The transforming power of these convictions is not adequately appreciated if they are understood only as academic dogmas. To thousands of sixteenth-century people they came as thrilling revelations of God's saving love towards then in the tragedy of their sin. We flavour their warmth and intensity in the words of Calvin's last will, dated 25 April 1564, when he acknowledged God's 'clemency and kindness' in receiving him into his mercy and goes on, 'I have no other defence or refuge for salvation than this gratuitous adoption, on which alone my salvation depends. With my whole soul I embrace the mercy which he has exercised towards me through Jesus Christ, atoning for my sins with the merits of his death and passion, that in this way he might satisfy for all my crimes and faults, and blot them from his remembrance.' It was precisely the same faith that supported Luther in his dying moments as he repeated again and again the words, 'God so loved the world, that he gave his only begotten Son . . .' (see John 3:16). The English martyrologist John Foxe (1516–87) spoke for all Protestants when he said, 'The foundation of all our Christianity is only this: The promise of God in the blood of Christ his Son, giving and promising life to all that believe in him . . .' Free grace in the Saviour, saving faith in the sinner's heart and a divinely authorized Bible form the three-fold cord upon which the eternal life of the sinner depends.

THE DYNAMISM OF THE BIBLE.

It was the German theologian, Isaac August Dorner (1809–

84) who first propounded the distinction between the 'material principle' and the 'formal principle' of the Reformation. The former, which points to the spiritual substance of the Reformation, is justification by faith alone. The latter, the shaping power, is Scripture alone. It is a useful distinction but more needs to be said to capture the impact made by the Bible.

The Bible was to play a massive role in the various Protestant Reformations. As the evangelical faith spread, it inspired translators to provide their respective nations with new renderings of the Bible. An astonishing number of such new translations appeared in the various languages of Europe. And the very best scholarship of the day was exploited to produce them. The consequence is that a surprising number of these translations were to become classics of prose writing in many European languages, so that many national cultures owe a large debt to the Reformation in the realm of literature.

As these translations circulated among thousands of people who had never handled a Bible in their life before, so they worked like a powerful leaven in the hearts and minds of readers. The Reformers insisted that the Bible was intended to be read by all Christians not by clergy alone, hence their passion for translating. Moreover, true Christians could read with the knowledge that the Holy Spirit would provide them with the necessary light to understand the Bible. But this did not preclude accepting guidance from fellow Christians. So a flood of commentaries and books about the Bible and its doctrines spread across Europe. Nothing was more characteristic of the Reformers than the enthusiasm with which they employed the printing press to spread their views. The result was that the Bible became an immensely potent instrument for the spreading of evangelical religion, for inspiring individual piety, and for provoking a lively variety of convictions, some of which did not meet with the approval of the Reformers themselves.

THE ROYAL PRIESTHOOD

The rich variety of Protestant Christianity is not rightly appreciated unless it is realized that 'faith alone' and 'Scripture alone' inevitably produced the emphasis on the

'priesthood of all believers'. Luther had propounded the
doctrine with characteristic forthrightness in the *Address to
the Christian Nobility* in 1520:- 'all Christians are truly the
spiritual estate, and there is no difference amongst them . . .
Thus we are all consecrated as priests by baptism, as St
Peter says, "Ye are a royal priesthood, a holy nation" . . .'
(*see* Peter 2:9). Jesus Christ, the great High Priest, by his
saving work has constituted all Christian believers into a
'royal priesthood'. This profound conviction asserts that all
Christians have direct access to God through the one
Mediator, Jesus Christ. The outcome was the dismantling
of the complex system of mediatorship upon which so
much mediaeval piety was erected. Belief in a host of
mediators, extending from the Virgin Mary to the local
saint, or from the pope to the local priest, was now
discarded. At the same time, the 'priesthood of all
believers' introduced a vision of spiritual equality among
Christians and dissolved that hierarchical distinction
between priests and laity which split the Roman Catholic
Church in twain.

What did the principle imply for church organization?
Here again the variety of Protestantism becomes evident.
For some, especially among the Anabaptists, the principle
implied a congregational polity in which authority was
vested in the whole congregation of believers. On the other
hand, the radical thrust of the doctrine was not realized in
the churches of the magisterial Reformation. Thus, it could
mean a purely spiritual status which permitted the organization and government of the church to remain in the
hands of the prince or his nominees, as in Lutheran
Germany. Or again, it could be interpreted to mean that the
Christian public should express its common priesthood by
exercising control over religious policy through parliament,
as in the Anglican system. The churches which embraced
presbyterianism sought a middle path and combined a
measure of autocracy through the church courts with a
strong democratic element which made it possible for
individual congregations to make their view known
through their elected representatives in these courts.
Although there was no unanimity among Protestants on
the question of church government, the differences
between them did produce in Christian Europe a variety of

organizations which contrasted vividly with the monolithic uniformity of the mediaeval church.

RECALL TO SIMPLICITY

The Reformation cut like a knife through the complexities of late mediaeval life. In the realm of thought it was a frontal attack on the tiresome complications of mediaeval scholasticism. In piety, it brushed aside indulgences, chantries, monasteries, pilgrimages, obits, images, sacred paintings and pictures and replaced them with a straightforward personal relationship between human beings and God. By the close of the mediaeval period, the Roman Catholic Church had become a vastly complicated structure, with a multiplicity of officers and offices, and its immense bureaucratic empire stretching to every corner of Europe, seeking by a confusing plethora of dues, tolls and taxes, to maintain its ramshackle structure. In this area too Protestantism meant a vigorous simplification. And, as Luther so powerfully insisted, all this meant that the Gospel gave the christian man an exciting freedom.

All in all, the Protestant Reformation was as fundamental a transformation as Christianity has ever experienced and for individuals, as in the case of Luther himself, it meant rediscovery of a gracious God and a saving Christ. It is this spiritual principle that lies at the heart of the Protestant Reformation.

38 Life is religion

We are not our own; therefore, as far as possible,
let us forget ourselves and the things that are ours.
On the other hand, we are God's; let us, therefore,
live and die to him (Rom. XIV.8). We are God's;
therefore, let his wisdom and will preside over all
our actions.

John Calvin (1509–1564) *Institutes* III.7.1.

The sixteenth century was suffused with a renewed sense
of God's presence. Many scholars have commented upon
this in the case of both Luther and Calvin. Luther gives
the reader of his works a vivid impression that he felt
himself to be living his life *coram Deo*, as he put it, – before
God. Similarly, there is no escaping Calvin's acute awareness of the presence of a glorious and sovereign God. But
this was true of thousands of people who had not the
means to express their feeling in books, yet they were
acutely concerned about the issues raised by the Reformers. The piety of such people, as well as the actions they
took in the light of their piety, were heavily coloured by
the Biblical teaching that was central to the Reformation.
They had learnt that God is both an omniscient God and a
gracious God who insists on making direct personal contact with those who seek him. Protestantism had sought to
correct those corruptions which had poisoned the piety of
the late mediaeval period. God is not a truculent heavenly
being to be manipulated and cajoled by esoteric ceremonies, nor is he a remote deity whose attention can be
secured only through the good offices of well-placed saints
in the celestial court. God in Christ seeks and saves sinners and those who have been privileged to be saved have
a direct access to the throne of grace. The constant nervous dread of a capricious God, and the morbid preoccu-
pation with death and dying, yield in private worship to

gratitude and certainty. And so it was also with public worship.

THE WORSHIPPING CONGREGATION

The central element in Roman Catholic worship is the celebration of the Mass. In its origins, it was a terse service, economical in words and ceremonial. With the passing of the centuries, however, it had become more elaborate. More serious were the accretions that it collected, not infrequently under the influence of folk piety.

The Eucharist became an 'unbloody sacrifice'. Jesus Christ was conceived to be corporeally present in the consecrated elements and these elements were offered to God as an actual sacrifice of the 'Holy Victim'. It was a re-enactment of the sacrifice of Calvary. Other concepts and practices followed. Since the sacrifice of the altar was pleasing to God, the mechanical multiplication of Masses was taken to be commendable. Nor was it necessary to have a congregation present. Communion, that is, partaking of the elements, became a rarity. Since 1215 it was required that people should take Communion at least once a year, at Easter, but that did not mean that the public complied with the rule. In any case, from about that time onwards the cup was withdrawn from the laity. The Mass became something to be seen and for many that meant seeing only the elevation without participating in the rest of the service. In the end, the Eucharist had become a parody of its New Testament progenitor and for the public in general it had become a magical rite for securing peace for the souls of the dead, or for ensuring safety on a journey, or success in a business transaction. But the Mass was not the only service of worship; the church had many others and in places like the monasteries, provided they were well ordered, these services were observed at the stipulated hours of each day.

The Reformers had to address themselves to the question of how best to restore the worship of the church to its original simplicity and glory.

LUTHER

Luther was both bold and hesitant, – bold in asserting

guiding principles but hesitant in introducing liturgical changes. By 1520 he had rejected the teaching that the Mass was a repetition of the sacrifice of Calvary. Nevertheless, he advocated the view that in the Eucharist believers identify themselves with the fellowship of Christs's suffering. This understanding of Communion as a fellowship meal was of great importance in Luther's doctrine. He insisted that it should be conducted in the people's language, the congregation should partake of both elements and they should do so frequently. But at the same time Luther adhered vehemently to the conviction that Jesus Christ is present bodily in the elements, although he rejected the Roman Catholic philosophical explanation of it. But Luther was in no hurry to introduce the changes at Wittenberg. Not until 1526 did he offer a German Communion Service and that was extremely conservative. His one great creative innovation was the introduction of German hymns.

ZWINGLI

Zwingli was more radical than Luther. He abolished singing, put the sermon in the place of honour in the Liturgy of the Word and in the Liturgy of the Upper Room – the Communion Service proper, – he severely simplified the traditional form of service. In fact, his service was very similar to that used in British nonconformist churches many years later. For Zwingli, of course, the Communion is a vivid memorial of Christ's sacrifice and so there is an emphasis in his liturgy on the completeness of his saving work.

BUCER

At Strasbourg a German evangelical liturgy had been introduced early in 1524 by Diebold Schwarz but changes continued to be made in the following years. The reformers there, under the guidance of Bucer, sought to retain as much as possible of the Roman Catholic liturgy, to ensure that the new liturgy was consistent with Protestant theology, to emphasize the congregational nature of worship by retaining responses and introducing hymn-singing, and by producing a choice of alternative prayers and confessions. The result was a rich liturgy which did full justice to the elements of fellowship, joy, repentance, thanksgiving and recollection. It is the felicitous combination of these elements that secures for the Strasbourg liturgies a place of honour in the history of Reformation worship.

CALVIN

Calvin approved of the Strasbourg liturgy and sought to produce a version of it at Geneva. In his attempt to reproduce the kind of worship which was to be had in the early church, he hoped to integrate Communion into the weekly Sunday service but that proved impossible except on the one Sunday every month when the city authorities permitted Communion. The Liturgy of the Word consisted of a call to worship, confession and prayer for pardon, a metrical psalm, prayer for illumination, Scripture reading and sermon. On Communion Sundays, the Eucharist followed without a break and it was a plain service in which the Lord's Prayer was said, the Apostles' Creed sung, the Words of Institution read followed by the Consecration Prayer, the delivery of the elements, Communion, then a short prayer and the Aaronic blessing. Calvin's services gave a large place to Scripture and the exposition of it in the sermon, and combined dignity with simplicity.

ANGLICANISM

In England Thomas Cranmer began to make his outstanding contribution to Anglican liturgy with the publication of his revised Breviary in 1538. It makes use of both Latin and English but later usage is foreshadowed in the way in which the traditional hours are distilled into two daily services, Mattins and Evensong. The translation of the Bible into English, with Matthew's Bible appearing in 1537 and the Great Bible two years later, was of the profoundest significance in the development of Anglican worship.

The reign of Edward VI proved to be the golden age in the production of the Anglican liturgy. Preliminary steps were taken by publishing the *Book of Homilies* on 31 July 1547 and *The Order of Communion* on March 1548. But the culmination came with the issue by Cranmer and his colleagues of *The Book of the Common Prayer and Administration of the Sacraments*. All the Church of England's services were now available in one book. The services were to be in English. They sought to preserve as much as possible of the Roman Catholic liturgy, even to the extent of earning the qualified approval of the conservative Stephen Gardiner. At the same time liturgical elements and implied theological doctrines that were offensive to Protestant consciences were omitted. The book did not meet with the approval of the more earnest reformers and so the second Edwardian Prayer Book was prepared and issued in 1552. This book owed much to the detailed criticism of Bucer and so shared some of the ideals of the Strasbourg liturgies. Altars became communion tables, the Communion Service was substantially modified, prayers for the dead deleted and eucharistic vestments banned. In a revised form this became the Prayer Book of the Elizabethan church in 1559 and continued in use, with minor modifications, until the twentieth century.

RADICALS

There was a wide variety of views about worship among the radical reformers. At one extreme there was the formalized worship of the Waldensians while at the other extreme a rationalist like Sebastian Franck argued for the elimination of audible prayer, preaching and the sacraments. The main body of radicals, the Anabaptists, stressed from the beginning the value of intense and prayerful study of the Bible in worship. They doubted the value of set prayers because they encouraged mechanical repetition and formalism. Yet, it is of interest that a radical like Thomas Münzer did pioneer a fundamental reformation of the liturgy. And Münzer, like Hans Hut and Melchior Hofmann and many others believed in the bestowal of charismatic gifts through the unction of the Holy Spirit upon worshippers. And this meant an emphasis on spontaneity. So the Protestant Reformation represents a wonderfully varied, but intensely influential, renewal of worship.

Nevertheless, for the Reformers in general the Bible did not warrant the restricting of religion to the cultic aspects of Christian life.

A RECOVERY OF UNITY

Calvin was imbued with a powerful conviction that we live in a coherent universe, subject in all its aspects to God's law and ruled by his sovereign will. Since it is the Christian's privilege and duty to exalt God's glory, it follows that all cultural activity, as well as the moral life and the practice of worship, is a way of serving God. Religion is not to be confined to church or monastery. The fundamental human passion for commitment is expressed in all that a person does. The commitment may indeed be to an image, or false idea, or to some created thing. In that case it is idolatry. If, however, through grace a person has been brought to the commitment of faith in Christ, then he can exercise his loyalty to God in his farming, or in business, as a parent, a schoolteacher, a craftsman, scientist, artist or politician. There is a profound unity in the Christian life, because the Christian acknowledges God's universal rule, sees the unity of all creation in Christ, and concentrates his own endeavours on the service of Christ's kingdom.

It is true that this theme emerges more clearly in the thinking of Calvin than any other Reformer. It is true also that Luther's teaching tended in the direction of differentiating too sharply between the spiritual life of the Christian and the sinful kingdoms of the world. And the Anabaptists for the most part were extremely critical of human culture as such and cherished the ideal of forming fellowships withdrawn from the world. Even so, the contrast between Calvin and other Protestants can be overemphasized for the simple reason that Calvin's thinking was to percolate into the minds of all Protestants. Thus it was that Protestantism was to inspire such a rich cultural contribution to the lives of so many nations.

MORALS

Almost from the beginning of his career as a reformer Luther was accused of promoting moral laxity by his teaching about justification by faith and not by works. He himself believed that the good news of justification by faith would produce an immediate improvement in morals. He was appalled when visitation reports showed how prevalent immorality was.

Protestantism has often been dogged by the problem of how best to integrate its stress on faith alone with good moral living. The radical Reformers, and especially the Anabaptists, were immediately conscious of this and insisted with passion that to believe in Jesus Christ is also to embrace the discipleship which he demanded of his followers. That meant embracing a simple style of living, using the Sermon on the Mount as a guide to the good life, and embracing pain and persecution as badges of discipleship. In the fine analysis of Christian living in Book III of his *Institutes* Calvin writes,

> Doctrine is not an affair of the tongue, but of the life; and is not apprehended by the intellect and memory merely, like other branches of learning; but it is received only when it possesses the whole soul, and finds its seat and habitation in the inmost recesses of the heart.

Again, Calvin's conception of the unity of the truly Christian life emerges. Doctrine is of crucial importance, but the truth of it must be apprehended with a warmth of feeling and it must flower in holy living. But such a unity, by God's grace, must be rooted in 'the inmost recesses of the heart'. With the development of Protestantism and the extension of Calvin's influence in the Puritan movement and later in the Evangelical Revival, the integration between the burning heart, correct doctrine and moral dedication was to be richly exemplified.

EXALTING THE LAITY

The Protestant Reformation indulged in an unparalleled flattering of the laity. The traditional status of the clergy was drastically modified; monks and nuns disappeared. In all Protestant countries the contribution of lay people to the Reformation was crucial, women as well as men. It was the best possible proof of the massive impact made by Luther's *Appeal to the Nobility of the German Nation*. The good health of the church was no longer a private matter for clerics; it was the concern of all Christians. In the realm of spirituality it was one of the most subtle achievements of the Reformers to produce a valid lay piety which proved attractive.

In that respect they provided a fruitful alternative to the
Roman Catholic idea that the only way to nurture lay
spirituality was to treat people as monks and nuns living in
the world. And then in the continuing government of the
churches produced by the Reformation, a wide variety of
means was adopted to ensure a place for lay people in the
government of the churches, through councils and parliaments in some countries, through appointment by princes
and kings in others, by participation in the work of church
councils in yet others and, among the Anabaptists, by
granting the ultimate authority under Christ to the whole
congregation. But whatever the method, the Reformation
meant a revival of lay participation in the government of
the churches.

POLITICS

The story of the reformations in the various countries of
Europe is itself sufficient proof that Protestants could not
evade the challenges of political life. Their attitudes to the
state varied considerably. Luther took a rather gloomy view
of the kind of service the Kingdom of Christ might hope to
get from any state. The Anabaptists were even more critical
for they raised the fundamental questions about the role of
the state. For many of them, Jesus Christ had specifically
prohibited the use of the sword and so pacifism was an
integral part of their Christian discipleship. How then
could the true Christian grant the state authority to wield
the sword and to wage war? Could it be acknowledged that
the state could properly use compulsion to ensure order
among those of its citizens who are not Christians? That
seemed to some Anabaptists a real possibility. But their
pacifism did not commend itself outside their own ranks.

So also it was with toleration. We have seen how a few
bold spirits made an open plea for toleration but it did not
persuade the leaders of the Reformation. Nevertheless, the
Reformation made a valuable contribution to the growth of
toleration without always intending it. The mere fact that
the unity of Christendom had been destroyed and several
faiths competed with one another in the same territory,
raised the question whether it was seemly for Christians to
indulge in senseless destruction of one another. It may well

be that for a minority was the sixteenth century reformation a struggle for individual liberty of conscience, but even so it was an issue that from then on disturbed the intolerance of an increasing number of Europeans.

That the Protestant Reformation were a great social upheaval in the countries of Europe is only too obvious and a large and fascinating literature has grown about this topic. How did Protestantism affect the class structure of European countries? What exactly was the relationship between Protestantism and the emergence of capitalism? Is there reason to believe that Protestantism was closely connected with urbanization? How did the Reformation help the growth of Dutch or English imperialism and contribute to the collapse of Spanish imperialism? These are all topics that have received close scholarly attention but consideration of them would take us beyond the scope of a modest introductory volume. But the mere fact that such questions engender extended debate is an indication of the impact made by the movement that opened with the nailing of Ninety-five Theses on the doors of a church at Wittenberg by the monk Martin Luther.

The Protestant Reformations together represent a momentous revival of Christianity, the greatest since the age of the apostles.

Further reading

SOURCES IN ENGLISH TRANSLATION

Several volumes in the S.C.M's 'Library of Christian Classics' are devoted to the Reformation period:
XV *Luther, Lectures on Romans* (1961).
XVI *Luther, Early Theological Works* (1952).
XVII *Luther and Erasmus on Free Will* (1957).
XVIII *Luther, Letters of Spiritual Counsel* (1955).
XIX *Melanchthon and Bucer* (1969).
XX-XXI *Calvin, Institutes of the Christian Religion* (1960).
XXII *Calvin, Theological Treatises* (1954).
XXIII *Calvin, Commentaries* (1958).
XXIV *Zwingli and Bullinger* (1953).
XXV *Spiritual and Anabaptist Writers* (1957).
XXVI *English Reformers* (1966).

The *Documents of Modern History* published by Edward Arnold provide an excellent selection of source materials with helpful notes. The volumes dealing with the Reformation period are:

Rupp, E.G. and Drewery, B., eds., *Martin Luther* (1970).
Potter, G.R., ed., *Huldrych Zwingli* (1978).
Potter, G.R. and Greengrass, M., ed., *John Calvin* (1983).
Dickens, A.G. and Carr, D., eds., *The Reformation in England to the Accession of Elizabeth I* (1967).

Other single volume collections are:
Hillerbrand, Hans J., *The Reformation in its own Words* (1964).
Hillerbrand, Hans J., *The Reformation* (1981).

Of the collections produced in the nineteenth century, the works of Calvin produced by the Calvin Translation Society and the works of the Anglican reformers reprinted by the Parker Society are of inestimable value to the student of ideas. Of more recent translations of the Continental reformers, the following are valuable:

Pelikan, J. and Lehman, Helmut T., eds., *Luther's works*, usually referred to as the 'American edition' in 55 volumes, from 1958 onwards.

Works of Martin Luther (Philadelphia edition, 6 volumes).

Torrance, D.W. and Torrance, T.F., eds., *Calvin's Commentaries* (1959 onwards).

For Protestant declarations of faith, *see*:

Schaff, Philip, *The Creeds of Christendom, III The Evangelical Protestant Creeds* (1877, reprint 1969).

Cochrane, A.C., *Reformed Confessions of the 16th Century* (1966).

Many bibliographies of the Reformation are available. Perhaps the most useful for the general reader is that produced by:

Wood, A. Skevington, 'A bibliographical guide to the study of the Reformation', in *Themelios*, January 1977 and January 1978.

GENERAL BACKGROUND

Elton, G.R., *Reformation Europe* (1971).
Green, V.H.H., *Renaissance and Reformation* (1952).
Hay, D., *Europe in the Fourteenth and Fifteenth Centuries* (1977).
Leff, G., *Heresy in the later Middle Ages* (2 vols., 1967).
McFarlane, K.B., *John Wycliffe and the Beginnings of English Non-conformity* (1952).
Mackinnon, James, *The Origins of the Reformation* (1939).
Oakley, F., *The Western Church in the later Middle Ages* (1979).
Oberman, H.A., *Forerunners of the Reformation* (1967).
Oberman, H.A., *Masters of the Reformation* (1981).
Ozment, Steven, *The Age of Reform 1250-1550* (1980).
Spinka, M., *John Hus* (1966).
Stacey, John, *John Wyclif and Reform* (1964).
Workman, H.B., *John Wyclif* (2 vols. 1926).

THE PROTESTANT REFORMATION IN GENERAL

Elton, G.R., ed., *The New Cambridge Modern History, II The Reformation* (1958).

Atkinson, James, *The Great Light: The Reformation* (Paternoster Church History, 1968).

Bainton, Roland, *The Reformation of the Sixteenth Century* (1953).

Brooks, P.N., ed., *Reformation Principle and Practice* (1980).

Buck, L.P. and Zophy, J.W., *The Social History of the Reformation* (1972).

Chadwick, Owen, *The Reformation* (Pelican History of the Church, 3, 1964).

Cunningham, William, *The Reformers and the Theology of the Reformation* (1862, 1967).

Dickens, A.G., *Reformation and Society in Sixteenth Century Europe* (1966).

Dickens, A.G., *The Age of Humanism and Reformation* (1977).

Grimm, H.J., *The Reformation Era 1500–1560* (1965).

Léonard, Émile G., *A History of Protestantism* (I, 1965; II, 1967).

Lindsay, T.M., *A History of the Reformation*, 2 vols. (1910).

Lortz, H., *The Reformation in Germany*, 2 vols. (1968).

Ozment, Steven, *The Reformation in the Cities* (1975).

Pauck, Wilhelm, *The Heritage of the Reformation* (1950).

Rupp, E.G., *Patterns of Reformation* (1969).

Spitz, L.W., *The Renaissance and Reformation Movements* (1971).

Sykes, Norman, *The Crisis of the Reformation* (1946).

Whale, J.S., *The Protestant Tradition* (1955).

MARTIN LUTHER

Atkinson, James, *Martin Luther and the Birth of Protestantism*, revised ed. (1982).

Bainton, Roland, *Here I Stand* (1950).

Dickens, A.G., *Martin Luther and the Reformation* (1967).

Dickens, A.G., *The German Nation and Martin Luther* (1974).

Ebeling, G., *Luther: an Introduction to his Thought* (1964).

Green, V.H.H., *Luther and the Reformation* (1964).

Kramm, H.H., *The Theology of Martin Luther* (1947).

Mackinnon, J., *Luther and the Reformation*, 4 vols. (1925–30).

Pelikan, Jaroslav J., *Obedient Rebels* (1964).

Rupp, E.G., *Luther's Progress to the Diet of Worms* (1951).

Rupp, E.G., *The Righteousness of God: Luther Studies* (1953).

Saarnivaara, Uuras, *Luther discovers the Gospel* (1951).

Schwiebert, E.G., *Luther and his Times* (1950).
Smith, Preserved, *The Life and Letters of Martin Luther* (1911).
Todd, J.M., *Martin Luther: a Biographical Study* (1964).
Watson, P.S., *Let God be God!* (1947).
Wood, A. Skevington, *Luther's Principles of Biblical Interpretation* (1960).
Wood, A. Skevington, *Captive to the Word* (1969).

ZWINGLI

Potter, G.R., *Zwingli* (1976).
Rilliet, J., *Zwingli, Third Man of the Reformation* (1964).
Walton, R.C., *Zwingli's Theocracy* (1968).

CALVIN

Beza, Theodore, *Life of Calvin*, ed. H. Beveridge (Tracts and Treatises of the Reformation, 1844).
Breen, Q., *John Calvin: A Study in French Humanism* (1968).
Hunt, R.N.C., *John Calvin* (1933).
McNeill, J.T., *The History and Character of Calvinism* (1954).
Monter, E.W., *Calvin's Geneva* (1967).
Niesel, W., *The Theology of Calvin* (1956).
Parker, T.H.L., *The Oracles of God: An Introduction to the Preaching of John Calvin* (1947).
Parker, T.H.L., *Calvin's New Testament Commentaries* (1971).
Parker, T.H.L., *John Calvin* (1975).
Wendel, F., *Calvin* (1963).

OTHER CONTINENTAL REFORMERS

Bainton, Roland, *Women of the Reformation in Germany and Italy* (1971).
Eells, Hastings, *Martin Bucer* (1931).
Harding, T., ed., *The Decades of Henry Bullinger* (4 vols. 1849–52).
Hildebrandt, Franz, *Melanchthon: Alien or Ally?* (1946).
Hopf, C., *Martin Bucer and the English Reformation* (1946).
Keep, D., *Henry Bullinger and the Elizabethan Church* (1970).
Manschreck, C.L., *Melanchthon: The Quiet Reformer* (1968).
Poll, G.J. van de, *Martin Bucer's Liturgical Ideas* (1954).
Steinmetz, D.C., *Reformers in the Wings* (1971).

Stephens, W.R., *The Holy Spirit in the Theology of Martin Bucer* (1970).

THE SPREAD OF THE REFORMATION

Baskerville, G., *English Monks and the Suppression of the Monasteries* (1949).

Bergen-dorf, C.J.I., *Olavus Petri and the Ecclesiastical Transformation in Sweden 1521–1552* (1928).

Blok, P.J., *History of the People of the Netherlands* (1970).

Brown, G.K., *Italy and the Reformation to 1550* (1971).

Chrisman, Miriam U., *Strasbourg and the Reform* (1967).

Church, F.C., *The Italian Reformers* (1932).

Clebsch, W.A., *England's Earliest Protestants 1520–35* (1964).

Dickens, A.G., *Thomas Cromwell and the English Reformation* (1959).

Dickens, A.G., *Lollards and Protestants in the Diocese of York 1509–1558* (1959).

Dickens, A.G., *The English Reformation* (1967).

Donaldson, G., *The Scottish Reformation* (1960).

Douglas, R.M., *Jacopo Sadoleto* (1959).

Edwards, R. Dudley, *Church and State in Tudor Ireland* (1935).

Edwards, R. Dudley, *Ireland in the Age of the Tudors* (1977).

Dunkley, E.H., *The Reformation in Denmark* (1948).

Fenlon, Dermot, *Heresy and Obedience in Tridentine Italy: Cardinal Pole and the Counter Reformation* (1972).

Fox, P., *The Reformation in Poland* (1972).

Geyl, P.C.A., *The Revolt of the Netherlands 1555–1609*, (1958).

Gray, J.G., *The French Huguenots* (1981).

Hughes, Philip, *The Reformation in England* (3 vols. 1950–4).

Hughes, P.E., *Theology of the English Reformers* (1965).

Hughes, P.E., *The Register of the Company of Pastors of Geneva in the Time of Calvin* (1966).

Hutchinson, F.E., *Cranmer and the English Reformation* (1957).

Hutton, J.E., *A Short History of the Moravian Church* (1895).

Kamen, Henry, *The Spanish Inquisition* (1965).

Kingdon, R.M., *Geneva and the Coming of the Wars of Religion in France* (1956).

Kingdon, R.M., *Geneva and the Consolidation of the French Protestant Movement 1564–1572* (1967).

Knowles, David, *The Religious Orders in England, III The Tudor Age* (1959).

Knox, John, *History of the Reformation of Religion within the Realm of Scotland*, ed. W.C. Dickinson, (1949).

Krasinski, W.S., *Historical Sketch of the Rise, Progress and Decline of the Reformation in Poland*, 2 vols. (1834–40).

Loades, D.M., *The Oxford Martyrs* (1970).

Longhurst, J.E., *Erasmus and the Spanish Inquisition: the Case of Juan de Valdés* (1950).

MacCurtain, Margaret, *Tudor and Stuart Ireland* (1972).

Moody, T.W., Martin, F.X., and Byrne, F.J., *A New History of Ireland III* (1976).

Motley, J.L., *The Rise of the Dutch Republic*, 3 vols. (1901).

Nieto, J.C., *Juan de Valdés and the Origins of the Spanish and Italian Reformation* (1970).

Parker, T.M., *The English Reformation* (1950).

Parry, Thomas (trans. Idris Bell), *History of Welsh Literature* (1955).

Pryce, I., *The Diocese of Bangor in the Sixteenth Century* (1923).

Renwick, A.M., *The Story of the Scottish Reformation* (1960).

Ridley, J.G., *Thomas Cranmer* (1962).

Ridley, J.G., *John Knox* (1968).

Roelker, *Queen of Navarre, Jeanne d'Albret* (1968).

Rothrock, G.A., *The Huguenots: A Biography of a Minority* (1979).

Rowen, H.H., *The Low Countries in Early Modern Times* (1972).

Rupp, E.G., *Studies in the Making of the English Protestant Tradition* (1947).

Salmon, J.H.M., *Society in Crisis: France in the Sixteenth Century* (1975).

Shaw, Duncan, *Reformation and Revolution* (1967).

Sutherland, N.M., *The Huguenot Struggle for Recognition* (1980).

Tedeschi, J.A., ed., *Italian Reformation Studies in Honor of Laelius Socinus* (1965).

Thomas, Lawrence, *The Reformation in the old Diocese of Llandaff* (1930).

Thomas, J.W., *The Wars of Religion in France 1559–1576* (1958).

Thomas, Isaac, *William Salesbury and his New Testament* (1967).

Wedgewood, C.V., *William the Silent* (1944).

Wiffen, B.B., *Life and Writings of Juan de Valdés* (1885).

Wilbur, Earl M., *A History of Unitarianism* (1946).
Williams, C.H., *William Tyndale* (1969).
Williams, David, *Modern Wales* (1950).
Williams, Glanmor, *The Welsh Church from Conquest to Reformation* (1962).
Williams, Glanmor, *Welsh Reformation Essays* (1967).
Willson, T.B., *History of Church and State in Norway from the Tenth to the Sixteenth Century* (1903).
Wilson, Charles, *Queen Elizabeth and the Revolt of the Netherlands* (1970).
Wood, J.C.F., *Icelandic Church Saga* (1946).
Wordsworth, J., *The National Church of Sweden* (1911).
Youings, Joyce, *The Dissolution of the Monasteries* (1971).

RADICAL REFORMATION

Armour, R.S., *Anabaptist Baptism* (1966).
Bainton, Roland, *Hunted Heretic: The Life and Death of Michael Servetus* (1953).
Bender, H.S. and Smith, C.H. eds., *The Mennonite Encyclopaedia* (1955–9).
Bender, H.S., *Conrad Grebel* (1950).
Clasen, C.P., *Anabaptism: A Social History 1525–1618* (1972).
Estep, W.R., *The Anabaptist Story* (1963).
Hillerbrand, H.J., *A Bibliography of Anabaptism 1520–1630* (1962).
Horsch, J., *Menno Simons: his Life, Labour and Teaching* (1916).
Horsch, J., *The Mennonites in Europe* (1950).
Jones, R.M., *Spiritual Reformers in the Sixteenth and Seventeenth Centuries* (1914).
Krahn, C., *Dutch Anabaptism* (1968).
Lienhard, M., ed., *The Origins and Characteristics of Anabaptism* (1977).
Littell, F.H., *The Origins of Sectarian Protestantism* (1964).
Maier, P.C., *Casper Schwenckfeld on the Person and Work of Christ* (1959).
Seypell, J.H., *Schwenckfeld, Knight of Faith* (1961).
Sider, R.J., *Andreas von Karlstadt: the Development of his Thought 1517–1525* (1974).
Vedder, H.C., *Balthasar Hübmaier* (1905).
Verduin, L., *The Reformers and their Stepchildren* (1964).
Verheyden, A.L.E., *Anabaptism in Flanders* (1961).

Williams, G.H., *The Radical Reformation*, 3rd ed. (1975).
Yoder, J.H., *The Legacy of Michael Sattler* (1973).
Zeman, J.K., *The Anabaptists and the Czech Brethren in Moravia 1528–1628* (1969).

THE ROMAN CATHOLIC REVIVAL

Brodrick, James, *The Origins of the Jesuits* (1940).
Brodrick, James, *The Progress of the Jesuits* (1947).
Daniel-Rops, H., *The Catholic Reformation* (1962).
Dicken, E.W.T., *The Crucible of Love* (1963).
Dickens, A.G., *The Counter Reformation* (1968).
Janelle, P., *The Catholic Reformation* (1949).
Jedin, Hubert, *History of the Council of Trent* (2 vols. 1957, 1961).
Kidd, B.J., *The Counter-Reformation* (1933, 1963).
Peers, E.A., *Mother of Carmel* (1945).
Peers, E.A., *Handbook of the Life and Times of Saint Teresa and Saint John of the Cross* (1954).
Schenk, W., *Reginald Pole, Cardinal of England* (1950).

Index

74078